A Practical Guide to Early Childhood Planning, Methods, and Materials

Related Titles of Interest

A Practical Guide to Early Childhood Planning, Methods, and Materials

The What, Why, and How of Lesson Plans

EVELYN A. PETERSEN

Allyn and Bacon
Boston   London   Toronto   Sydney   Tokyo   Singapore

Library of Congress Cataloging-in-Publication Data

Petersen, Evelyn A.
    A practical guide to early childhood planning, methods, and
materials : the what, why, and how of lesson plans / Evelyn A.
Petersen.
        p.   cm.
    Includes bibliographical references and index.
    ISBN 0-205-17404-3
    1. Early childhood education—Curricula—Handbooks, manuals, etc.
2. Lesson planning—Handbooks, manuals, etc.   I. Title.
LB1139.4.P48   1996
372.21—dc20   95-36548
                                                                  CIP

Printed in the United States of America
10   9   8   7   6   5   4   3   2   1   99   98   97   96   95

Contents

10   Priorities in Early Childhood Lesson Planning   142

Preface

The Purpose of This Guidebook

When early childhood teachers get together, what do they talk about? Most of the time, they are busy sharing ideas to try out in their lesson plans. Teachers in our field probably spend as much outside time working on and writing up their lesson plans as they do in the classroom. Despite this reality, college classes spend little time preparing teachers to do lesson planning, and specific inservice on lesson planning is minimal. Many early childhood teachers have been frustrated by a lack of direction in this important area.

Sometimes this frustration leads to desperation; teachers may purchase or use inappropriate "canned curriculum" resources that set forth lesson plans that are already completed and do not take the differences of programs and children into consideration. That's why this book has been written.

The purpose of this guidebook is to help teachers organize lesson plan ideas, methods, and materials in order to write effective lesson plans. This guidebook will not do your lesson plans for you, but it will present you with a system that will help you do appropriate lesson plans more easily and quickly. This system should help improve the quality and content of your lesson plans, and help you to document the good work you are doing with young children.

The system presented here is flexible. It supports individual choices and teaching styles, and it has been field-tested in a variety of centers to ensure that it protects the autonomy of programs. I hope the information shared in this book will also help teachers maintain compliance with the standards of quality that are accepted in the field.

This system incorporates a practical, step-by-step process for doing long-range, monthly, and daily lesson planning. It covers two kinds of planning: the kind of planning that deals with themes based on children's interests, and the kind of planning that incorporates the practice of many skills we want children to learn.

In classrooms serving three- to five-year-olds, children may start out the year as threes or young fours, and end the year as much more skillful and "grown-up" four- and five-year-olds. Seeing children grow and change, and being excited about every small miracle of this process, is an enjoyable aspect of our work! But whether early childhood programs run for twelve months or only nine, there are many changes in children in the course of a program year. This is why our lesson plans should look very different at the beginning of the year than they do at the end.

The lesson planning system in this guidebook is designed to help teachers get from point A to point B, from the beginning to the end of a program year, in a way that meets the continuously changing needs and skills of three- to five-year-olds. Lesson plans, methods, and materials need to be appropriate to the development of children at every skill level throughout the year. Skill-focused planning for the practice of specific thinking, reasoning, and psychomotor skills is the emphasis of this system.

When we do lesson plans, many things affect what we write. The settings in which we work, the materials in our centers, the diversity of children and their needs, and our programs' priorities all affect our lesson plans. Our methods of assessing and working with children, and even the kinds of forms we use, affect the kind of lesson plans we create. The first half of this guidebook presents the lesson planning system; the second half includes chapters that summarize the ways other aspects of early childhood methods and materials affect lesson planning.

This guidebook, used as a daily tool, can be very helpful to teachers already practicing in the field, regardless of their background and experience. It can also be a helpful resource on lesson planning, methods, and materials for administrators, supervisors, and college educators.

Acknowledgments

Because this guidebook represents many years of experience with programs, teachers, children, and colleagues in the field, there are many people to thank. First and foremost, thanks must go to the staff with whom I worked in developing this system, the parents of the Traverse City, Michigan, Cooperative Preschool Center. Without their interest and support, this system would not have been developed, refined, and used successfully with children.

Next, my thanks go to the teachers in programs who have examined the concept and system in this guidebook and used excerpts from it prior to publication. Their input and feedback helped clarify written strategies and add information to the guidebook on issues that are important to early childhood teachers. These teachers and programs are as follows:

Northwest Michigan Human Services Agency Head Start, Traverse City, MI
Teacher: Midge McCreedy, Cadillac Intermediate School District

Hualapai Nation Head Start, Peach Springs, AZ
Teacher: Drusilla Clarke

Garfield-Fraser Elementary, Pinconning, MI
Teacher: Lynette Frankovich, Kindergarten

Mahube Head Start, Detroit Lakes, MN
Teachers: Sara Hoffert and Dawn Leeseburg

Garrett County Head Start, Oakland, MD
Teacher: Debbie McCroskey

Hoosier Valley Child Care, Jeffersonville, IN
Teachers: Tonya Spall and Melinda Brock

Thanks also go to two programs that have examined some of the manuscript materials and given me helpful feedback: Navajo Nation Head Start, Window Rock, AZ, Gloria Clark, Education Coordinator; and Cincinnati Public Schools Head Start, Jennifer Cottingham, Director.

I could not have shared a broad range of practical ideas and information with readers without the experience of my roles as an early childhood consultant and trainer, Child Development Associate Representative and advisor, and Head Start peer review team member. I am grateful that I have had the opportunity to work with specialists in the Head Start Bureau, in CDA programs, and in various regions of the country served by Head Start, including tribal nations. I feel very lucky to have been able to work with teachers and programs in many states.

Many of the issues and the activity ideas shared in this guidebook are the result of these experiences in the field, as well as my own teaching experiences.

Thanks must go also to the editors and reviewers whose input made this book possible: Mary Langenbruner, East Tennessee State University, and Florence Wilson, Eastern New Mexico University. The feedback of colleagues Laura Dittmann, author and early childhood advocate, and Lillian Sugarman, who trained me as a CDA representative, was especially helpful, as was the input of Patricia J. Belter, disabilities specialist.

Finally, special gratitude is expressed to my entire family for their patience and support. Special thanks go to my husband, Jon, for helping on the home front and occasionally wrestling with the quirks of the computer and printer.

Very special appreciation goes to our daughter, Karin Petersen, graphic designer, who worked with me for many months creating and designing all the illustrations, tables, and forms for this guidebook.

This guidebook is dedicated to the children who attended the Traverse City Cooperative Preschool Center when I was teacher and director. When we observe children with focused interest and unconditional regard, we discover what they need and how best to deliver it. The children taught me what I needed to know in order to develop this lesson planning system and this book.

*Evelyn Petersen resides in Traverse City, Michigan. For information about this book and her other work with early childhood programs and parents, call her home/office at 800-748-0213. E-mail will reach her at **Petersen 13@AOL.com***

About the Author

Evelyn Petersen has over thirty years' experience in the field as an early child-hood instructor, consultant, and Head Start trainer. She has worked with children, teachers, and parents in over five hundred programs across the country, and in varied settings from homes to early childhood centers to college class-rooms. Her degrees in Child Development–Family Life and in Early Childhood Education were granted from Purdue University and Central Michigan University. As a member of the expert panel of The National Parenting Center, America Online, and as a weekly parenting columnist for the Knight Ridder Tribune Wire, she is a strong advocate for children, teachers, and parents.

1 Introduction to This Guidebook

LIKE ANY OTHER EARLY childhood teacher, I have spent many nights working on lesson plans until the wee hours. But after I developed and used the system of planning that I will share with readers in this book, my daily lesson plans took very little time. Moreover, I was confident that they were developmentally appropriate and could be fully understood by both my supervisors and my staff. Readers will surely understand why I wanted to make lesson planning simpler and faster, but they may wonder how I did it. Understanding this lesson-planning system will be easier if readers know how it came about. Just as necessity is the mother of invention, so a problem can be the mother of a solution.

A Lesson Planning System—Concept and Development

As a teacher-director of a cooperative preschool program, I evaluated my program and curriculum at the end of each program year. My curriculum themes were based firmly in children's and families' interests, and each program day was rich in concrete and enjoyable learning experiences. However, at the end of the year I found myself wondering whether I had really done my best in planning skill-focused activities—those activities that are planned to help children practice specific skills.

My long-range, yearly plan of thematic units was written out in a flexible format, but I did not have a written plan stating my long- and short-range goals for skill-focused activities. Two questions kept nagging me: Did I really plan a good balance of activities throughout the year so that every child had enough practice in motor, perceptual, language, memory, and problem-solving skills? And did I plan the practice of those activities at the right times of the year in terms of the children's development?

In addition to the problems posed by these two questions, I often felt smothered and overwhelmed by the number of choices for curriculum activities that were available to me. Like most early childhood teachers, I faced continually expanding choices. I was growing more experienced and wanted to try ideas emerging from parents and children, from workshops and conferences, and from the ever growing number of excellent early childhood resources in the field. Choices, choices, choices! Answering those two nagging questions about skill-focused activities kept getting put on the back burner in favor of the avalanche of new ideas to try.

Like many other teachers, I was making choices about what ideas to use and where to put them in my lesson plans, but I was not seeing these ideas for what they really were—information that I could manage more effectively. Instead, most of the time, the wealth and variety of information was managing me. When it came to thorough planning for skill-focused activities, I felt as if I were in a kitchen chock full of wonderful ingredients and recipes, but I was not quite sure of what to cook and when to cook it. There was so much stuff in my kitchen that I could not see whether or not I was planning consistently good "menus" or lesson plans every day, all year long.

Then something remarkable happened. I was studying several college textbooks, and while reading *The Whole Child* by Joanne Hendrick, I suddenly saw that all the ideas, activities, and learning experiences I was using, whether they were spontaneous, thematic, or skill-focused, could simply be viewed as a huge pile of information—information that could be sorted into three parts and then organized, prioritized, and used in long-range, monthly, and daily lesson planning.

Lesson planning would include three kinds of curriculum: the *spontaneous curriculum,* which would be based on the ongoing contributions and interests of children; the *horizontal curriculum,* which would be based on expanding those interests with further learning experiences in thematic units; and the *vertical curriculum,* based on activities for practicing specific skills and thinking processes. In the vertical curriculum a teacher could build on the experiences and factual content of the horizontal curriculum, and use them as a medium for practicing skills.

For example, if children become fascinated by playing with the falling leaves of autumn, and if a teacher builds on this interest with a thematic unit on fall, he or she would be using spontaneous and horizontal kinds of curriculum information. If further learning and skills are encouraged by having children order the leaves by size or sort them by color or shape, the teacher would be using vertical curriculum information.

It was not until I saw my skill-focused activities in this perspective, as "vertical curriculum information," that I understood that there was a way to do a better job of teaching specific skills to children through better lesson planning.

However, in order for these skill-focused activities to be effectively used in long- and short-range planning, they had to be prioritized and organized. In prioritizing ideas for these activities, I had to decide what particular mental abilities or cognitive and psychomotor skills I thought were the most important for children to practice.

My choices of skills to be practiced were based on whether or not the skills were truly important in providing children with lifelong thinking and doing skills that would serve as a foundation for success in future learning during the forthcoming school years.

In organizing these ideas, it was necessary to know what types of skills these were. Into what categories could they be placed? In listing and sorting all the classroom activities from lesson plans covering several years, I found that every activity offered or encouraged in our center fell into one of five major learning categories: motor, perception, literacy or language, memory, or problem solving. These were also the five basic categories of the Santa Clara Inventory of Developmental Tasks, the screening instrument I was using at that time.

The use of these five categories in my lesson-planning system would give me a way to provide a daily balance of all these skills in every lesson plan. I would be able to answer "yes" to that old question: am I giving children enough practice in each type of skill?

The next organizational task was to discover the sequence of development of each of these skills, and figure out how children could practice them gradually. This was a much more time-consuming and complex procedure because every skill-focused activity had to be sequenced. I had to think about what activities would have to be put into the lesson plan when children first began to practice a particular skill, and what activities would be put into the lesson plans gradually throughout the year until children gained mastery of the skill.

By combining basic child development knowledge with what I knew from ongoing observations of children, it was possible to sequence most of the skills I wanted children to practice and put them into logical and gradual time frames. When the sequencing for every skill-focused activity was done, I had my system for vertical curriculum lesson planning. I had a system that answered "yes" to the other old question: Am I planning the practice of skills at the right times for children throughout the year?

It was fairly easy to see why this third type of curriculum information, the vertical curriculum, was the type that many teachers do not carefully and consistently organize and preplan. Organizing and planning all the skill-focused activities of the vertical curriculum was not only hard work; it also presented me with many uncomfortable eye-openers about my own teaching.

I found that many skill-focused activities had been occurring, but not always at the right times or in the best balance for the skill levels of children being served. I could see that if teachers are not careful in preplanning the vertical part of the curriculum, certain skill-focused activities might be put into lesson plans too early in the year, when most children would not be ready for them. As a result, sometimes children might be expected to practice skills at the beginning of the year that would be better practiced midyear or in the last months of the year.

I also discovered that I had been placing more emphasis on certain types of skills and not enough on others. I had planned many science and math activities throughout the year, but I had not planned the practice of enough visual and auditory memory activities or enough auditory perception activities to meet children's needs. The system quickly helped me correct these aspects.

As I was refining and using the system with children, I was pleased to find that the sources from which I drew my curriculum ideas did not affect the system, nor did the system affect my resources. Like most early childhood teachers, I use an eclectic approach in gathering curriculum information. This is necessary in meeting the diverse and changing needs of children. I found that teachers would be able to use ideas and approach methods from Head Start curriculum guides, from The Creative Curriculum, from High Scope, from Montessori, from professional journals, from college textbooks, from workshops and conferences, and from virtually any curriculum module or past teaching experiences right along with this lesson-planning system.

The system does not define or restrict curriculum information; it merely organizes it for use in lesson plans. Like developmentally appropriate practice, it is not a rigid or restrictive system, but an approach to lesson planning and teaching based both on what we know and on what we are constantly learning about children.

The phrases *developmentally appropriate* and *standards accepted in the field* will be used frequently in this guidebook. It may be helpful to readers if we take some time to define these terms more clearly.

Developmentally Appropriate Practice

Developmentally appropriate practices and the acronym DAP have become such buzz words in our field that sometimes it is easy to forget what DAP really means. It simply means that our work should always incorporate both basic child development knowledge and sensitivity to individual and changing children's needs.

Developmentally appropriate programs are those that are planned and implemented on the basis of a basic knowledge of how children grow and what they can do, as well as on what teachers learn about individual children as they work with them. DAP is not only what is appropriate for an age group, but also what is appropriate for individual children. Sue Bredekamp of the National Association for the Education of Young Children, author and advocate of DAP, reminds us that children develop at their own pace and that they bring to every learning experience individual personalities, learning styles, family backgrounds, and family values. We must address these individual needs and differences.

> Human development research indicates that there are universal predictable sequences of growth and change that occur in children during the first nine years of life. . . . Knowledge of typical development of children within the age span served by the program provides a framework from which teachers prepare the learning environment and plan appropriate experiences. (Bredekamp, 1992)

Teachers should use basic child development knowledge of the sequences of growth in their long-range planning, but they should also be able to use these same sequences of growth to individualize their daily planning for children. The system of lesson planning in this guidebook includes strategies to help teachers plan developmentally sequenced activities relating to specific skills that individual children or groups of children can practice in the classroom. Goals for the practice of these skills are both age-appropriate and individually appropriate.

Another major element of developmentally appropriate practice is play, in which children explore concrete learning materials first-hand. Play is a primary vehicle for growth and further development because play helps children to progress from a sensorimotor stage of development as infants, to the stage of preoperational thought when they are preschoolers. "Child-initiated, child-directed, teacher-supported play is an essential ingredient of developmentally appropriate practice" (Bredekamp, 1992).

I believe that the "child-initiated" time of the day in which children explore materials of their choice is not only "teacher-supported" but is a period of the day in which choices of materials for learning may have been carefully planned by teachers in order to allow a broad range of both spontaneous and guided learning. In this guidebook, when I refer to this period of the program day, I will most often use the term *free choice,* but I will also use the phrases *activity time* and *child-initiated time* interchangeably.

Even though there is agreement in the field that DAP promotes methods and approaches that we know are good practices for teaching young children, some misconceptions about DAP still persist. In *Reaching Potentials: Appropriate Curriculum and Assessment for Young Children, Volume I,* the authors try to clarify some of these misconceptions (Bredekamp, 1992, pp. 1–13).

• DAP is not a curriculum with a rigid set of expectations. It is a framework, or a philosophy; it is an approach for all children and families, based on both what we know about children and what we learn about their individual needs and interests.

• DAP's approach is both age-appropriate and individually appropriate. It is based on child development knowledge, but it adapts for individual needs and diversities, and it respects the cultural values of children's families and communities. DAP supports curriculum ideas that emerge from the children, their families, and from teachers.

• DAP does *not* mean that teachers abdicate their roles as adult leaders and simply allow children to take charge and control the classroom. DAP supports the use of ongoing teacher and program goals and objectives in a framework of careful planning, which is appropriate for children's age levels and also helps children reach their individual potentials (Bredekamp & Rosegrant, 1992, pp. 4–26).

To me, DAP just means that in the early childhood field, we are continually striving for teachers, children, and families to work together to find and to use the best practices of teaching and learning for all children. The system in this guidebook for organizing curriculum ideas and activities in order to write appropriate daily lesson plans is firmly based in the principles of DAP and is strongly supportive of this approach.

Standards in the Field

Despite the wide diversity of early childhood programs and individual practices in those programs, there is a consensus in the field as to accepted standards of quality and the indicators of best practice. What are these indicators?

- Developmentally appropriate practices based on basic child development knowledge and individual differences and needs.
- Child-initiated play within the framework of teacher planning.
- Ample time for children to make choices for learning among those offered by the teacher.
- Active exploration and experimentation with concrete learning experiences in which children construct their own knowledge to add to the base of knowledge that teachers impart to them.
- Methods that support all areas of growth in the child, including self esteem and physical and social-emotional development.
- Enhancement of the child's thinking and reasoning abilities, and other cognitive and psychomotor skills.
- Methods that help children develop and gain mastery of skills through supportive interactions, stimulating questions, and positive reinforcement.
- Respect and support of children's parents and families, and a commitment to work as a team with parents, building positive relationships, and including parents in decisions about their children's care and education.

Standards of quality including these criteria have been established, published, and used for some time by the early childhood profession. These standards include the following publications, all of which are listed at the end of this chapter along with brief but pertinent information about each publication.

1. "Developmentally Appropriate Practice in Early Childhood Programs Serving Children from Birth through Age 8."
2. "Head Start Program Performance Standards."
3. "Accreditation Criteria and Procedures of the National Academy of Early Childhood Programs."
4. "Right from the Start," Report of the National Association of State Boards of Education Task Force on Early Childhood Education.

5. "Standards for Quality Programs for Young Children: Early Childhood Education and the Elementary School Principal."
6. "Guidelines for Appropriate Curriculum Content and Assessment in Programs Serving Children Ages 3 through 8: A Position Statement of the National Association for the Education of Young Children and the National Association of Early Childhood Specialists in State Departments of Education."
7. "Essentials for Child Development Associates Working with Young Children."

In addition to these publications on accepted standards in the early childhood field, teachers and students in various states will find that in cases where state departments of education fund and monitor early childhood at-risk programs, the published standards of quality for such programs follow very similar guidelines to the criteria for the standards in the publications listed above.

When this guidebook refers to *accepted standards in the field,* it means the consensus of agreement found in all of these publications concerning accepted standards of quality.

Overview of the Contents of This Guidebook

This is a guidebook about early childhood lesson planning, methods and materials. Chapter 2 is about those for whom we are doing the planning—the children. It includes information about child development that affects our lesson planning. Examples are given to show how a knowledge of child development specifically affects lesson planning entries on health, nutrition, safety, and other curriculum areas. Developmental information about two- to five-year-olds is also included so that teachers will have a summary of pertinent developmental information at their fingertips during lesson planning.

Chapter 3 discusses ideas, activities, and experiences based on the interests of children and teachers. These interest-based ideas are used in lesson planning for the horizontal part of the teacher's curriculum. This chapter will also include an example of a year-long horizontal plan, in outline form; teaching strategies for using a horizontal plan in daily lesson planning are presented.

Chapter 4 presents a system for organizing and using ideas and activities that are skill-focused, rather than interest-based. This chapter includes a comprehensive discussion of vertical planning and of developmentally sequenced skill-focused activity ideas. It presents strategies for helping teachers plan activities sequentially, so that they match the ongoing and changing skill development of children as they move through the program year. The system organizes skill-focused activities for lesson planning in the areas of motor, perception, literacy, memory, and problem solving.

Chapter 5, on daily schedules and daily lesson plans, emphasizes the practical aspects of lesson planning, or getting teaching ideas down on paper. It also examines the ways the lesson plan format itself can help teachers to document compliance with program priorities and accepted standards.

Chapter 6 presents the ten steps in the lesson-planning process and important details regarding each step. The steps summarize the management process presented in chapters 3 through 5 of this guidebook.

Chapters 7 through 11 review other important topics that specifically affect the teacher's daily lesson plans and daily work with children. These chapters provide information on individualizing, documentation, the setting, child-initiated time, national priorities in early childhood education, and integrated activities.

Appendix A provides teachers with seven consecutive time blocks containing a variety of developmentally sequenced skill-focused activity examples for children's practice in the areas of motor, perceptual, literacy, memory and problem solving. The activities in the seven time blocks follow the gradual and natural growth of children's skill development throughout a nine-month program year.

Appendix B is a self-assessment tool for the teacher's use concerning appropriate lesson plans and practices. In checklist format, it is based on accepted standards in the field.

Appendix C is a list of early childhood books and resources divided into common categories for quick reference. Some, but not all, of the references in Appendix C are also listed in particular chapters of the guidebook because of their relevance to the chapter's topic.

Now that we have introduced this guidebook and its purposes, discussed the origins of the lesson-planning system, and defined some of the terms that will surface frequently, let's get into the fun part—the rest of the book!

Self-Study Activities

1. Think about your vertical curriculum and some of the skill-focused activities you plan. List these to discover which of the five major skill categories your activities fall into—motor, perception, literacy, memory, or problem solving.

2. Look at the list of publications of accepted standards in the field at the end of this chapter. Which of these publications do you have in your own personal professional library? If you have not seen or read any of these publications, arrange to obtain, read and compare at least two of them.

References and Resources for Further Reading

Bredekamp, Sue, ed. *Developmentally Appropriate Practice in Early Childhood Programs Serving Children from Birth through Age 8,* expanded ed. Washington, DC: National Association for the Education of Young Children, 1992. *This book puts into writing the consensus of the early childhood field concerning appropriate practice. For information on obtaining this book, call NAEYC at 800-424-2460.*

Bredekamp, Sue, & Rosegrant, Teresa, eds. *Reaching Potentials: Appropriate Curriculum and Assessment for Young Children,* Vol. 1. Washington, DC: National Association for the Education of Young Children, 1992.

Brewer, Jo Ann. *Introduction to Early Childhood Education: Preschool through Primary Grades.* Boston: Allyn and Bacon, 1995.

Head Start Bureau, Administration for Children and Families, Department of Health and Human Services. *Head Start Performance Standards.* Washington, DC: Department of Health and Human Services, 1975. *This document sets forth core goals and standards for the implementation of the Head Start program. For a copy, send a request to ACYF, Head Start Bureau, Box 1182, Washington, DC 20013.*

Hendrick, Joanne. *The Whole Child: New Trends in Early Education.* St. Louis: C. V. Mosby, 1975. (Out of print; available through interlibrary loan.)

Hendrick, Joanne. *The Whole Child: Developmental Education for the Early Years,* 5th ed. Columbus, OH: Merrill/Prentice-Hall, 1992.

Hohmann, Mary, & Weikart, David, P. *Educating Young Children: Active Learning Practices for Preschool and Child Care Programs.* Ypsilanti, MI: High/Scope Press, 1995.

Koralek, Derry, G., Colker, Laura, J., & Dodge, Diane Trister. *The What, Why, and How of High Quality Early Childhood Education: A Guide for On-Site Supervision.* Washington, DC: National Association for the Education of Young Children, 1993.

National Academy of Early Childhood Programs. *Accreditation Criteria and Procedures of the National Academy of Early Childhood Programs,* rev. ed. Washington, DC: National Association for the Education of Young Children, 1991. *NAEYC accreditation is an award that designates high quality in a program that has been evaluated voluntarily through a comprehensive accreditation process and has been found to meet accreditation standards. For information on accreditation or this book, call National Association for the Education of Young Children at 800-424-2460.*

National Association for the Education of Young Children and National Association of Early Childhood Specialists in State Departments of Education. *Guidelines for Appropriate Curriculum Content and Assessment in Programs Serving Children Ages 3 through 8.* "Young Children." Washington, DC: National Association for the Education of Young Children, March, 1991. *This is a position statement of the NAEYC and the National Association of Early Childhood Specialists in State Departments of Education. Reprints are available from NAEYC, 1509 16th Street, Washington, DC 20036-1426.*

National Association of Elementary School Principals. *Standards for Quality Programs for Young Children: Early Childhood Education and the Elementary School Principal.* Alexandria, VA: National Association of Elementary School Principals, 1990. *This publication puts developmentally appropriate practices and criteria into an action plan for principals. It is written in a management-by-objectives format stating early childhood standards and quality indicators. For information on this book, write NAESP, 1615 Duke Street, Alexandria, VA 22314.*

National Association of State Boards of Education. *Right from the Start: The Report of the NASBE Task Force on Early Childhood Education.* Alexandria, VA: National Association of State Boards of Education, 1988. *This approximately fifty-page document sets forth a policy agenda to promote the development of young children and design supportive services for families. For information on this book, write to NASBE at 1012 Cameron Street, Alexandria, VA 22314.*

Phillips, Carol Brunson, ed. *Essentials for Child Development Associations Working with Young Children.* Washington, DC: CDA Professional Preparation Program, Council for Early Childhood Professional Recognition, 1991. *This book sets forth and incorporates in its narrative both standards for staff competence and standards of quality as defined by the Council for Early Childhood Professional Recognition. The Child Development Associate certificate awarded by the council is a national competency-based credential that is awarded to those CDA candidates successfully completing the CDA training and credentialing process, thereby meeting the standards of the council. For information on this book or the CDA credential, call 800-424-4310.*

Phillips, Deborah, ed. *Quality in Child Care: What Does Research Tell Us?* Washington, DC: National Association for the Education of Young Children, 1987.

Spodek, Bernard, & Saracho, Olivia. *Right from the Start: Teaching Children Ages Three to Eight.* Boston: Allyn and Bacon, 1994.

Schweinhart, Lawrence, J., Barnes, Helen V., Weikart, David P., Barnett, W. Steven, & Epstein, Ann S. *Significant Benefits: The High Scope Perry Preschool Study through Age 27,* Monograph Number 10. Ypsilanti, MI: High/Scope Press, 1993.

Taylor, Barbara J. *A Child Goes Forth,* 8th ed. Englewood Cliffs, NJ: Prentice-Hall, 1994.

2 Child Development Knowledge and Planning for Young Children

Introduction

Many teachers and caregivers believe they will always remember perfectly all the stages of development of young children. In fact, the details of growth and development, no matter how many children we have taught (or birthed), are usually blurred in our memories. When teachers do lesson planning, it is important that they do not just trust their memories; they should check references to sequences of child development to ensure that they are planning age-appropriate learning activities and appropriate strategies for children's health and well-being. Sometimes teachers do not take time to check references, simply because they do not have a developmental checklist at their fingertips. To address this problem, developmental milestones for ages two to five are listed in this chapter.

Rather than propelling the reader directly to a list of developmental milestones, this chapter will begin with several examples highlighting some of the ways child development knowledge specifically affects lesson plans. What we know about children and how they learn influences our planning for the health and well-being of the children in our classrooms and also affects our planning for children's other learning activities.

Planning for Children's Health and Well-Being

All teachers who work with young children know that children have not yet developed strong skills in health and hygiene. They need to learn these life skills with the guidance of adults who teach them such things as, "Germs make you catch cold or get sick." Children need adult guidance to learn that the spread of germs can be controlled by keeping things we handle clean, by keeping ourselves clean, by washing our hands with soap before eating and after toileting, by covering our sneezes and coughs, and by properly disposing of tissue paper.

Early childhood teachers know that young children do not come to them with these skills in hand! They know, from both observation and their knowledge of basic child development, that children put things in their mouths, take off their coats in winter weather at the first sign of sunshine, forget to wash their hands, blow their noses, or cover their sneezes. They know that young children do not come into classrooms understanding the cause-and-effect aspects of good hygiene and illness, and that if they, as teachers, do not teach children about health and hygiene, children are likely to pick up and pass on germs, get sick, and miss school. Teachers also know that if we begin teaching and practicing these skills at an early age, good health habits in children are likely to become life-long skills.

Two ways to teach children these skills are by doing appropriate adult modeling and by praising children for using good health habits. Basic child development knowledge tells us that this works, because we know that young children copy adult modeling and repeat behaviors for which they are praised. Another effective method for teaching health and hygiene is through regularly planned health education activities and demonstrations of good hygiene. These should be seen regularly in the teacher's lesson plans.

❖❖❖❖

Along the same lines, early childhood teachers know that most young children will not understand cause-and-effect connections about eating healthy foods instead of junk foods, or brushing their teeth after meals. This is why teachers must also put focused activities on nutrition and dental education into their lesson plans throughout the year. What we know about children and what we want them to learn about dental health has an additional impact on the content of lesson plans.

Since teachers or caregivers of young children usually provide meals and/or snacks, it is also important for them to include in lesson plans ways to involve children in the preparation of nutritious foods. Not only will this experience encourage children to eat the foods, but the children's hands-on involvement will simultaneously provide ongoing opportunities to teach them about the nutritional values of foods and to teach other skills. During foods experiences, children will practice skills in sanitary food handling, estimating, pouring, mixing, measuring, counting, and cause and effect. The ways children learn food and nutrition concepts also affects the content of daily lesson planning.

Since health and nutrition are important aspects of both the early childhood setting and lesson planning, it is also wise for teachers share nutritional information with staff and parents whenever possible. Recommended nutritional guidelines from the U.S. Department of Agriculture (USDA) can be used as a resource. Recipes for healthful snacks can be gathered and distributed, and can even be the topic of a parent meeting. Sometimes dentists can be persuaded to visit the classroom to talk about and demonstrate ways to maintain healthy teeth, or to talk about why too much sugar in our foods can damage teeth.

Good resources for interesting and current information on nutrition can be obtained from any program's county Extension Office. Materials in county Extension Offices are developed, gathered, and distributed to the counties in each state by state land grant universities. Other resources can be found in materials from such organizations as the American Dairy Council and the American Heart Association.

Working with parents regarding good nutrition, good health habits, and common health problems is an important part of the early childhood teacher's job. Teachers, like parents, care about children's health and well-being, and teachers know that healthy children are better able to learn. Early childhood teachers demonstrate their commitment to children's health and well-being with comprehensive lesson plans that include focused activities on health education, with appropriate modeling, with praise for good health habits, with knowledge of what to do in health emergencies, and with ongoing health information that they share with parents.

Certain other aspects of health and hygiene in young children also affect early childhood teachers, their planning, and the information they share with parents. In some classrooms, teachers may discover head lice in individual children, and this problem can quickly spread to an entire group. Teachers need to develop a policy and procedure for communicating to all parents what to do about this problem. In the same way, teachers need to know the symptoms of common early childhood diseases, so that if a child is found to have "pink eye," chickenpox, or measles, teachers can quickly communicate necessary information to all parents.

An outbreak of contagious disease can affect the teacher's long-range planning and daily lesson plans; it is difficult to accomplish one's goals when half the children are absent. Therefore, another important kind of information early childhood teachers may wish to share with parents is an immunization schedule. Up-to-date recommendations on immunization can be obtained from any pediatrician's office. Parents should be encouraged to take both preschool children and younger siblings and infants to a doctor or clinic for all recommended immunizations. Preventing those illnesses that can be prevented will save children's lives. In addition, immunizations will keep children healthy; children with health problems are absent more often and have more difficulty in learning. For the convenience of teachers and the parents with whom they work, the most current immunization schedule from the American Academy of Pediatrics and the National Center for Disease Control should be requested from a pediatrician and posted in the classroom.

Height and weight measurements should be taken regularly by early childhood teachers. Children love to see their own growth, and taking these measurements can help prompt teachers to investigate unusual growth spurts or lags. Since children learn so much through their senses, vision and hearing screening or checkups should begin by age three.

Dentists recommend that dental checkups or screening begin by age three, because good care of baby teeth is important to healthy permanent teeth. Dental education among families served by early childhood programs can also help prevent baby bottle tooth decay in infants and toddlers.

Planning for Children's Safety

Safety is another aspect of lesson planning that is affected by what we know about basic child development. Young children know very little about danger or its cause-and-effect relationships. They don't know that certain behavior (not looking before crossing a street, playing with matches, or drinking water from an open pond) can put them in danger. Young children move quickly and impulsively; they can be distracted from seeing a potential hazard because they are busy playing. Children rarely know how to handle themselves in an emergency. Without adult guidance, they might not know what to do or to whom to go for help if they were being abused or molested.

It is because early childhood teachers know that young children come to them with so little knowledge of personal safety that teachers plan learning activities relating to safety throughout the year. Safety activities are planned and entered into lesson plans in a variety of ways.

Some of these planned safety activities involve large-group discussions (group safety rules), large-group practice (fire drills; traffic safety during outdoor walks), and dramatic play concerning safety during free choice or children's activity time (stop, drop, and roll if clothes are on fire; camping safety; beach safety; wearing seat belts). In addition, teachers make entries in lesson plans regarding the times they are going to introduce and explain the safe use of new materials and equipment. Teachers also reinforce safety through incidental learning experiences about working and playing safely throughout each day.

Planning for Other Learning Activities

A knowledge of children's development also affects the way that teachers plan other learning activities and carry out these plans. Young children have not yet developed abstract thinking skills; they learn through concrete experiences. These facts are of the utmost importance when teachers are planning themes and thematic unit activities, and great differences can be seen between the lesson plans of teachers who consider child development in their planning and those who do not.

Planning for Thematic Activities

Let's examine two hypothetical examples in which teachers want children to learn more about frogs. One teacher disregards basic child development knowledge about the ways three- to five-year-olds learn. The other bases her plans on what she knows about child development.

The early childhood teacher who disregards child development knowledge about children's thinking processes might decide to have young children sit for thirty or forty minutes in a large-group circle time while she explains the life cycle of a frog with charts and pictures.

The early childhood teacher who understands basic child development might stimulate an interest in frogs by bringing frogs into the classroom in an aquarium and showing them to children in large group. Then she would explain safe ways in which children could observe and talk about the frogs during free-choice or activity time.

Additionally, the children might take a walk to a pond and find tadpoles to put in the science area for future observation and dictation about the changes they see in the tadpoles. The teacher might even plan to play some instrumental "frog-jumping" music during large-group music time so children can practice creative movement and jumping skills.

In the first example, where attention was not given to basic child development knowledge, the lesson plan would simply reflect thirty to forty minutes for the teacher to talk about frogs in large-group time.

In the other example, the lesson plan would reflect that the teacher had motivated an interest in frogs during large-group time, followed by observation of the frogs and literacy activities during free-choice or children's activity time. The lesson plan would reflect a walk to the pond by the whole group during outdoor time to gather some tadpoles, and would state that children would observe and tell about either the tadpoles and/or the frogs during free-choice time. Finally, the lesson plan would reflect the teacher's plans for large-group music and movement, including "frog jumping." Using basic child development knowledge and checking developmental milestones has a definite impact on the kinds of lesson plans a teacher creates.

Planning for Physical Activities

When early childhood teachers understand the developmental need for children to engage in active play in order to develop physical strength and large-muscle skills, teachers include in their lesson plans specific ways to practice these skills, both indoors and outdoors.

If teachers value the things children learn from the outdoor environment, and understand the health benefits of fresh air and activity, they will always enter activities for outdoor time in the daily lesson plan. This may mean that children will take a walk around the block (practicing safety skills at the same time), walk on a nature trail, practice using skis and snowshoes, or use outdoor equipment in an outdoor play area. If a teacher does not understand, developmentally, that growing young children need fresh air and exercise, it is likely that either the lesson plan will reflect no outdoor activity or that no outdoor activity will occur in actual practice, even if it is listed on the daily schedule.

When teachers understand the developmental need for children's daily practice of large-muscle skills, lesson plans will also reflect these experiences indoors, during free-choice or children's activity time. Some of these activities might be to encourage walking on a balance beam, tossing a pillow filled with crumpled newspaper, or using tumbling mats. If there is enough space in the setting, the lesson plan might show that children will be practicing safe climbing skills on a climber or practicing a variety of skills in a planned obstacle course. No matter how small the classroom space, the lesson plan should reflect the teacher's plans for indoor large muscle activity of some kind.

Planning for the Use of Manipulatives

One of the most important areas of lesson planning that is affected by a knowledge of child development is planning for the use of manipulatives. A teacher who has a classroom of three-year-olds would not start the year by planning to offer fifteen-piece puzzles, very small pegs and boards, small beads for stringing, or tiny Lego blocks. Young threes are likely to put small objects in their mouths, which would make such plans dangerous, and threes would be frustrated by trying to manipulate materials that are too difficult for their skill levels. The teacher who is aware of the developmental needs of threes would offer jumbo Lego blocks, large bristle blocks, large pegs and pegboards, very large beads, and simple three- to five-piece puzzles in both rubber and wood.

Teachers of mixed groups of three- to five-year-olds would give detail in their lesson plans which would state that a variety of three- to ten-piece puzzles would be offered, as would both large and small beads, and/or both jumbo and small Lego blocks. Lesson plans would also specify that an adult should be in the manipulatives area for safe supervision and assistance.

Planning for the Use of Art Media

A variety of creative art media and materials is also important in developing children's manipulative and fine motor skills. In the creative art area, when teachers' lesson plans reflect open-ended art media such as crayons, markers, paper, glue or paste, painting materials, playdoughs or clays, and various collage materials, three- to five-year-olds will not become frustrated with activities or materials that do not match their skill levels. Children will use open-ended materials like these according to their own skill levels. With adult supervision and reinforcement, children will keep using the materials and keep becoming more and more skillful.

Teachers who keep basic child development in mind will have newspapers on the floor or at the easel for paint splashes, because they know that young children are just beginning to learn to control this medium. As they learn, children will also drip and splash, but this gives teachers an opportunity to help children to learn responsibility for cleaning up after using art media materials. Small buckets or dishtubs of soapy water, sponges, and toweling (with instructions for their use) should also be part of the teacher's plans for the creative art area.

Teachers who understand basic child development also know that unless children are shown carefully how to use glue bottles, they will use great gobs instead of small dots of glue. Lesson plans should specify the introduction of such materials as glue bottles and eye droppers for painting. This can be done either with children in a planned small-group time, or with children during free-choice time as they enter the art area and sit down with an adult to explore the media.

Teachers who are attentive to children's learning processes will also know that giving children practice in the process of using these open-ended materials, and guiding and encouraging such practice instead of focusing on an expected product or result, will allow children to learn naturally to be more skillful with art manipulatives and media, and to be delighted with their own creations.

Unfortunately, at times teachers become so excited about something "cute" that can be created as a product in the art area that they may forget basic child development knowledge and the varied skill levels of three- to five-year-olds. For example, a teacher who wants all the children to cut out a predrawn turkey, or even a facsimile of a turkey made by tracing around the child's hand, forgets that while some four- and five-year-olds might have no problem creating this "product," some fours and most threes would be very frustrated in trying to create it. If such turkeys are really important to the teacher, varied options and materials for creating them should be available to the mixed group to match all skill levels and allow for individual creativity.

In these situations, teachers should keep in mind that children will probably be cutting out turkeys, making identical Christmas trees, and fashioning daffodils with nut cups over and over again for years in elementary school. Why do it when they are three and four? With such products, the focus is on small motor skills and following directions. In the early childhood center, there are many other opportunities for children to learn small motor skills and how to follow directions. With young children in the creative art area, the developmental focus in the lesson plan should be on learning to use various art media to plan and problem-solve in order to create their own art.

There will always be certain times of the year when teachers encourage children to create something "special" for a holiday or a gift. However, teachers should always remember that differences in the skill development of three- to five-year-olds must still be considered in lesson planning. No gift or special project, whether it is a turkey or a piece of driftwood decorated with moss and pebbles the children have collected, should be made with all the children sitting together at tables, following step-by-step instructions. The skill levels of children in most early childhood settings vary too widely for this to be effective or enjoyable.

It is far easier for teachers and better for children if teachers plan this sort of activity to occur for several days as one of the regular choices in the art media area. After several days, with the encouragement of adults, all the children would have had time to complete the creation at their own skill level and pace. A separate "art project" time scheduled for all children in the lesson plan usually indicates that the teacher prefers product over process in the use of art media, and, if children are three to five years old, that their individual developmental needs are not being met by the teacher's plans.

Planning for the Use of Sensory Materials

In closing these examples of some of the ways child development knowledge affects the lesson planning of learning activities, we cannot neglect to mention that young children learn both through their active interactions with materials in the learning environment and through all their senses. Lesson plans that take this basic knowledge of child development into consideration will always show sensory learning taking place. Daily lesson plans should contain entries such as listening to sounds or matching sounds; planned tasting of healthy foods, and the use of tactile materials such as sand, water, and playdough or other clays made by the teacher and children.

Some of these experiences might take place and be seen in the lesson plan in large-group time, such as listening to sounds; some might take place in small-group time, such as the planned tasting of healthy foods. Many of these sensory experiences, along with the skills of observing, telling, pouring, estimating, counting, sorting, and seeing cause and effect will take place during free-choice time.

When early childhood teachers plan activities for learning and for the well-being of children, they should not enter these activities into lesson plans because they feel vaguely that these are the "right" things to do or "because these are things we always do" with children. Reasons for entries in lesson plans should be based on sound principles of child development and a knowledge of how young children learn.

Let's take a closer look at what three- to five-year-olds are like. In these brief descriptions of threes to fives, please think about specific ways the teacher's lesson planning will be affected by children's development.

Three-Year-Olds

Threes are more relaxed and cooperative than they were at two; they are eager to please adults, rather than engage in power struggles with them. They are more verbal and social than they were at two, and are beginning to be interested in other children. However, their world still revolves around themselves and their home and family. Teachers are most likely to find threes at play in the housekeeping area, where they feel comfortable and secure. They strongly prefer simple field trips, such as walks in the outdoors or in the neighborhood, over complex trips where they would have to travel to new places.

Three-year-olds have difficulty taking turns and sharing, and this is one of the things they will learn to do in very small groups in work and play situations planned by teachers throughout the year. Threes are beginning to express their ideas, needs, wants, and identities to others. They begin to pretend, and they sometimes have imaginary friends with whom they talk, practicing their growing language skills.

Three-year-olds love to explore the world with their senses; sensory materials, including open-ended art media, are a must in planning for threes. Three-year-olds like to be independent and can do many things for themselves if adults are patient with their dawdling, but threes have difficulty doing more than one thing at a time, such as talking while dressing themselves. Threes are delightfully laid back most of the time and need lots of praise, cuddling, and hugs. What they want most is to feel loved and to feel pride in their growing accomplishments.

Four-Year-Olds

While teachers usually find threes relaxing, fours will keep them extremely busy with new challenges. Four-year-olds seem to be in a constant state of motion, eager for new experiences of any kind. The are very active and extremely verbal; this is the age of constant questions. It is an age of hands-on experimenting and curiosity about everything, including the give and take of cooperative play.

Fours are "workaholics" about play, which is their "work" in learning about the world. They frequently try to do too much because they do not understand their own capabilities or their need for rest. When they become overtired, they get grouchy. Teachers often need to plan strategies to teach fours to calm themselves, relax, and take quiet breaks. A variety of transition activities must be planned in order to move fours smoothly from one activity to another.

Fours are insistent about doing everything for themselves, are often boastful about what they can do, and often bite off more than they can chew. They love to pretend and role-play, incorporating their growing knowledge of the world. However, they are not always sure of the difference between reality and fantasy, and they sometimes have new fears based on their new knowledge. They are friendly and outgoing with adults and are interested in everything adults do. They are interested in their bodies and their gender.

Fours love to help out if they are praised. They also love name-calling, naughty words that get a reaction from adults, silly jokes, and tattling. They are beginning to develop empathy; they can take turns, and sometimes they are both generous and loving to peers, even though they may have had a verbal battle with those same peers within the past hour. Fours require from their teachers a great deal of energy and excellent planning and management skills. They are sometimes exasperating, but they are always interesting and exciting.

Five-Year-Olds

Five-year-olds are more likely to tell you they are five than tell you their names. They are excited about new experiences, but they are still vulnerable; sometimes they need support in facing new situations. Calmer, more confident, and more cooperative than they were at four, fives want to be liked by others; they thrive on adult praise. While they are very practical and industrious little people, fives also love fun and jokes. They love to learn and love to laugh, but hate to be embarrassed or wrong. They are beginning to like rules, especially if the rules are for other people.

If they started the habit of whining or tattling at three or four, and if they have not yet learned that this is inappropriate behavior, some fives will still whine and tattle. Generally, however, fives have good self-control, they have mastered many skills, they can easily share and take turns, they like to help and "teach" younger children, they can understand and follow through on adult expectations, and they are usually quite happy to do so.

Developmental Milestones

Now that we have examined the general characteristics of three- to five-year-olds, we need to consider the ways each child's personal and individual development can impact lesson planning. To do this, we need to look at some developmental milestones in several areas of growth and development for these age groups.

Do not look at these developmental milestones as "achievements." Instead, think of them as signposts along a road or path of continuous and gradual human development. All children are following the same road or path, but each individual child will reach each of these signposts in his or her own way and at different times. Some children will go through these sequences and pass these milestones at a much faster than average rate, and others will proceed much more slowly. These deviations are not abnormal; they are simply individual differences. Watching individual differences with focused interest will help teachers make appropriate adaptations or modifications in lesson planning.

It is important to remember that all children grow and develop at their own pace. The indicators listed in this chapter for each age group (two to three, three to four, and four to five) are based on average behaviors for most children. Observations of three- to five-year-olds, and basic child development information on these age groups such as is taught at the college level are the basis for the developmental indicators in Tables 2-1, 2-2, and 2-3.

When a teacher sees that most children are developing "normally"—that is, following the steps of developmental sequences at about the same times as most other children—or that, whether slower or faster, they are still moving forward in the sequence of growth and development, there is little cause for worry. However, when certain children lag far behind the others in moving through the developmental milestones in an area of growth, teachers should discuss the need for more information with the child's parents. Parents may need assistance in arranging for more in-depth observation or screening by a qualified diagnostician. They should be reassured that there may not be a problem at all, but that the earlier a problem is found, the more quickly it can be addressed successfully.

Developmental Sequences and Lesson Planning

While the general category "age two to three" in Table 2-1 will tell the teacher much about this age group, individual children will move through these developmental milestones at different speeds. Therefore, it is just as important for the teacher to note the sequences of events or milestones of growth within each developmental category (physical, social-emotional, intellectual) as it is to note basic knowledge about a certain chronological age group. In fact, for daily, ongoing lesson planning, the sequences through which the milestones occur has a far greater impact.

For example, all skills are learned bit by bit, in sequence. A child learns the skill of building with blocks in a series of small events. As infants or toddlers, children handle (and probably taste) the blocks. Next they put them into a container and take them out. Then they carry them about, or lay them flat on the floor, or stack a few. Later they will bridge three blocks and set blocks in a pattern to enclose a space. Still later, by the time they are four or five, they will build taller, more complex structures, repeat patterns, and eventually name their buildings and plan ways to build them together.

An understanding of the sequence of block play development is important for early childhood teachers who plan the use of blocks during children's free choice or work/play time. During this time, teachers can encourage and guide children's construction and thinking skills by helping them to notice bridges, spaces, shapes, sizes, and patterns. By knowing the sequence of development of these skills, teachers can more effectively ask appropriate questions of children who are at different skill levels, and assist them in problem-solving skills as they gradually grow more skillful.

The teacher might praise a three-year-old for a flat "road" she built all by herself, and might ask questions of a four-year-old to help him discriminate shapes or see repeated patterns. The teacher might also praise a group of older fours for their construction, take a photo of it, and mount the picture on a poster, along with printed dictation of what the children said about their building and how they built it. In other words, when teachers know the steps of developmental sequences, it helps them both in lesson planning and in interacting with children as they carry out these lesson plans.

Similarly, knowing developmental sequences affects other areas of planning. Understanding motor skill development helps the teacher to plan the kinds of large-muscle experiences that will take place indoors and outdoors with three- to five-year-olds. Knowing the differences in the attitudes of threes and fours about field trips will affect teacher planning about field trips during the beginning of the year. Knowing that threes dawdle and dress themselves slowly will mean that the teacher needs to allow more time in the lesson plan for threes to dress for outdoors or going home. Readers will be able to find many more such examples if they think about these developmental sequences in terms of actual lesson planning.

Table 2-1   Developmental Milestones, Ages Two to Three

Physical:
- Scribbles
- Much body activity and climbing.
- Walks, runs, falls easily, jumps, rolls.
- Needs help in dressing; dwadles.
- Begins to toilet self (frequent accidents).
- Drinks from a cup, uses spoon (many spills).
- Needs fresh air and exercise.

Intellectual:
- Uses two- to three-word sentences; usually hard to understand.
- Very curious; likes to examine and explore with all senses.
- Good observer, listener; understands more than adults realize.
- Growing interest in books; loves "lap stories."
- Names familiar objects, people, and pictures.
- Can associate functions of familiar objects.
- Tries to take things apart.

Social-emotional:
- Often watches other children, but plays alone.
- Little interest in peers; hits, pushes, grabs.
- Is very possessive; needs help in defining personal space.
- Begins to play "house" or pretend.
- Watches and copies family or caregivers' modeling.
- Suspicious of new situations.
- Power struggles and tantrums are common.
- Needs security of consistency in routines and guidance.
- Shows independence of spirit.
- Loves praise.

Note: Successful adult interactions and guidance encompass tact, calmness, diplomacy, and a combination of ignoring and praising. Rigid schedules for play are not appropriate. Adults must safety-proof environment.

Table 2-2   Developmental Milestones, Ages Three to Four

Physical:
- Still eats small servings.
- Some still need naps; some do not.
- Helps dress self; undresses fairly well.
- Toilets self; accidents still common.
- Climbs steps alternating feet; loves to climb on and over/under things.
- Runs well; pulls, pushes or steers wheel toys; jumps.
- Throws, catches, and begins to be able to balance on one foot and hop.
- Walks on balance beam or line.
- Can do simple puzzles or stack a few blocks or rings.
- Takes things apart.
- Enjoys using dough, clay, paint, etc., and movement with music.
- Tears paper; with practice, tears shapes.
- Begins to snip edges of paper with blunt scissors.

Intellectual:
- Listens to and repeats stories, rhymes, songs.
- Talks in simple sentences; can be understood.
- Knows age and name; talks a lot; sometimes has imaginary friend.
- Begins to recognize (match) colors.
- Tells about own "artwork" after it's done (product-oriented art is not appropriate).
- Begins to ask questions and make associations.
- Uses blocks and compares differences in simple shapes.
- Understands "today" and often, "tomorrow," but lives in the NOW.
- Learns through hands-on activity and the senses.
- Loves sand, water, mud, clays.
- Loves repetition.

Social-emotional:
- Plays well with one or two peers sometimes.
- Often participates well in group activity for short time.
- Learning to use words to tell own wants or needs to others.
- Plays with same toys as others in a small group.
- Sometimes will take turns or share.
- Watches and copies adult modeling.
- Pretends; plays house or imitates family; notices sex differences.
- Enjoys own birthday and simple celebrations, especially at own home.
- Begins to show sympathy.
- Still fears new things; likes rituals and consistent routines.
- Wants to please; generally cooperative with adults.
- Can become jealous and revert to babyhood for attention.
- Wants to try to do things independently (self care).
- Thrives on praise, hugs and positive reinforcement.
- Has sense of pride in accomplishments.

Note: Successful adult interactions and guidance encompass tact, calmness, diplomacy, and a combination of ignoring and praising. Rigid schedules for play are not appropriate. Adults must safety-proof environment.

Table 2-3 Developmental Milestones, Age Four to Five

Physical:
- Handles blunt scissors and simple tools safely with adult guidance.
- Very active; uses slides, climbers, tunnels, and balance beams in many ways.
- Begins to do simple jump rope.
- Hops, gallops, begins learning to skip.
- Pumps a swing.
- Throws and catches balls easily.
- Toilets self; washes self; helps clean up toys; helps with "jobs."
- Enjoys using variety of open-ended art media, and creative movement to music (all kinds).
- Workaholic about learning through play; often becomes overtired.
- Builds vertical block structures.

Note: Sequence of scissors skill development: (1) tearing, (2) snipping, (3) cutting apart, (4) cutting on a straight line, (5) cutting curved lines, (6) cutting crooked lines. In all physical areas, fives progress very easily.

Intellectual:
- Talks a lot; uses compound sentences and increased vocabulary.
- This is the "age of questions."
- Loves to experiment; wants to know *how* and *why.*
- Learns by doing and can tell others own observations.
- Likes books, stories, and acting them out.
- Can make up own stories, songs, and jokes.
- Interested in own forms of writing words.
- Designs and constructs; uses original ideas with art and blocks.
- Still confused about "real" versus "pretend."
- Understands yesterday, today, and tomorrow.
- Responds well to "what if" and open questions.
- Can match and sort; makes many associations.
- Enjoys nature and cooking activities.
- Still loves sand, water, mud, and clays.

Note: In all areas above, fives become more skillful and verbal.

Social-emotional:
- Enjoys peers, makes "friends" and plays cooperatively
- Often plays or builds with a purpose and delegates roles.
- Interested in world outside of the family.
- Can share and take turns, but sometimes teases or calls names.
- Enjoys participating as member of group.
- Enjoys "jobs" and holidays.
- Enjoys imitating adults and using positive social language and manners (copies "bad" words, too).
- Empathy, sensitivity, and conscience start to develop.
- Fours show many emotions, most of them loudly.
- Fours can separate from parents fairly easily for child care.
- Fours are impatient and change moods often; test limits.
- Fours want to be more independent then they are able; still resist unpredictable changes.
- Fours still need lots of praise and reassurance.

Note:
- Fives are more even-tempered and cooperative than fours.
- Fives can accept change more easily now, and are comfortably independent.
- Fives do less "showing off" and begin to have a comfortable sense of who they are and what they are able to do.
- Fives begin to like rules, especially for others.
- Fives can play simple group games and can accept group experiences. They can play cooperatively most of the time, taking turns easily.

Source (Tables 2-1, 2-2, and 2-3): Evelyn Petersen, Parent Talk: The Art of Parenting Video Series—The Young Child. Traverse City, MI: Platte River Printing, (1990), *Leader's Guide,* pp. 48–51.

Summary

In this chapter, what we have really been talking about is those for whom we are planning when we do lesson plans. We have covered the ways lesson planning relates to the well-being of children (their health, nutrition and safety) and have presented some examples of lesson planning as it relates to thematic activities, physical learning activities, manipulative activities, art media activities, and sensory activities. We have looked at both the general characteristics of three- to five-year-olds and the developmental milestones that occur in this age group's physical, social-emotional, and intellectual growth, as seen in Tables 2-1, 2-2, and 2-3.

Developmental sequences in the practice of skills affect lesson planning. This will be a subject that surfaces again, in more detail, in Chapter 4 of this guidebook. In Chapter 3, we will return to the subject of organizing and managing the horizontal curriculum (content or interest-based curriculum information) for lesson planning.

Self-Study Activities

1. Plan a way in which you can observe varied ages of children in public. You may decide to go to a mall, to a family fast-food restaurant, or to pediatrician's office waiting room. If so, identify yourself and your reasons for being there, and obtain permission from the doctor or receptionist. Take notes on the physical appearance, behaviors and skills you observe being performed by various children. See if this information helps you estimate the ages of the children you are observing. Then, if possible, check to see how close you were to being correct.

2. Arrange to visit a child care center (but not one in which you are already involved and know the children) and engage in the same process. Check with the child care provider or teachers to see if your determination of ages is correct. You may also wish to make notes, for your own personal use only, on whether or not planning in the center matched skill levels of the children.

Resources for Further Reading

Ames, Louise Bates, & Ilg, Frances L. *Your Three Year Old: Friend or Foe.* New York: Dell, 1985.

Ames, Louise Bates, & Ilg, Frances L. *Your Four Year Old: Wild and Wonderful.* New York: Dell, 1976, reprinted 1994.

Ames, Louise Bates, & Ilg, Frances L. *Your Five Year Old: Sunny and Serene.* New York: Dell, 1979.

Berk, Laura E. *Infants and Children: Prenatal through Early Childhood.* Boston: Allyn and Bacon, 1994.

Bredekamp, Sue, ed. *Developmentally Appropriate Practice in Early Childhood Programs Serving Children from Birth through Age 8.* expanded ed. Washington, DC: National Association for the Education of Young Children, 1992.

Dodge, Diane Trister, &nd Colker, Laura. *The Creative Curriculum for Early Childhood,* 3rd ed. Washington, DC: Teaching Strategies, Inc., 1988, 1992.

DeVries Rheta, & Kohlberg, Lawrence. *Constructivist Early Education: Overview and Comparison with Other Programs.* Washington, DC: National Association for the Education of Young Children, 1987.

Elkind, David. *A Sympathetic Understanding of the Child: Birth to Sixteen*, 3rd ed. Boston: Allyn and Bacon, 1994.

Elkind, David. *Images of the Young Child: Collected Essays on Development and Education.* Washington, DC: National Association for the Education of Young Children, 1993.

Engstrom, Georgianna, ed. *The Significance of the Young Child's Motor Development.* Washington, DC: National Association for the Education of Young Children, 1971; 8th printing, 1994.

Forman, George, & Hill, Fleet. *Constructive Play: Applying Piaget in the Preschool.* Reading, MA: Addison-Wesley, 1984.

Forman, George E., & Kuschner, David S. *The Child's Construction of Knowledge: Piaget for Teaching Children.* Washington, DC: National Association for the Education of Young Children, 1983.

Katz, Lillian, Evangelou, Demetra, & Hartman, Jeanette. *The Case for Mixed-Age Grouping in Early Education.* Washington, DC: National Association for the Education of Young Children, 1990.

Kendrick, Abby, Kaufman, Roxanne, & Messenger, Katherine. *Healthy Young Children: A Manual for Programs,* revised ed. Washington, DC: National Association for the Education of Young Children, 1994

McAfee, Oralie, & Leong, Deborah. *Assessing and Guiding Young Children's Development and Learning.* Boston: Allyn and Bacon, 1994

Peterson, R., & Felton-Collins, V. *The Piaget Handbook for Teachers and Parents.* Williston, VT: Teachers College Press, 1986.

Phillips, Carol Brunson, ed. *Essentials for Child Development Associates Working with Young Children.* Washington, DC: Council for Early Childhood Professional Recognition, 1991.

Thompson, Eleanor, D. *Pediatric Nursing: An Introductory Text,* 5th ed. Philadelphia: W. B. Saunders/Harcourt Brace Jovanovich, 1987.

3 Interest-Based Planning

The Spontaneous and Horizontal Curriculum

Introduction

In this chapter, we will explore some of the ways teachers translate their ideas from thought to paper and then to classroom activities. Many of these ideas are based on factual content about topics in which the teacher or the children have an interest. How do teachers get interest-based information and ideas into their lesson plans?

To answer this question, we need to focus on the spontaneous and the horizontal curriculum, two of the three parts of curriculum information discussed in Chapter 1. The spontaneous and horizontal parts of the curriculum are interest-based because, in both cases, the information used as grist for the mill of lesson planning is based on the interests of the children and teachers.

We will examine the kind of lesson planning that is almost purely spontaneous in nature, and compare this to long-range horizontal planning, which is based on emerging interests that are expanded with factual content through thematic units. Appropriate ways to use themes in one's planning will be discussed, and an example of horizontal planning, in which themes and subthemes appear in outline form for a nine-month program year, will also be examined.

One of the marks of competency in an early childhood teacher is the ability to organize, preplan, and manage interest-based curriculum ideas. These ideas should be visible in lesson plans and in the implementation of those plans, flowing smoothly throughout the program year. The flip side of this coin is that good early childhood teachers must also be flexible, always ready to change or modify their plans to meet the needs of their children, and/or to respond to "teachable moments" with unplanned, incidental teaching. Competent teachers plan carefully, but maintain flexibility.

Spontaneous Curriculum Planning

In some classrooms, curriculum and lesson planning seem to be based entirely on the changing daily interests of children. In such classrooms, the teacher might use a very general plan for the day, or post a schedule that allows ample time for children to explore and experiment in all learning centers of the setting. The children's interests are daily sources for impromptu learning, such as the study of a fuzzy caterpillar that wanders into the classroom.

Sometimes this sort of teachable moment is expanded into further examination of the topic, such as the addition of a terrarium and caterpillars to the setting, or the placement of a cocoon in a jar in the science area. The children might paint or draw caterpillars, and they might read or act out the story of "The Hungry Caterpillar."

The advantages for basing all of one's curriculum and lesson plans on the spontaneous and changing interests of children are considerable. The teacher and children are enthusiastic; learning is concrete and hands-on. It is both relevant to children's interests and very enjoyable. However, excessive reliance on spontaneous or spur-of-the-moment curriculum often results in the inability of the teacher to do advance planning or to document in the lesson plan the kinds of skill and content learning that are actually occurring.

As readers can imagine, if the program is funded by an agency that requires compliance and documentation of certain performance standards, the supervisor of a teacher using only spontaneous lesson planning might face a dilemma. On the one hand, the supervisor sees that the learning is fun and appropriate to the children's interests and skill levels. On the other hand, there is usually no evidence that the teacher has long-range or short-range goals and objectives, or a plan to develop certain skills that children may need.

Although children do gain many bits and pieces of knowledge and skills, there is a lack of overall integration and direction in what they learn. It is almost as if the teacher comes into the setting saying, "Well, what do we feel like doing today?" Sometimes the opportunity of expanding and developing specific content learning, or of practicing cognitive and psychomotor skills, is not taken. Sometimes it happens sporadically, but is not developed to full advantage for children's learning.

Spontaneous curriculum and the lesson planning that is related to it is always a valid part of the teacher's total curriculum information. It is definitely interest-based, and it has value, but it is not, in my opinion, strong enough to stand on its own as the only kind of curriculum information (ideas, activities, experiences) to use in one's lesson planning.

Horizontal Curriculum Planning

Most teachers use the spontaneous interests of children, along with their own interests and goals, as a springboard for the development of further factual or content learning. Horizontal curriculum information and the lesson planning related to it is also interest-based, but it is more fully developed and expanded than is purely spontaneous curriculum information.

Ideas, activities, and experiences emerge from both the children's and the teacher's interests. Sometimes ideas are sparked by the children's parents. When genuine interests are identified, they are developed into themes or thematic units which include many related ideas and activities. The themes the teacher develops carry the children from the beginning to the end of the program year.

As long as early childhood teachers use the interests and skills levels of the *children* as determining factors in choosing and developing their themes, they will find that they have little difficulty in successfully pursuing this avenue of curriculum and the lesson planning related to it.

One way of organizing and expanding one's thinking about themes or thematic units is by seeing them as teaching and learning webs. Ideally, these theme ideas would be drawn not only from the teacher's ideas but also from those that emerge from the children's own interests.

For example, if children are digging outdoors and become interested in the earth, the teacher might expand what they are experiencing and learning about soil. Many related topics with accompanying activities could be developed, as in the following (by no means all-inclusive) list.

1. Ways to clean up soil or dirt
2. Experiments with soil (look at it with magnifying glass, smell it, see if it dissolves, see what disappears in it over time)
3. Exploration of different kinds of soil (sand, topsoil, clay, gravel-mixed, etc.)

This list could lead naturally to even more topics and related activities. For example, examining topsoil could lead to planting things in dirt to see if they grow or to see what they need in order to grow. Examining clay might lead to exploring different kinds of clay and to making things from clay. In turn, this might lead to examining clay pottery of different cultures.

Figure 3-1 presents an example of a simple teaching and learning web that could have evolved from either the children's spontaneous interests in soil or the teacher's goal to motivate the children's interest in studying soil. There are many ways to expand this web in new directions. Other webs will be found in Chapter 11 of this guidebook, which concerns integrated activities.

Whether the teacher plans his or her thematic units with notes, lists, or drawings of webs, at some point they should appear as a written, long-range, horizontal plan for the year that should be flexible enough to allow for changing needs and interests. When teachers organize their thematic units in this way, they have created a *horizontal plan*. Horizontal planning follows an ongoing timeline for the program year; the teacher's themes and thematic units serve as consecutive guideposts or milestones in the timeline.

Teachers may develop their own themes, or use resource books for thematic unit ideas. They may use themes they have seen as examples in textbooks or in various curriculum modules, themes they have heard about from other teachers or in workshops, and themes they have developed by brainstorming with other adults.

For the purposes of the lesson-planning system in this guidebook, the sources of thematic ideas are not relevant. Our purpose is to help the teacher conceive of

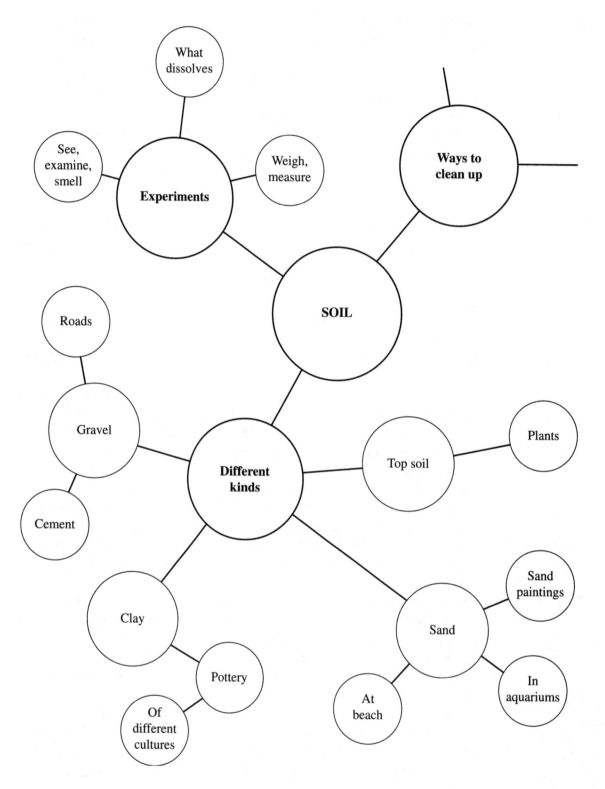

Figure 3-1 Teaching Web Example—Soil

all thematic curriculum ideas, activities and experiences as *horizontal curriculum information,* and help the teacher understand how to organize this information and use it systematically in lesson planning.

A few important points about themes bear mentioning. Although teachers draw thematic unit ideas from many sources, best practice indicates that teachers should choose among themes that are the most relevant to program priorities and to the children and families with whom they work. Teachers must sometimes hold their own interest in a particular theme in check until the children's interest is realistically evaluated. Teachers should not merely choose a theme they think is "neat" or "cute."

In addition, teachers should ask themselves what the children will learn from experiencing activities related to a particular theme. When evaluating a theme for possible introduction to the group, teachers would be wise to write down what children might actually learn from a particular thematic unit or a teaching and learning web.

In other words, as a teacher, you can choose any themes you wish, as long as they reflect your children's interests and are age-appropriate. Usually, simple themes are explored at the beginning of the year and become more complex as the year progresses. When you put appropriate themes on paper, starting at the beginning of the year and proceeding to the end, you are doing a written, long range horizontal plan.

The best horizontal planning begins with several overall or primary themes that reflect program priorities for children and that reappear regularly throughout the year. Secondary themes and subthemes should frequently mesh with these overall themes. These subthemes, often called *thematic units,* can be varied. Their content depends on the ongoing or changing interests of children and their families, the teacher's and program's priorities or values, cultural influences, and the geography that influences curriculum choices.

The Written Horizontal Plan

Now we must get down to the brass tacks of meshing the long-range horizontal plan with the daily lesson plan. The teacher's horizontal plan should be accessible and available each day when the teacher does the daily lesson plan, and also whenever the teacher spends time thinking ahead to the following days or weeks.

When the teacher does his or her daily lesson plan, activities and learning experiences relating to the current theme or teaching and learning web are entered into the lesson plan in various spaces. Many of these will be entered in the child-initiated or free-choice section of the lesson plan, and others may be entered in the teacher's small-group or large-group time spaces.

For example, if the group is involved in a unit or a teaching and learning web about apples, the teacher may have planned a story about apples or creative movement about apple trees growing for large-group time. In free-choice or activity time, the teacher may have planned that children will cut up apples, make applesauce, and do tempera apple prints. In small-group time, the teacher may have planned that children will use food mills to strain and eat the applesauce they have cooked during free-choice time, and will discuss and dictate written words about the ways apples change during cooking.

When the teacher has his or her long-range horizontal written plan in plain view during daily lesson planning, the long-range plan also helps the teacher to see other thematic or webbing possibilities that might emerge during the following days. In addition, seeing the overall direction of the plan as a timeline helps the teacher do advance planning for future thematic units. This advance planning might include arrangements for visitors, field trips relating to the unit or web, or notes on special items that the teacher may want to gather to bring into the learning setting.

Horizontal Plan Outlines

I believe an outline method works best in organizing a written horizontal plan on paper, for the following reasons:

1. The outline format presents a natural, gradual flow of ideas.
2. It clearly shows primary, secondary, and subthemes.
3. Thematic units can easily be changed to match children's needs and interests. New webbing resulting from children's interests can easily be incorporated.
4. No dates or weeks for themes are rigidly set in stone; time frames are flexible.
5. Seeing the entire horizontal plan helps the teacher in advance planning of visitors and field trips, and in gathering particular items that may enrich the thematic unit.

The teacher and staff can move along the horizontal plan outline without deadlines, staying in tune with the changing developmental needs and interests of children in the group. Outlines are flexible; flexibility is a must for the early childhood professional.

In the example of horizontal planning found in Table 3-1, the overall or primary themes of self-esteem, caring for and learning from others, and caring about the world we live in reappear throughout the year in secondary and subthemes. Because I chose the themes in this horizontal plan, these themes also reflect my own values, just as your choices as a teacher would reflect your values. Please skim over the example of the horizontal plan that follows, and note some of the themes that recur.

In this example of horizontal planning, we see that the positive self-esteem of the child is the overriding goal. The themes incorporate activities that help chil-

Table 3-1   Example of a Horizontal Plan

  I. Me and My World (September/October)
     A. Me
        1. My body
        2. My health and fitness
        3. My senses
        4. My feelings
        5. My safety
     B. Families
        1. My family
        2. Brothers and sisters
        3. Other families
     C. Homes
        1. My home
        2. Other kinds of homes
        3. Family fun (leisure interests, hobbies)
        4. Family routines (rules, eating sleeping, beds)

 II. My Expanding World (October/November)
     A. Friends
     B. Changes
        1. In air, weather, sky
        2. In the water around us
        3. In things that grow in the earth around us
     C. Foods
        1. Of the orchard (fruits and seeds)
        2. Of the water (lakes or sea)
        3. Of gardens or farms (squashes, corn)
        4. Breads—food everyone eats

III. Special Days in My World (November/December)
     A. Changes in seasons and special days
     B. Holidays—what they mean to us
        1. Family fun and family traditions
        2. Friends and company
        3. Shopping and gifts
        4. Traveling
        5. Special foods

 IV. Learning More about My World (January/February)
     A. How I learn best
        1. Senses, questions
        2. Experiments and changes
     B. Shapes are all around us
     C. Staying healthy keeps me learning
     D. Learning from friends

  V. Learning More about My World (February/March)
     A. Adults help me learn (include snow plowers, trash collectors, linemen, etc., not just
        professionals)
     B. Important places where I learn
     C. Staying safe and healthy as I learn

 VI. Sharing My World (March/April)
     A. My world is always changing
     B. Seasons and timelines
     C. Changes in the environment

VII. Sharing My World (April/May)
     A. Plants grow, change, and share my world
        1. Baby plants (seeds, cuttings, care)
        2. Big plants (trees, flowers, food plants, care)

(Cont.)

Table 3-1   *(Continued)*

3. Plants help us and need our help
B. How animals grow, change, and share my world
  1. Animal babies (and human babies)
  2. Animal "clothes" or coverings (and ours)
  3. Animal homes (and ours)
    a. Animals that fly
    b. Animals in the sea, water, and mud
    c. Animals in the woods, forests, and meadows
    d. Animals in the desert and mountains
    e. Animals on farms or in zoos
  4. Animals help us and need our help

dren to feel special and competent, and help them to understand and proud of their own capabilities. Underlying these basic themes is the unspoken but implied basic human question, "Who am I and how do I fit in to a changing world?"

Look again at the seven main parts of the horizontal plan in this outline. The concept of caring about oneself is incorporated in I, II, and III of the outline ("Me and My World," "My Expanding World," and "Special Days in My World"). The concept of caring about both oneself and others in one's world is incorporated in parts IV and V, "Learning More about My World." The concept of caring about our world is incorporated in parts VI and VII, "Sharing My World."

All seven of the sections in this outline include concepts on *caring* and *changes,* which are recurring subthemes, as are *health* and *safety.* Health and safety are integral parts of caring about oneself, and coping with change is a necessary life skill, important to self-esteem. These themes on self-esteem, health and safety, and caring are variations in this horizontal plan that repeat themselves as would certain patterns of threads or colors in a design.

As teachers develop written horizontal plans, they may arbitrarily decide just how long each theme or subtheme should last. However, putting down highly specific days or weeks for each theme may end up putting a teacher in a bind. In actual practice with young children, flexible time frames are easier to work with than specific dates.

In the example of the horizontal plan presented here, the time frames during which themes might occur is implied in suggested time blocks, but the dates are flexible; for example, the children may become so entranced with a particular subtheme or thematic unit that the teacher will want to spend more time expanding it or may even wish to repeat it. A new teaching or learning web might emerge from the children's interests, and this could alter the time frame. These additional emergent curriculum ideas can be easily incorporated into an outline format.

On the other hand, the children may have little interest in a subtheme planned by the teacher. Such a theme could easily be suspended, or cut from five or six days to two days. In these ways, the outline format for horizontal planning helps the teacher become much more open and responsive to children.

Comments on the Horizontal Plan Example

Teachers will always need to modify their horizontal plans to fit the interests, culture, climate, and geography in which they find themselves. The example presented was based on the interests, climate, and geography of a program in northern Michigan. The choices for time frames for learning about plants and animals are reflective of that geographic area and the families that live there.

Please look at IIC on "Foods." In some geographic locations, teachers might emphasize foods of the water and sea and disregard orchards because they would want to concentrate on themes with which their students have real experience. For the same reasons, in VIIB teachers might focus only on those animals that live in their own geographic area.

It is also important to note that many of the themes on plants and animals would have been introduced in various incidental teaching throughout the entire year as children made ongoing observations about plants and animals, such as how they look, where they live, and what they need.

Certain parts of the example presented can obviously be extended, and, in actual practice based on children's emerging interests, they were. For example, Part VA and B, on "Adults Help Me Learn" and "Important Places Where I Learn," led to other interesting subthemes or thematic units, such as the exploration of tools adults use to help us and the many ways we can travel to particular places. (In any travel unit, an awareness by children of modifications such as wheelchairs and ramps should be included.)

Here is another example of a modification that occurred in pursuing this example of a horizontal plan. The intense interest of children in their own hearts emerged during the exploration of heart shapes in Part IVB on "Shapes" in our world. This naturally led to activities about our bodies and our hearts. Resource materials obtained to pursue this interest were the American Heart Association's package of early childhood learning materials about the heart, which provided a natural transition to Part IVC, "Staying Healthy."

The point is that the use of a horizontal plan in outline format is flexible enough to allow teachers to include, expand, and build on the emerging interests of their own children in long-range and daily lesson planning. The pace of the steps in such an outline might be altered, but in an outline format, changes in pace will not detract from the overriding goals and direction of the teacher's horizontal plan.

One more comment on the horizontal plan in Table 3-1 should be made. The seven parts of the outline in this plan increase in pace and complexity as the year progresses. Children in a mixed group of three- to five-year-olds could not comfortably handle the complexity and pace of the thematic units or webs in Parts VI and VII at the beginning of the year, but could do so eagerly and easily at the end of the year.

Teachable Moments

Teachable moments are discussed in this chapter because they are a part of the spontaneous curriculum. The term *teachable moments* refers to teaching and learning opportunities that usually occur in response to an interest that emerges spontaneously from a child or from the children in the group. As an observer and frequent evaluator of competence among early childhood teachers, I feel that the ability to think on your feet, respond, and expand learning appropriately when a spontaneous opportunity occurs is the mark of an excellent early childhood teacher.

The ability to use teachable moments to do incidental teaching is an important skill. These moments cannot be preplanned and written in a lesson plan. Early childhood teachers need to be open and ready at all times to capture teachable moments and capitalize on these teaching opportunities. Many teachers naturally do this kind of on-the-spot teaching. In observing and evaluating teachers, I have found that the ability to respond to children in teachable moments is most often demonstrated by teachers who create careful and comprehensive lesson plans.

These are teachers whose lesson plans demonstrate that they are doing both horizontal and vertical planning. They have carefully thought out their long-range and monthly goals as well as their daily objectives. Lesson plans include both thematic content that is appropriate to children's interests, and activities that are appropriate for practicing specific skills at varying skill levels.

Readers may wonder how such careful planners could also be spontaneous teachers. Detailed and comprehensive planning might also characterize a person who has rigid expectations, or one who lacks the creativity and divergent thinking skills necessary to respond spontaneously to incidental teaching moments. Assuming that a person who creates careful lesson plans is one who never could be spontaneous is just as biased as assuming that a "free spirit" sort of teacher will always be able to respond to teachable moments. Conclusions on this interesting issue, if any, must be based on real experience and not on assumptions.

The best way to explain what I have seen in practice—that most teachers who do detailed lesson plans are also those most likely to risk changing their plans to capitalize on a teachable moment—is the way a college instructor once explained it to me as a student: Those who have a strong, healthy tree with strong roots and strong primary branches are those who are the most likely to go out on a limb.

Strong horizontal and vertical planning are the strong roots and the tree of the teacher's curriculum. Teachers who have mastered these elements can always risk going out on a limb or a smaller branch (leaving the lesson plan to capitalize on teachable moments) because the tree is strong and will always be there for them, whenever they want to return.

Summary

In this chapter we have discussed the spontaneous and the horizontal curriculum, or the interest-based parts of the teacher's curriculum information. We have seen that much more content learning can occur when teachers expand and build on the children's spontaneous interests, develop themes and units based on these interests, and put these plans in written form. Daily lesson planning and advance planning relating to the values and priorities of the children, teacher, and program are easier to accomplish when one has a horizontal plan in writing.

We have also examined one way to put the teacher's horizontal curriculum ideas into writing in a long-range plan for the year. A horizontal plan in outline format was suggested and discussed in terms of its many advantages. An outline format is more flexible and more in tune with the changing interests of children than are horizontal formats that are dependent on rigid timelines and dates.

The horizontal plan presented in this chapter (Table 3-1) is only an example. Horizontal planning among teachers can and should differ on the basis of personal values; program priorities; the interests of children, parents, or the community; and the geographic nature and culture of the program's location. The concepts presented Table 3-1 can be used in helping teachers to develop their own long range or horizontal plans for the year. Any elements of the example presented can be incorporated into the planning of teachers who find them appropriate.

Books that particularly emphasize themes and emergent curriculum are recommended at the end of this chapter. Whether or not teachers use resource books to plan thematic units, they should be sure to include themes that will really interest children, not just themes they think are "neat." Teachers should give careful thought to what children will be learning from the themes chosen.

As themes and their related activities are used in horizontal planning, they will make an ongoing written appearance on lesson plans. Many activities chosen for daily and weekly lesson plans will mesh with and reinforce a theme. However, other activities in daily lesson plans may be chosen because they help the children learn particular skills. These skill-focused activities, occurring regularly throughout the year, are another very important kind of planning which proceeds simultaneously with the teacher's horizontal plan. These skill-focused activities are the *vertical* part of the curriculum, which is the subject of the next chapter.

Self-Study Activities

1. Critique a thematic unit you have written or used in terms of the children's parents and the community in which you live. Would adults be interested and supportive of your choice? What additional ideas might they want you to add?

2. Choose one thematic unit that you have done. Now imagine your program and classroom in an entirely different geographic location and climate, and find ways to modify your web or thematic unit to fit that new culture. For example, what would change if you lived in the desert of the Southwest, or on the tundra near Nome, Alaska?

Resources for Further Reading

Note: Many resources for activities in specific areas of the curriculum are listed in Appendix C. Those listed here are more specific to the subject of this chapter.

Becker, Joni, Reid, Karen, Steinhaus, Pat, & Wieck, Peggy. Themestorming: *How to Build Your Own Theme-Based Curriculum the Easy Way.* Beltsville, MD: Gryphon House, 1994.

Berry, Carla F., & Mindes, Gayle. *Planning a Theme-Based Curriculum: Goals, Themes, Activities, and Planning Guides for 4's and 5's.* New York: Goodyear Books/HarperCollins, 1993.

Brewer, Jo Ann. *Introduction to Early Childhood Education—Preschool through Primary Grades.* Boston: Allyn and Bacon, 1995.

Fortson, Laura Rogers, & Reiff, Judith. *Early Childhood Curriculum: Open Structures for Integrative Learning.* Boston: Allyn and Bacon, 1995.

Gryphon House. *The Giant Encyclopedia of Theme Activities for Children 2 to 5.* Beltsville, MD: Gryphon House, 1993.

Jones, Elizabeth, & Nimmo, John. *Emergent Curriculum.* Washington, DC: National Association for the Education of Young Children, 1994.

Katz, Lillian, & Chard, Sylvia C. *Engaging Children's Minds: The Project Approach.* Norwood, NJ: Ablex, 1989.

Kostelnik, Marjorie, Howe, Donna, Payne, Kit, Rohde, Barbara, Spalding, Grace, Stein, Laura, & Whitbeck, Duane. *Teaching Young Children Using Themes: Ages 2 to 6.* Glenview, IL: Good Year Books/Scott Foresman and Company, 1991.

Schiller, Pam, & Rossano, Joan. *The Instant Curriculum.* Beltsville, MD: Gryphon House, 1990.

Warren, Jean. *Theme-A-Saurus.* Everett, WA: Warren, 1989.

4 Skill-Focused Planning: The Vertical Curriculum

Part 1: The Need for Planning and Management of Skill-Focused Activities

Introduction

The two interest-based parts of the curriculum tend to emphasize interesting factual content, which adds to the child's body of knowledge. The vertical part of the curriculum, on the other hand, emphasizes planning that helps children develop their cognitive and psychomotor skills and helps them in the process of thinking and constructing their own knowledge.

Planned activities based on vertical curriculum information would include many types of problem-solving learning experiences in observing, describing, measuring, experimenting, and comparing. They would include matching, grouping, pairing, ordering, and cause and effect; they would also include many types of perceptual-motor experiences, as well as memory and language activities.

When teachers use only spontaneous and horizontal or interest-based ideas and information in lesson planning, children may have many concrete and enjoyable hands-on experiences and learn many facts about things that interest them. If learning experiences are appropriate, children may also learn many skills. However, when teachers plan primarily with the spontaneous and horizontal curriculum, and "work in" the practice of skills (the vertical curriculum) without long- and short-range planning, children may not have enough opportunities to increase their thinking and psychomotor skills in every area of skill-focused learning, every day. This chapter will address this issue by presenting a management system for skill-focused planning that is tied to the sequential development of skills.

Why Is a Management System Needed?

Some readers may believe that a management system for the vertical curriculum is not necessary. They might say that if teachers do a really great job of offering a rich and varied learning environment, encourage children to use all learning centers, and give them ample time to use the materials in these centers, the problem of increasing all the children's thinking and psychomotor skills will take care of itself. They may think that all children will gain mastery of all skills simply by working with appropriate materials and activities each day.

Actual experience tells us that this is not always true. Most of the time, some children who are actively involved in experiences in all areas of the setting do get enough practice in most of the skills we want them to develop. However, many other children do not get enough guidance, reinforcement, and practice in every skill area to reach their full potentials.

There are several reasons for this. One reason is simply the preferences of children making choices during free-choice or child-initiated time. Some children want to spend most of their time in the art or fine motor manipulatives areas, and avoid the large-muscle area and its opportunities for building large-muscle physical and perceptual-motor skills. Other children might be particularly inventive, skillful, and verbal in using the literacy and dramatic play areas, but may spend very little of their time in the fine motor and manipulatives areas.

Another factor that inhibits the ability of children to gain enough practice in all the skills they need in all areas of the setting is inherent in the makeup of many of today's early childhood classrooms, which are becoming more diverse in nature. This diversity creates a need for greater attention to individualized teaching.

Although many early childhood classrooms continue to maintain age divisions for three- and four-year-old groups, in other centers we find mixed groups of children from young three's to age five. These demographics are more prevalent in day care centers, which tend to serve children from ages two and a half or three to school age, but there also seems to be a trend to integrate more three-year-olds into classrooms that were formerly homogeneous groups of four-year-olds. For example, the Head Start program has full authorization to serve three-year-olds as well as fours. On fall enrollment dates in the 1989–1990 to 1993–1994 school years, Head Start classrooms averaged 62 percent four-year-olds and 28 percent three-year-olds.

In addition to the chronological mixture of children beginning to appear in early education classrooms, children enter today's centers with far more diverse backgrounds and skill levels than they did a decade ago. Although some children have reaped the benefits of more sophisticated and skilled parenting, others have stressful home lives or may even come from abusive homes. Many more children in today's centers have been identified as having special needs, learning deficits, and disabilities. This is partly because educators working with qualified diagnosticians have become more skillful at identifying such children.

The bottom line for early education teachers is that the children being served, whether they are in mixed groups or homogeneous age groups, present far greater challenges in individualized teaching than they did in the past. Groups of young children with different ages, backgrounds, needs, and skill levels need ample time to explore materials and an ample number of adults to encourage and help them practice skills. Today's teachers are finding that they need to make stronger efforts to do individualized teaching during free choice time, and that they must usually schedule small group times for the practice of various skills.

To help today's children reach their full potentials, teachers now need to develop and use better management systems for the lesson planning of the vertical curriculum. A lesson-planning system can help ensure that all basic skill areas are covered, that skill practice activities are introduced gradually throughout the year, and that they are practiced in meaningful ways that mesh with children's natural development. This is the kind of system presented in this chapter. To use this kind of system, it is necessary for teachers to understand fully what is meant by skill-focused and developmentally sequenced activities.

Skill-Focused Activities

There are certain skills that every teacher wants children to master before they leave the program. These are skills agreed on in the early childhood field as appropriate to the development, limitations, and capabilities of the children with whom the teacher is working. They are probably skills that the early childhood program and the children's parents believe are important for teachers to teach. These skill-focused activities should consistently appear in daily lesson plans.

Skill-focused activities are activities or situations planned by the teacher in which children use particular materials to practice specific skills. For example, children might practice tearing or cutting, practice walking on a balance beam; or practice sorting and matching items by category, color, shape, or size. Sometimes the practice of a specific skill will take the form of a literacy activity, such as dictation by the child about a painted creation, or about a block structure, or about words to be put into a personal journal. At other times, the practice of a specific skill such as problem solving might be accomplished by a teacher's plans to have children help plan a field trip, prepare and eat vegetable soup, measure and graph objects, or do a science experiment and tell what happened. In each case, the teacher's lesson plans reflect a desire for specific skills to be practiced by children.

In planning the practice of specific skills, many teachers ask themselves these two questions: "When and in what order do I have children practice these skills?" and, "Am I really planning enough practice of each kind of skill activity?" Planning developmentally sequenced skill-focused activities throughout the year that reflect a daily balance of all skill areas is the basic challenge of vertical curriculum planning. To examine management ideas that will help teachers cope with this challenge, we need to take a deeper look at what *developmentally sequenced* means.

Developmentally Sequenced Activities

Developmentally sequenced activities are those activities that are planned in order to mesh with the ongoing and changing development of children as they grow and learn. Such activities are always planned to provide children with success; children should practice skills that match their skill levels. But these activities should also provide an element of challenge; opportunities to grow gradually even more skillful or use more advanced thinking processes should also be included in the planning of developmentally sequenced activities.

❖❖❖❖

Very little written guidance has been available to early childhood teachers for addressing the comprehensive daily planning of developmentally sequenced skill-focused activities. Most teachers do this sort of planning on the basis of fundamental child development knowledge, what they have learned from their own observations and experience, and what they have learned from other teachers.

Sometimes, the only guidance teachers have as to which activities to practice are lists of various skills that are found in screening and observation instruments. These lists usually show skills in terms of achievement-level milestones and are written as behavioral outcomes: "Can cut paper with scissors on straight line," "Can pair two items by a common relationship," "Can remember and follow two oral directions," "Counts 8 cubes," "Tries several methods to solve a problem and is highly persistent."

The achievement-level milestones in these publications are used as indicators to help teachers see "where each child is," either in achieving mastery or in needing help in practicing skills within the growth areas that are covered in screening and assessment tools. These tools may tell the teacher which skills individual children need to practice, but they do not give specific help to teachers in *breaking down these skills into sequenced hands on activities that can be entered in daily lesson plans from the beginning to the end of the year.*

Often, early childhood texts provide lists in which certain skills are broken down into gradual developmental steps on the basis of fundamental child development knowledge. In these lists, teachers may find an indication that a three-year-old can walk and run, will probably be about four years old before being able to gallop, and will be much nearer to five years old before being able to skip.

When early childhood teachers read or use developmental milestones, they should keep in mind that deviations from these milestones are not abnormal but are simply based on individual differences. These individual differences in children are interesting, worthy of watching, and well worth individual attention in lesson planning. The purpose of developmentally appropriate lesson planning is to help all children reach their full potentials.

Early childhood texts usually list consecutive developmental milestones in the areas of the child's physical, social, emotional, and intellectual growth and development. However, sequences of specific, activity-related skill development that could be incorporated into daily lesson planning are not broken out into detail. Each milestone may describe a skill at a certain level of growth and development, but the information provided rarely tells teachers how to help individual children to *arrive* at that particular milestone.

Here is an example of what a textbook might tell us: "By four years most children can make one full cut with scissors but have trouble cutting on a straight line." This information is helpful because it tells us generally what to expect from four-year-olds, but it does not tell us what to do with a group of 4 year olds to help them practice the skill of cutting if many children are at different skill levels. *There is not enough detail about developmental sequencing to tell the teacher how to practice cutting with diversely skilled four-year-olds on a daily and weekly basis from the beginning to the end of the year.* To do this kind of individualized planning, the teacher needs more sequential information about the skill of cutting.

Despite these limitations, early childhood texts are helpful in providing basic child development knowledge for general and long-range planning for different age groups. Several books that might be of particular help to teachers who are attempting to find developmental sequences that could be organized into planning strategies are listed at the end of this chapter, accompanied by a brief description of information in each book.

Frequently, early childhood teachers buy and use trade books that purport to include complete curriculum-planning activities for the program year. These should be examined very carefully. Many of the ideas included in such books are excellent. However, if a book simply proposes that "cutting and pasting" should be done during the first three months of the year, the direction to cut and paste does not give teachers enough sequential information about the skill of cutting to allow teachers to address individual differences in children's skill levels. Similarly, a book that directs the teacher to do specific activities for the entire group of children for each day of each week of the year will not be of much help to teachers who want to address *individual* needs and differences .

❦❦❦❦

To sum up, developmental milestones do not tell us how the child learns each skill, gradually, bit by bit, by practicing an activity that the teacher incorporated into his or her ongoing lesson plans. To do lesson planning that incorporates sequenced skill practice, teachers need to look at what should be happening for children *in between the developmental milestones,* instead of focusing on the milestones themselves.

Whether developmental milestones are written as achievement levels in screening inventories or as steps of growth and development in early childhood texts, they can be used as guidelines in planning long-range objectives. However, in order to do daily and weekly lesson planning that more effectively addresses individual differences, teachers need to figure out and plan skill-focused activities that help children practice all the steps that come between the milestones. When teachers do this kind of thinking and planning, they are doing developmental sequencing of skill-focused activities, or vertical planning.

❦❦❦❦

Because so little is available to teachers that tells them how to do developmental sequencing and vertical planning, many teachers simply plan their skill-focused activities on the basis of final cognitive and psychomotor goals for the year. Others base their planning on "What do I feel like having them practice today?" or "What haven't we practiced lately?" Even worse, some teachers may choose a skill that a child is to have mastered by the end of the year and, inappropriately, simply start practicing the "finished skill" the first week of school and practice it every day thereafter.

Teachers do not intend to plan skill-focused activities at inappropriate times, but they may not be aware of more appropriate alternatives. In discussing these alternatives, it would be helpful to examine what we might call *natural* developmental sequencing, *guided* developmental sequencing, and *planned* developmental sequencing.

Natural Sequencing

An example of natural developmental sequencing is the gradual sequence in which a baby learns to control and strengthen the muscles and movements of its body in order to learn to walk. If you allow a baby safe and normal opportunities to move about, and do not unduly restrict movement, the baby will learn to lift its head, then learn to roll over, then gradually learn to sit without support, then learn to creep and to crawl, then learn to pull itself up to stand with support, then learn to stand without suport. Then, finally, after learning to walk a few steps by holding on to an object or a person, the baby will learn to walk independently.

Guided Sequencing

Guided developmental sequencing occurs in several ways during free-choice time in most early childhood programs. In a center for three- and four-year-olds, if adults offer crayons, markers, and paper every day, and if they encourage and praise the open-ended use of these materials, the children who use them will gradually improve their skills in using crayons, markers, and paper. By the end of the year, they may able to do a drawing and print their first names with a large pencil, a crayon, or a marker. This method allows children's skills with crayons and markers to develop gradually and comfortably at the developmental pace of each child, but the skills are encouraged and reinforced, or "guided," by adults.

An example of inappropriate planning for this skill-focused activity would be a scenario in which a teacher provides paper and pencils on the first day of school and insists that children practice printing their names every day until the end of the school year. In this example, the natural developmental sequence in learning the skill is neither guided or planned; it is ignored.

Similarly, in programs following appropriate practices in the field, adults guide the developmental sequence of painting skills by emphasizing the process of painting, not the product that might emerge. They guide by offering bright, thick paint and large brushes. They encourage children to experiment with paint, and the children start by mixing the colors up and covering the entire paper. Then, as adults continue to offer painting experiences, the children start to separate some colors and leave some empty space. Next they enclose some spaces with planned strokes and begin to see emerging shapes. Next, children paint planned shapes, and finally they learn how to plan and put together some of their painted shapes and spaces so that a "picture" recognizable to adults emerges. Daily painting opportunities provide guided developmental sequencing for the skill-focused activity of painting.

A third example of guided sequencing can be seen in the use of unit blocks. When early childhood teachers provide unit blocks, the time and space to use them regularly, and the praise, encouragement, and questions that nurture further skill development, they are providing guidance to the developmental sequence of skills that children acquire during block building.

Children begin by laying the blocks flat in "roads"; they put blocks into containers and carry them about. Later they will discover that they can make a "bridge" with blocks and that they can enclose spaces with blocks. Still later they will notice and repeat patterns and build vertically, not just horizontally. Complex structures will emerge that will sometimes be named. Finally, children will work together as a group to build something they have planned. When teachers see block building as a skill-focused activity that can be practiced and encouraged with attention, questions, and accessories, they are guiding the developmental sequence that occurs when children use blocks.

Planned Sequencing—Motor Skills

Think about the example provided earlier of guided sequencing in using crayons, markers and paper. There is a way for teachers to expand their teaching methods to do "planned sequencing" of this skill-focused activity.

If the opportunity to use crayons and markers were offered only as a guided activity during free-choice time, some children who might need extra practice in this skill might not choose this area and this activity very often; they might not get enough of the practice they need. However, if the teacher could identify which children were not using this area and these materials, and which of these children needed more opportunities to practice the skill of using crayons and markers, then the teacher could plan several ways for those children to practice this skill.

The teacher could plan to sit with a child one-on-one during free-choice time and use the materials, encouraging the child to participate. Or the teacher could plan to work with two or three children who needed this practice during free-choice time, keep notes on their progress, and keep examples of their work in their files or portfolios.

The teacher could also provide this practice by planning for it to happen regularly in a scheduled, short, small-group time for all the children. This method would not single out any children as being less skillful than others. All the children in a small group could enjoy scribbling or drawing, regardless of skill level. The children could tell the adult leading the group about their drawing, and the adult could write down their dictated words and date the drawing; this would also nurture literacy skills. In five to ten minutes, children in a small group could make two drawings, one to take home and one for the teacher to keep in the file or portfolio. This would give the teacher an ongoing and planned method to assist the children who need individual encouragement, as well as a way to observe children's progress in the skill of handling crayons, markers, and paper.

❖❖❖

Here is a second example of planned sequencing. In a mixed age group of three- to five-year-olds, children may start the year at ages three and a half or four and end the year at ages four and a half or five. Teachers may want children to end the year with the ability to use scissors to cut on a line or to cut out a large, simple shape.

Most three- and four-year-olds are not adept with scissors when they enter preschool programs. They should not all be expected to start practicing cutting with scissors at this time, and certainly should not be expected to cut pictures from magazines, in which the thin paper slips and bends. Cutting pictures from magazines in the first month of the program year is a good example of the inappropriate practice of practicing the "final result" of a skill at the wrong developmental time.

The developmental sequence of mastering skills leading to the use of scissors should be planned, and should begin with experiences that strengthen the hand muscles, like using clays and playdough, tongs, hole punches, and pinch clothes pins. The next step in the sequence is to plan many experiences in tearing paper, so that the child's hands learn the feeling of opposition, and so that the fingers learn how to begin controlling the medium of paper.

TRY THIS NOW To understand exactly what is meant by the "feeling of opposition" and "controlling the medium of paper," get a scrap piece of paper right now and tear it in half. You will see that your two hands did opposite things: One hand moved away from you and one toward you. Now, try to tear the scrap paper into a shape. Again, your hands do different things as you turn the paper and control it as you tear it.

In cutting with scissors, the hands also do different things. One hand holds and turns the paper, and the other hand cuts. Enjoyable activities in tearing various papers and sometimes using glue to make torn paper collages will lead naturally to children's interest in tearing shapes out of paper. When the child can tear out shapes, he or she has learned that the hand that holds and turns the paper being torn does something different than the dominant hand, which will eventually do the cutting.

This is why experiences in tearing paper should be planned to precede the use of scissors, especially if the practice of this skill is to occur in a scheduled small-group time in a mixed-age group. During free-choice time, children who are already adept at using scissors will have plenty of opportunity to use their skills. But in a mixed-age group during small-group time at the beginning of the year, tearing paper (not using scissors) should be the planned, developmentally sequenced activity, because it will be successful and helpful to every child in the group. Those who are more adept with scissors will not mind tearing (all children love to tear paper), and the activity of tearing and turning the paper will still help children who can cut to improve their scissor skills.

Skills in using the scissors themselves can also be developmentally sequenced and planned. Appropriate vertical lesson planning should gradually incorporate the following steps in the skill-focused activity of using scissors:

1. After tearing experiences, children practice snipping the edge of the paper.
2. Next they practice cutting into the paper, making fringes.
3. Next they practice cutting the paper apart at random.
4. Then they practice cutting it apart by following a straight line drawn on the paper, and then a curved line.
5. Next, they practice cutting on a line drawn on paper which incorporates angles or zig-zags.
6. Then they practice cutting out a large circle or oval of paper by following a continuous line.
7. Finally, they practice stopping and changing direction with the scissors as they follow a line that is not continuous; for example, they might practice cutting out a square or triangle.

The developmentally sequenced steps listed here for the skill of cutting with scissors could easily be put into monthly or daily lesson plans in a planned, consecutive, and gradual order for practicing and learning.

Most of the skills we want children to attain by the end of the year could be practiced in guided and/or planned developmental sequences, starting very simply and gradually becoming more challenging or complex. Motor, perceptual, memory, language, and problem-solving skills can all be practiced gradually, with planned and developmentally sequenced activities that match children's changing skill levels.

Planned Sequencing—Perceptual Skills

Here is an example of a perceptual activity that can be sequenced for the purpose of lesson planning. Young children begin to internalize the concept of the shape of a triangle or square through real experiences, such as playing a triangle instrument or sitting on a carpet square. Learning that adults have names for colors and shapes and that they want children to learn these names is comfortable and acceptable to children, who want to please adults and who want praise for their accomplishments. However, learning colors and shapes (and many other such concepts) can and should proceed in planned, sequenced, "match, find, and label" activities that move from concrete to abstract.

In elementary education university math methods courses, directions given to students include the use of the "match," "find," and "label" sequence in teaching methods, as well as the directive that teaching and learning experiences should always proceed from concrete to gradually more abstract activities.

Let's examine the way these sequenced methods could be used in teaching a child about a square. The first step in the perceptual skill of learning a shape is for the child to experience the shape with his or her senses, physically and kinesthetically. In learning what a square is, the adult would start the year with observations and meaningful verbal comments whenever a child is using or handling something square—a carpet square, a square cracker, a window square, or a square enclosure made of blocks.

The adult would also use questions in small-group or one-on-one time to help a child understand the concept of a square shape, starting with "Can you find one that is just the same shape as this one?" The child would be matching the shape, not naming it. Later, the adult would name the shape, saying, "Can you find a square one like this?" The child would find a square and also hear the name, which would be the "finding" stage. Later, the adult would be able to ask the child to look at a group of various shapes and tell which ones were square. When the child can isolate and name the shape, he or she has reached the "label" stage. After the match, find, and label stages, the child's learning about a square does not stop; it continues to develop.

What has been learned about a square with practice in hands-on perceptual experiences now becomes committed to memory. At this point, when an adult asks what a square is, the child will be practicing a *memory skill* as well as a *perceptual skill* whenever he or she tells the teacher the name of the shape. The concept of that shape is something the child has already learned through hands-on perceptual experiences.

Further, when the child uses this learning about what a square is in creating a pattern or design, the child is synthesizing the information from hands-on experiences in both perceptual and memory activities and putting this information to a new use. He or she is now demonstrating a *problem-solving skill.* When we see the child using information in this new way, it shows a change in behavior; we not only know the child has "learned" what a square is, but the

child is now using and integrating new problem-solving skills, along with formerly acquired learning, to construct new knowledge about the square.

This particular example, skill practice with shapes, was given to illustrate something interesting that happens when teachers do long-range planning for certain skill-focused activities. At the beginning of the year, activities in which children practice recognizing shapes would be categorized as perceptual activities. But as the year progresses and children integrate their learning, skill-focused activities concerning shapes would encompass other skill areas. Tracing shapes would be a motor activity, remembering names of shapes would be a memory activity, and creating designs with shapes would be a problem-solving activity. Readers are asked to remember this point when we begin to look at the management plan for vertical activities that will be presented in this chapter.

Similar planned developmental learning sequences can also be used in teaching three- to five-year-olds the colors. Again, the learning activities or experiences should move from concrete to abstract and from matching to finding to labeling. For example, a child learns what *red* is by actual experience with things we call *red*—by playing with paints, playdough, and other things that are red; by consuming foods and liquids that are red; or even by seeing that blood from a cut is red.

The child would see and handle real red objects first, (real red apples) then see the color red in pictures of these real objects, (pictures of red apples), and then recognize the color red in more abstract symbols for the objects (pictures of red spheres or circles).

Young children may also eventually be able to learn *red* by an inappropriate method, the method of rote practice. In this unfortunate case, they might be expected to practice saying the name *red* and seeing the color word *red* combined with pictures of red objects every day. They might also be able to learn the name for a shape such as a triangle in the same rote practice manner, but this is not an appropriate or pleasant way for children to learn. Learning should not be difficult or uncomfortable; it should be filled with the joys of discovery and success.

In the field of early childhood, we want children to develop the lifelong skill of learning to love learning, and we do this, not with rote practice, but by helping children gain skill mastery through meaningful, enjoyable learning experiences and active engagement in planned, guided, and spontaneous hands-on activities.

Part 2: A System for Skill-Focused Planning

Sequenced Skill-Focused Planning

In addition to those skills already mentioned in this chapter, complete sequences for nurturing the development of many motor, perceptual, memory, literacy, and problem-solving skills are presented to readers in Appendix A of this guidebook. The two tables that follow, which we will look at in detail, are the first two of the seven time blocks or tables that will be found in Appendix A. These tables provide the teacher with a lesson-planning system for vertical planning.

When teachers examine the information in Tables 4-1 and 4-2 (and later Appendix A) they will find that most of the skill-focused activities they practice with children on a daily basis are already sequenced and inc the seven time blocks. Each time block is approximately four to five length. These time blocks can be thought of as navigational charts for planning in the seven consecutive periods of a nine-month program will provide a system for organizing vertical curriculum information long-range plan, containing seven four- to-five-week plans. This help teachers place already sequenced skill-focused activities into da plans more easily and quickly.

Tables 4-1 and 4-2 will give the reader examples of sequenced skill-focused activity ideas that could be used in lesson plans during the first eight weeks of the program year. We will use them in this chapter to learn more about the system and how it works.

General Notes on Format

The first thing readers will notice about Tables 4-1 and 4-2 is that each of these time blocks is organized into five categories under the headings "Motor", "Perceptual", "Literacy", "Memory," and "Problem Solving." All the activities that occur in an early childhood classroom will fall into one or more of these five general categories.

Seeing these five categories of skill areas simultaneously as each time block is viewed is helpful to teachers who are concerned about planning a balance of activities in all five skill areas. This format helps the teacher see all the basic skill activities that are important for children, not just choices of activities that the teacher might enjoy doing most often.

The next thing readers will notice is that a comprehensive list of already sequenced, skill-focused activity examples is suggested in every one of the five skill categories. If teachers choose activities from each of these five categories regularly each day over the course of a month or five weeks, they will be providing a balance of practice all skill areas in their lesson plans.

When readers examine these two tables more closely, they will also see that in the "Motor" category, both small and large motor activities are listed. In the "Perception" category, tactile, auditory and visual perception experiences are included. Both visual and auditory memory activities are included in the

"Memory" category. Comprehensive lesson planning for young children should include all these areas of development.

❋❋❋❋

Each of the five categories are further divided into three subcategories: large-group, free-choice, and small-group. This has been done to precipitate easier and quicker placement of these examples (or alternative activities of the teacher's choice) into a daily lesson plan. The title "Free Choice" is used because of its brevity; readers should bear in mind that *free choice* means that children will make choices of materials that may have been preplanned by the teacher with specific goals in mind.

Please notice also that meal and snack activities are listed under "Small Group," because, whenever possible in early childhood programs, children do eat in small groups, where conversation and learning are guided and led by an adult.

Teachers who do not schedule a daily small-group time may still use or modify the "Small Group" examples presented in the tables. For example, these small-group activities could be used with individuals or small groups during free-choice time or at other times in the program day.

❋❋❋❋

As readers examine the examples of activity ideas, they should bear in mind that these lists are comprehensive but are purposely not all-inclusive. To present this system, it is necessary to provide examples of developmentally sequenced skill-focused activities in five major skill areas. In Tables 4-1 and 4-2, however, and in the complete set of time blocks provided in Appendix A, what is emphasized are the sequential steps in practicing each activity or skill, not the specific methods or materials the teacher would use in implementing the activities.

The steps in skill sequencing and the method of organizing the activity examples are far more important than the examples themselves, because it is the steps and the method that give teachers a system for organizing and using their own ideas in the vertical curriculum. As they become familiar with the system, teachers are urged to add their own ideas and skill sequences, and to modify the examples presented in order to address individual or program priorities.

For example, a kindergarten teacher might have different long- and short-range goals and objectives than a teacher of four- and five-year-olds, but kindergarten goals could still be broken down and sequenced, and the method presented here could still be used. In addition, the kindergarten teacher may be required to use different semantics; categories might be titled "Physical" instead of "Motor," or "Science and Math" instead of "Problem Solving."

As we further examine these two tables, we will be discussing several aspects that will help teachers use the system effectively. Readers may ask: "Why are some activity ideas general and some specific?" "What are the reasons they are placed in certain categories or sections?" "What do I do first?" "How fast should I move through a time block?" "How can I individualize this system?"

MOTOR

Large Group
Body Movement:
Copy and/or create to music, songs,
　　chants, rhymes.
Act out prepositions.

Free Choice
Using Blocks:
Use unit and large hollow blocks.
Stack, lay, carry, build.
Active Play Inside/Outside
Use all types of locomotion, including
　　wheel toys.
Follow line or path with body or toy.
Practice climbing and rolling.
Jump with both feet.
Toss, catch, and pass with big, soft
　　beanbags, or paper-stuffed pillow-
　　case.
Use hammer with pegs or *soft* wood
　　or Styrofoam.

Clays and Playdough/Sand and Water:
Use freely; fill, pour, float, sink, mold
　　and dig.

Dressing and Undressing:
Practice with outer wear, dress-up,
　　and zipper/button toys.

Art Media:
Use crayons, markers, chalk, paper.
Use easel paint and fingerpaint.
Paint at tables.
Use varied collage materials.

Manipulatives, Table Toys, Floor Toys:
Use large, easy puzzles.
Use large pegs/pegboards.
Use large lego blocks.
String large beads.
Use stack and nest toys.
Use shape box toys.
Use snap and bristle blocks.

Small Group
Games:
Follow object with eyes.
Tear paper at random.
Use tongs and pinch clothespins.
Trace simple templates with fingers;
　　free form, one line.
Practice pouring water.
Practice any manipulatives.

Meals and Snacks:
Pour, pass, serve, spread.
Clean up, brush teeth.

PERCEPTUAL

Large Group
Music and Circle:
Use instruments.
Recognize body parts.
Listen to sounds and identify some.
Notice what we are wearing.

Free Choice
Blocks:
Use all types.
Handle and match types.

Exploring with Senses:
Use clays, playdough, water, sand,
　　earth.
Explore and match textures.
Handle and match recycled items.
Handle collage items.
Match familiar objects.
Use various paints.
Compare colors used in art media.
Notice smells, tastes.

*Manipulatives, Table Toys, Floor
　　Toys:*
Use simple, large puzzles/parquetry.
Use face–body parts activities.
Match textures.
Match familiar silhouette shapes.

Cleanup:
Use pictures and perceptual labels.
Recognize sound cues.

Small Group
Games:
Compare sounds; high, low, loud,
　　soft.
Tell direction of sound source.*
Compare ourselves regarding sizes,
　　hair, eyes.
Guess a hidden object by touch
　　alone.
Match some primary colors.
Compare objects; big, small, like,
　　unlike. Match like objects.
Examine/match circles and ovals.
Identify simple sounds.*
Recognize familiar shape sil-
　　houettes.

Meals and Snacks
Perceive colors, textures, tastes,
　　smells and temperatures.

LITERACY

Large Group

Literature:
Hear stories and books.
Do fingerplays and rhymes.
Do songs and chants.
See flannelboard stories.
Use/talk with puppets.

Conversations:
About work and play choices.
About plans and routines.
On simple rules for safety.
About friends and names.
On things that make us happy or sad.

Body Language:
Move to music.
Imitate animals and nature.
Act out prepositions with music, rug
    squares.

Free Choice

Talk/Listen/Do:
Use books and pictures.
Use people's names.
Name items and equipment.
Talk about healthful ways.
Use friendly words.
Use, talk about safe ways and rules.
Play with puppets.
Talk about art and creations.
Use picture recipe to make playdough.
Use tape recorder.
Use listen station.
Use play telephones.
Examine computer.

Dramatic Play:
Converse spontaneously.
Use materials creatively.

Writing Center:
Do creative "writing" and communi-
    cating.

Small Group

Games:
Discuss "me," my home and family.
Start a "me" book.
Discuss pictures about feelings.
Discuss work and play choices.
Use puppets together.
Discuss health and safety.*
Read a picture book.*
Discuss visitors/helpers.*
Discuss outdoor walks.*

Meals and Snacks:
Discuss and name foods. Tell
    preferences.

MEMORY

Large Group

Learning Together:
Copy adult modeling.
Imitate in simple games of "Do What I
    Do."
Hear and talk about stories.
Sing songs in unison and call and
    response.
Enjoy and learn fingerplays.
Try counting by rote up to 5 in songs,
    rhymes, birthdays.
Learn daily schedule, routines, limits.
See picture sequence of daily
    schedule.
Use names of friends in songs, rhymes
    and games.
See own name in print.

Free Choice

All Area Learning:
Learn names of areas, materials and
    equipment.
Learn how we use materials and
    equipment.
Learn names of friends.
Learn limits, expectations and routines
    with practice and helpful visual
    cues.
Learn helpers' jobs with practice and
    helpful visual cues.
Use healthful habits at snacks and
    meals, when toileting, and in
    cleaning to prevent spread of
    germs.
Use safety habits with materials,
    movements, fire drills.

Cleanup:
Learn adult cue to start.
Learn where things go.

Small Group

Games:
Talk about fire and tornado drills.
See sequenced pictures of the daily
    schedule.
Recall today and what I liked best.
Repeat own and each other's names in
    rhythmic chant.
Remember summer and family fun.*
Recall one or two objects when these
    are removed from a group and
    hidden.
Guess names of areas from adult
    clues.
Sometimes recognize own printed
    name.
Recall some friend's names.

Meals and Snacks:
Learn the routine.
Copy positive social language.

PROBLEM SOLVING

Large Group

Conversations:
On work/play choices from day's
    options.
On the schedule of the day.
About nature, the weather, and its
    changes.
About our body parts and their use.
    (demonstrate)
On what makes us feel happy or sad.

Free Choice

Blocks:
Stack, lay, connect.
Compare different structures.

All Area Learning:
Begin to know areas and materials by
    use.
Make work/play choices.
Begin to plan the use of time.
Ask questions and use senses to gain
    information.
Negotiate turns with materials.
Explain wants and needs with words.
Match, sort, and tub materials.
Manipulate materials.
Examine computer.
Observe properties of sand, water,
    paint, playdough/clays.
Observe changes resulting in mixing
    colors.
Make playdough; measure, mix; see
    changes.

Dramatic Play:
Choose items for role play and
    pretend.
Plan and carry out play.

Science and Math:
Observe and handle nature items.
Observe our plants and animals.
Measure and weigh ourselves.
Estimate in pouring and filling.

Small Group

Games:
Discuss play choices and plan one
    choice for next time.
Tub and sort items.
Count own body parts.
Count heads and noses of those in
    group.
Blow bubbles with individual cups/
    straws; observe.

Meals and Snacks:
Set table with one-to-one match.
Help prepare snack when possible.
Problem-solve when using utensils.
Estimate in pouring, filling.

MOTOR

Large Group
Body Movement:
Copy and/or create to music, songs, chants, rhymes.
Act out prepositions.

Free Choice
Using Blocks:
Use unit and large blocks freely.

Active Play Inside/Outside:
Use varied locomotion, including wheel toys.
Follow line with body or toy.
Try balance beam, FLAT.
Use steps/rocking boat.
Use indoor climber.
Use mats to jump and roll.
Balance on one foot; try to hop.
Toss/catch large, light items.
Jump over a low rope; rake, jump in leaves.
Use hammer and soft materials or pegs.

Clays and Playdough/Sand and Water:
Use freely; add variety.
Pour, fill, float, sink, dig, mold.

Dressing and Undressing:
Outer wear, dress-up, and zipper/button toys.

Art Media:
Use crayons, markers, paper, and scissors.
Do varied painting, fingerpaint, and collages.
Try spray painting.
Try dripped-glue designs.
Try hole punch designs.
Try rubbings from nature.

Manipulatives, Table Toys, Floor Toys:
Use all appropriate manipulatives freely.

Small Group
Games:
Tear paper with purpose.
Use simple templates with curves; one line.
Fold paper; either one or two folds.
Learn about eye dropper painting.
String paper tubes, big pastas, or cereals.
Snip or fringe with scissors.
Practice any manipulatives.

Meals and Snacks:
Pour, pass, serve, and spread.
Carry, clean up, brush teeth.

PERCEPTUAL

Large Group
Music and Circle:
Use instruments.
Match sounds of like instruments.
Identify other sounds.
Compare ourselves; sizes and other characteristics.
Guess hidden objects by touch alone.
Notice what we wear.

Free Choice
Blocks:
Use all types.
Handle, match, and find types.

Exploring with Senses:
Use clays, playdough, water, sand, mud.
Match textures and recycled items.
Mix and match paints.
Do more smelling and tasting.
Sort items found in nature such as leaves, stones, seeds.
Use some musical instruments in play.

Manipulatives, Table Toys, Floor Toys:
Use materials fully.
Use blocks, flannel pieces, beads, pegs, and parquetry to create own patterns.

Clean Up:
Use perceptual labels.
Recognize sound cues.

Small Group
Games:
Match primary colors, unnamed.
Hum together; match a pitch.
Recognize a voice.
Identify familiar sounds on tape.
Match familiar shapes.
Match simple objects to their pictures.
Reproduce easy three-part patterns with model in view using cubes, beads, or other objects.
Find or match circles, ovals, squares.
Guess objects by touch.*
Match big and small objects.

Meals and Snacks:
Perceive and discuss tastes, smells, textures, colors.
Perceive that some foods have shapes.

LITERACY

Large Group
Literature:
Hear stories and books.
Do fingerplays and rhymes.
Do songs and chants.
Use flannelboard and puppets.

Conversations:
About choices and plans.
On rules for our room and group.
About feelings and fears.
About friends and names.
About new toys and equipment.

Body Language:
Move to music.
Use gestures and imitations.
Try signing a simple word or phrase.
Add to actions with prepositions.

Free Choice
Talk/Listen/Do:
Use books/pictures.
Use names of people and materials.
Use and talk about healthful ways.
Use friendly words.
Use and talk about safe ways/rules.
Use puppets and flannelboard.
Answer open questions.
Do artwork dictation.
Try new recipe cards.
Use the computer.
Tape record/listen.
Use play telephones.

Dramatic Play:
Use new props and materials.
Converse spontaneously.

Writing Center:
Create original communication.
Try new materials.

Small Group
Games:
Continue "me" book as a personal
    journal.
Discuss foods, health, safety.*
Discuss feelings of self and others.
Discuss visitors, trips, and walks.*
Discuss our plants and animals.
Begin simple dictation or experience
    stories.

Meals and Snacks
Discuss and describe food. Talk with
    peers and adults.

MEMORY

Large Group
Remembering Together:
Copy adult modeling.
Imitate in simple games of "Do What I
    Do."
Hear stories and songs.
Do fingerplays/rhymes.
Know what comes next in schedule.
Try rote counting to 5 in non-
    stereotyped songs, rhymes.
See and discuss pictured sequence of
    routines such as fire drills, meals/
    toothbrushing.
See visual cues for limits/rules and
    helper jobs.
Know many names of friends and
    adults.
Recognize and name familiar sounds.
See own name in print (name tag,
    creations).
Remember summer or past events.
Remember fun times with friends/
    family.
Recall name of a person hidden when
    adult gives clues.
Repeat simple oral or clapped rhythm.

Free Choice
All Area Learning:
Know names of areas, equipment, and
    materials.
Know how to use these appropriately.
Use names of friends.
Know rules and expectations.
Remember helpers' jobs; use visual
    cues.
Practice health habits.
Practice safety habits.

Cleanup:
Remember light or sound cues.
Know where things go.

Small Groups
Games:
Recall two things I did today.
See, match own name in print.
Remember walks, trips, visitors.*
Recall two or three objects removed
    and hidden.
Recall/do one or two tasks while
    seated.
Find one primary color when named.
Find circles and ovals.
Repeat a simple clapped or oral
    rhythm.

Meals and Snacks:
Remember the routine.
Use positive social language.
Begin to talk about food groups.
Talk about foods for healthy teeth.

PROBLEM SOLVING

Large Group
Conversations:
About work and play choices.
About the daily schedule.
About weather changes and how these
    tell us seasonal changes.
On rules developed by the group.
On "last time" or "next time."
On body parts and their use.
About ways we can relax.

Free Choice
Blocks:
Stack/lay, connect, enclose.
See parts of whole.
Compare differences in structures.

All Area Learning:
Know areas by use.
Make work/play choices.
Ask questions and use senses to gain
    information.
Negotiate wants, needs, and turns with
    words.
See step-by-step process in use of
    media and manipulatives.
Begin to see parts of whole in puzzles,
    designs.
Match, sort, and tub materials.
Use computer.
Try new multisensory media; colors,
    clays.

Dramatic Play:
Plan and carry out play.
Do safety and health habit role play.

Science and Math:
Notice and handle new items; count
    some.
Observe/tell about nature and our
    plants and animals.
See changes mixing, cooking and
    grinding.
Use the balance scale and measuring
    tools.

Small Group
Games:
Use minilight and a magnifier to
    examine nature items found.
Blow bubbles with individual cups/
    straws; add drops of food color;
    observe and tell.
Sort nature items in two ways.
Graph selves by size or in other ways.
Guess, find out what floats or sinks in
    cup of water.
Match three or four items one to one.

Meals and Snacks:
Continue to help in set up and
    preparation.
See changes in foods experiences.

General and Specific Activity Ideas

Most activity examples listed are general in nature so that teachers can engage in their own teaching styles and use their own materials with the activities they choose. For example, look at Table 4-1. In the "Motor" category, one "Large Group" activity is to "Copy and/or create to music, songs, chants, rhymes." In motor, free-choice time, another is "Use crayons, markers, chalk and paper." In the "Literacy" category, one large-group activity is "Hear stories and books"; another is "Talk about plans, rules and routines." Specific music, books, materials, and "plans, rules, and routines" would be up to the individual teacher. Necessary details would be noted by the teacher in the lesson plan.

A few general activities are seen repeated in every time block, such as "Copy adult modeling" in the "Memory" category. This is because children at every age and stage will remember and copy adult modeling. We need to remind ourselves that our adult modeling helps children practice memory skills, even when we don't realize it.

Very specific activity examples are given in the "Small Group" sections of Tables 4-1 and 4-2. These specific activities have been included either to help children practice skills that are important to the teacher's horizontal and vertical plans (in this case, my own plans) or because they are skills that are best practiced with adult guidance. During planned small-group time, children usually practice skills that teachers want to observe closely, or skills with which teachers may want to assist.

Manner of Sequencing

Please note the manner of sequencing that has been done in the tables by looking at some examples. In Table 4-1 "Motor, Small Group," you will see "Tear paper at random." In Table 4-2, "Motor, Small Group," you will see "Tear paper with purpose," as well as "Snip or fringe paper with scissors". In Table 4-1, "Motor, Free Choice," you will see "Follow a line or path with body or toy" (such as a taped line), and in Table 4-2, "Motor, Free Choice," you will see "Try the balance beam laid flat."

If you would look at the time blocks that follow Table 4-2, (Tables A-3 to A-7, "Motor," in Appendix A), you would find continuous steps in the sequential development of skills with both scissors and the use of the balance beam.

Look at the "Perception" category in Table 4-1. In "Small Group," you will find "Tell direction of sound source." In Table 4-1, "Perception, Large Group," you will find "Listen to sounds and identify some." In Table 4-2, these activities are more challenging. See Table 4-2, "Small Group," "Hum together and match a pitch," "Recognize a voice," and "Identify familiar sounds on tape." In Table 4-2, "Large Group," see "Match sounds of like instruments" and "Identify other sounds."

Please compare Tables 4-1 and 4-2 in the "Literacy" category. You will find that the conversations and materials become slightly more complex in Table 4-2. For example, in the "Free Choice" section, children move from examining the computer in Table 4-1 to using the computer in Table 4-2. They move from naming equipment to using the names of equipment; children move from telling about their art to doing simple dictation about their art.

In "Literacy, Large Group, Literature," children move from seeing and hearing the teacher do flannel board stories in Table 4-1 to using flannelboards themselves during "Large Group" and "Free Choice" in Table 4-2. In "Literacy, Large Group, Conversations," children move from discussing a few simple safety rules in Table 4-1 to talking about rules for the room and the group in Table 4-2.

Similar examples can easily be found by examining the sequences in the "Memory" and "Problem Solving" categories. In Table 4-1, "Memory, Large Group," we see that children "Enjoy and learn fingerplays" In Table 4-2, "Memory, Large Group," they "Use fingerplays and rhymes." In Table 4-1, "Memory, Free Choice," children "Learn helpers' jobs with practice and helpful visual cues." In Table 4-2, "Memory, Free Choice," they "Remember helpers' jobs."

Please examine the "Problem Solving" category in the "Blocks" section of free-choice time to compare Tables 4-1 and 4-2. Readers will see that children move from "Stack, lay, connect" and "Observe differences" in Table 4-1 to "Stack, lay, connect, enclose; compare differences" and "See parts of whole" in Table 4-2. The examples listed in the "Blocks" section will remind teachers to guide block building skills during free-choice time with focused interest and appropriate questions. If readers examine all seven tables or time blocks, they will see that all the steps of skill development in block building have been planned for practice.

As these tables are used throughout the year, each activity becomes more challenging, meshing with children's growing skills. For example, in Table 4-2, "Small Group," readers will see "Recall/do 1–2 tasks while seated." In the time block table corresponding with the end of the year, or seven months later, readers would see "Recall/do 3 tasks which include movement." Recalling tasks while moving about is a much more complex memory skill than recalling and doing tasks while remaining in place. Careful sequencing of these activity examples was attempted in every section of these tables, not only in teacher-directed sections such as large group and small group, but also in the work that teachers do with children in free-choice time.

Placement of Activities within Categories

The placement of activities in the particular subcategories of "Large Group," "Small Group," and "Free Choice" in these tables is based on my own experience with three- to five-year-olds. These were the places and times where these activities fit best in my own daily lesson plan. However, every teacher has an individual style and works with different kinds of groups. Flexibility is important. The time blocks are not a "canned curriculum" but a method of organization for lesson planning. When teachers become familiar with this system, they not only should experiment with new sequenced activities, but also should experiment with the placement of activities in their lesson plans.

Readers should, however, be provided with some insight into the reasons for the placement choices seen in the subcategories of these tables ("Large Group," "Small Group," "Free Choice").

Please examine Table 4-1, "Literacy." In "Large Group," suggestions are made to talk about friendships, safety, and routines. In "Small Group," the skill-focused activities suggested are "Discuss me, my home and family," "Discuss pictures about feelings," and "Start a me book." The reason for this placement is that children with little experience talking in front of others will usually talk much more openly about self and family in a small group than in a large group. This is why it is important to place personal discussions in small group during the first time blocks, and in large group during later time blocks.

Another reason for placing certain activity examples in the small-group section of these tables is so that the teacher can more easily guide and reinforce the sequential development of particular skills. A similar reason for placing activity examples in the small-group section is so that the teacher may appropriately introduce them to children. Many skill-focused activities, especially those that incorporate new materials or pieces of equipment, should be introduced by adults in small group before they are fully available for use during free-choice time. A few examples are the use of eye droppers for painting, the use of magnets, the use of dry cell batteries, and the use of musical instruments.

Please notice in Table 4-1, "Perception," that instruments were introduced in large group, as "Use instruments," and also inferred as potential suggestions in small group, as "Compare sounds . . . Tell direction of sound source," and "Identify simple sounds." In Table 4-2, "Perception, Free Choice," you will see the suggestion to "Use some instruments in play." Children need to know how to use instruments and other materials safely and in the manner for which they are intended. This is why readers will see some activity examples listed in "Small Group" in a particular time block or table, and then see these activities moved into "Free Choice" in the following table.

Readers will notice that an asterisk (*) has been placed next to certain small-group activities. Some examples will be found in Table 4-1, "Small Group, Literacy." Whenever an asterisk is placed next to an activity, it indicates that this activity might also be appropriate for large-group discussions. Some teachers might prefer to place these asterisked activities in large group on their lesson plans; I chose to introduce these activities in small group before placing them in large group.

In a final word regarding placement, please recall the information presented earlier in this chapter which described practicing perceptual activities with shapes. Some activities regarding particular skills will be found in one category in the earliest time blocks, but in later time blocks, as children use the skill in different ways, the activity may be placed in another category. If you were to look at the activities on shapes and colors in all seven tables in Appendix A. you would see that these activities begin in the perceptual category; but later (after children conceptualize the shapes or colors and learn their names), practicing with shapes and colors would be found in the memory category.

Individualizing the Use of the System

The main advantage of this time block system for individualized planning is that the examples of skill-focused activities are already sequenced. This factor helps the teacher to maintain control of the system, the information, and his or her choices.

The teacher can easily move forward or backward in the steps of the sequence for any of the skills in order to meet the needs of the group, or of individuals in the group. Teachers can also move forward to the next time block in any skill area (any one of the five major categories) or move backward in any skill area of a time block to repeat activities within that category.

If a teacher finds that certain skills in a particular category have not been "practiced enough" for all children to have been successful, the teacher can simply repeat those activities before moving on to the next time block for new activities in that category. If children "simply love" a certain activity, the teacher is free to choose to stay in a time block or go back to a previous time block to repeat it.

In using small-group time activity examples, the teacher may find that some children in the group are far more skillful than others in a particular activity. This means that those children have moved through the steps in the sequential development of that skill much faster than others. In this case, the teacher can simply move forward in the sequence of that particular skill-focused activity example to find ideas from the next time block (in the same category) to suit that particular child or children in the group.

Teachers should pay particular attention to children who move through developmental sequences very quickly. Sometimes teachers tend to be less aware of the needs of children who need challenge than they are of those children who are "challenged" and/or move very slowly through sequences of development.

If a child in the small group needs to repeat skill-focused activities from a previous time block, the teacher can go back to the previous table and offer those activities as alternatives for that child. These alternatives from previous steps in a sequence could be used either during the small-group time itself, or whenever the teacher might work with the child individually during another part of the day.

Another scenario might be that some children in a mixed-level small group might only be able to "match" a color or shape, while others may be able to "find" the color or shape. The teacher could simply pose his or her questions differently to the children in the group, depending on each child's skill level. This why readers will see that in some of the activity examples, the wording is "match OR find", or "recall two OR three objects." Readers will also often see the word *try* instead of *do* as children begin practicing a new skill.

The Pace of the Teacher or Group

Just as the pace of children within the group differs, the pace of each teacher or classroom group may differ. The system presented here is flexible enough to allow for these differences. In some groups, or at particular times of the year, children seem to have growth spurts where they will practice all the activities in a particular time block very quickly and will be eager for new challenges. If so, the teacher can move on to ideas in the next time block whenever children are ready. In other groups or at other times of the year, teachers will find that children will need or want more time to finish the activities of a particular time block. No problem. The teacher can continue to practice any activities in any categories of his or her choice, going on with the sequence later, when children are ready.

Integrating Themes with Skill-Focused Activities

When possible, teachers should take advantage of the opportunity to integrate skill practice with meaningful and interesting thematic content. When skill-focused activities mesh naturally and easily with thematic units, integration enhances interest, motivation, and skill development. However, this does not mean that every single skill-focused activity must be done within the context of a theme. This is not necessary; "theme overkill" can sometimes stifle the joy of children in just doing some things because they like to repeat doing them and get better at them.

However, some teachers live in areas where the seasons change; they often plan thematic units about fall, and the children usually collect leaves from outdoors. Sorting and matching these items from nature; telling about them, and grouping them by shape, color or size would be an excellent and appropriate way to integrate theme content experiences with perceptual, literacy, or problem-solving skill-focused activities (Table 4-2 "Perception, Free Choice").

Readers may have noticed that many of the skill-focused activity examples in Tables 4-1 and 4-2 relate to the primary and recurring themes of the horizontal plan that was shared with you in Chapter 3—caring about myself, about others, and about my world. Here are a few examples from Tables 4-1 and 4-2 that demonstrate a logical integration of these three themes with skill-focused activities.

In the motor category, children practice self-help skills including health and nutrition skills, and engage in active play and creative movement. In the perceptual category, they enjoy the use of their senses, observe characteristics of self and others, recognize body parts, and help care for the setting. In the literacy category, they talk about themselves; they sign a simple word or phrase; they talk about their health and safety, their friends and families, their choices, and their feelings. In the memory category, children remember what they enjoyed doing at school, remember each other's names, recall family fun, remember group rules and jobs, and remember safe and healthy habits. In the problem-solving category, children plan choices and the use of their time; develop group rules; observe nature and changes in our world; weigh, measure, and graph themselves; count body parts, and learn to problem-solve with words.

Using the System in Lesson Planning

To begin using this system for managing skill-focused activities, all teachers need to do is look at the appropriate time block as they are doing their daily lesson plans. If it is the beginning of a nine-month program, this is Table 4-1, September–October.

Next, teachers would make choices from the examples of skill-focused activities listed in each of the five categories, and enter them in their lesson plans in large-group, small-group, or free-choice time, adding whatever specific detail is necessary. Teachers may always add their own ideas or experiment with different placements in the lesson plan. The emphasis would be on sequencing the activities in practicing any skill and on using a balance of activities from all skill areas.

Teachers should remember that these activities are designed to be used over four or five weeks' time. It is best to begin working with each time block by choosing ideas for the lesson plan that teachers believe are easiest for all children to accomplish successfully, then proceed to more challenging activities during the later weeks of the time block.

It is wise for teachers to keep a simple tally of the activity examples that have been used in lesson plans as they work with each time block. Place a check mark or a date next to each activity example as it is used. This will not only help document the use of skill-focused activities; it will help ensure a daily balance in activity choices. Teachers will find that most of the time they will use all the activities listed in each time block within the four- or five-week period. Activities that may not have been used in a particular time block can usually be used at the beginning of the next one.

To sum up, here are the main points for teachers to remember when they use this system in lesson planning.

1. Use the appropriate time block to plan the practice of presequenced activities in all skill areas.
2. Modify activities to fit one's own program and geographic location when necessary or appropriate.
3. Add appropriate detail to the activity examples presented when entering them in the lesson plan.
4. Experiment as desired with new ideas for sequenced activities, and with the placement of activities in the lesson plan.
5. Use activities from previous time blocks or from forthcoming time blocks, depending on the pace of the group.
6. Use activities from previous or forthcoming time blocks to meet children's particular and individual needs, and to provide both challenge and success for each child.
7. Use the time blocks with any curriculum methods, modules, or resources, and with any appropriate themes.

Parent Education: Sharing Information and Time Blocks with Parents

While my purpose for the detail in this chapter was primarily to introduce the time blocks to teachers as a system to use in lesson planning, these time blocks have another very important function. The time blocks also can be extremely useful in the area of parent education and involvement. It is particularly vital for teachers to understand, developmentally, how children learn particular skills, so that they can explain to parents how children learn these skills.

Many of today's programs for young children build in the requirement that parents be involved on an ongoing basis with their children's progress and learning. At the beginning of the year, and regularly thereafter, parents are often asked for input on the goals they have for their children.

When parents give input on skills they want their children to accomplish, teachers may think that what some parents want is in conflict with what teachers and programs want. Some parents do not know a great deal about the sequences of child growth and development or the specifics of children's intellectual skill development. At times, they may seem to have unreasonable expectations for their children.

In reality, however, parents want the same things for their children that early childhood professionals want. They want their children to have strong self-esteem and skills that will help them be successful when they leave the program. Parents want and deserve reassurance that the program will teach their children skills that will help them to be more successful in school. Because parents and programs want, essentially, the same things, the conflict is not so much in the skills that should be mastered as in the *ways* they will be mastered.

It is the responsibility of the early childhood professional to explain to parents the ways children learn to master skills gradually, over time, by hands-on participation in planned, sequenced, skill-focused activities.

Parents need to know that some children, though not all, may have difficulty understanding and following a line on a printed, two-dimensional page if they have not first experienced what a line is, in three dimensions, with their bodies. When parents understand how children learn what a "line" is by gradually learning to follow a line with their bodies and then with their eyes, they will better understand why we want children to use balance beams, balls, crayons, paintbrushes, and scissors.

When parents are made aware of the many steps in the sequence of learning to cut with scissors or to print with a pencil, they are far less likely to demand to know why teachers are not practicing letters and numbers or cutting out squares with scissors at the beginning of the year.

We need to help parents understand that playing with parquetry and puzzles helps train children's eyes to focus on one point while they continue to see what is in the background, and that this may help them later in focusing on one word or one line of print found on a whole page full of print.

Parents need to know that children need to experience books and stories every day, at school and at home, and that children are excited about seeing their own words in print. When children see that adults value their thoughts and ideas enough to put them down as words on paper, children are proud and will become motivated about reading and about communicating with written words.

We need to help parents understand that dramatic play can help children practice language and safety and health habits, and that involvement with meals and snacks not only helps children learn about nutrition, but also helps them learn math and science skills.

Parents need to understand that when we help children listen carefully to sounds and play matching sound games, we are training their ears to hear the differences between sounds, and that this can help them later to hear the small differences in the sounds of letters.

Additionally, when teachers understand the relationships of skill-focused activities to cognitive and psychomotor development, and learn ways to sequence the practice of these skill-focused activities, they will not only do lesson planning that is more beneficial to children; they will also know how to explain to parents what they are doing and why they are doing it.

Here is how the time block pages in this chapter and in Appendix A can be used in parent involvement and parent education. Sharing copies of these time block pages with parents at the beginning of each four- or five-week period will help parents know what will be experienced by their children during the current or coming month. Better still, parents will see, over and over again, that all these activities are learning activities, and that all of them teach their children specific skills in motor, perception, literacy, memory, and problem solving. After I began to use the time blocks in this way, I never, never again heard a parent ask, "Why are they just playing?"

Summary

In this chapter, we have discussed the increasingly diverse nature of today's early childhood classrooms, and the corresponding need for today's teachers to spend more time addressing children's individual needs. We have examined the ways that the developmentally sequenced practice of skills can be effective in helping all children reach their full potentials.

A more effective system of managing the vertical curriculum can help ensure that teachers plan skill-focused activities that can be practiced in gradual and meaningful ways as children grow and change throughout the year. Such a system will also help ensure that teachers will plan activities that cover all major skill areas.

Teachers who want to do a really competent job of planning and implementing the vertical curriculum with today's children need to need to do all of the following:

1. Offer a rich and varied learning environment full of appropriate materials.
2. Give children enough time to use them freely, and guide them in this process by adding interest, by providing reinforcement, and by using open questions that challenge children's thinking.
3. Schedule small-group times and one-on-one time for the further practice of sequenced skill-focused activities.
4. Use a system that ensures that you will plan a balance of developmentally sequenced activities in all five skill areas.

I believe readers will agree that when teachers have ways of organizing information, they can always use it much more efficiently and quickly. The analogy used in this guidebook is that if you have hundreds of great recipes, but you can't find the one you want and your kitchen is a mess, it's pretty hard to prepare the recipe.

Understanding the differences between horizontal and vertical planning, and being able to organize and do vertical planning more easily, will save teachers time, energy, and paperwork. They will be able to put that time and energy to use in better ways. They will have more time to "float" in all areas of the room to observe, interact, individualize, and really enjoy their work with young children.

This chapter has focused on planning that helps children practice specific skills, but the other entries in the teacher's lesson plan will depend on the teacher's themes, other things that are happening in the classroom, and the teacher's other priorities. In Chapter 5, we will review the purposes and basic elements of daily schedules and daily lesson plans, and see some ways that the lesson plan form itself can help teachers document the quality of their varied work with young children.

Self-Study Activities

1. If you have thoroughly read and digested all the material in this chapter, you deserve a break! After your break, and in light of your new understanding about vertical curriculum information and the use of the time blocks to manage it, read the tables in Appendix A that present all seven time blocks for the program year. Choose one activity and follow its sequence through all seven time blocks. One example that you might find interesting is temporal ordering, or the gradual introduction and use of time concepts and the calendar with young children.

2. Find some time to reflect on some of the activities you like best to do with your children. List ten such activities. Then categorize your list by the five major skill categories presented in this chapter. Find out where your ideas fall: motor, perceptual, literacy, memory, or problem solving. Do the activities you chose reflect a balance of all five major areas?

3. Without looking at the tables in this guidebook, think about one skill that you want children to master by the end of the program year. Write a list of all the activities you would use in order to provide mastery of this skill through hands-on activity. Now list the activities as you would use them in consecutive order, or the order in which you would put them in lesson plans. Check the tables in Appendix A to see if your sequence for each skill meshes with the sequences found there.

References and Resources for Further Reading

Bredekamp, Sue, ed. Developmentally *Appropriate Practice in Early Childhood Programs Serving Children from Birth through Age 8,* expanded ed. Washington, DC: National Association for the Education of Young Children, 1992. *Developmental milestones for children from birth to age three are presented and are listed in seven areas: interest in others; self-awareness; motor and eye–hand skills; language and communication; physical, spatial, and temporal awareness; purposeful action and use of tools; and expression of feelings. Each of these seven areas is divided into three general age categories: birth through eight months, eight to eighteen months, and eighteen months to three years. (pp. 30+31).*

Forman, George, & Hill, Fleet. *Constructive Play: Applying Piaget in the Preschool.* Reading, MA: Addison-Wesley, 1984. *This book includes open-ended activities and games developed from Piaget's principles of child development. Although the activities are not sequenced, strategies encourage children to move at their own pace in developing skills.*

McAfee, Oralie, & Leong, Deborah. *Assessing and Guiding Young Children's Development and Learning.* Boston: Allyn and Bacon, 1994. *This book contains five comprehensive appendices which list "developmental patterns" of growth and development for ages two to seven or eight in large-muscle development, small-muscle development, cognitive development, language development, and personal and social development. This text also contains developmental red flags or child behaviors that the teacher should consider carefully as possible indicators that the child might have special needs. Red flag behavior information is included in the social-emotional, perceptual-motor, language, and hearing areas of development for three- to five-year-olds (pp. 231–274).*

Phillips, Carol Brunson, ed. *Essentials for Child Development Associates Working with Young Children.* Washington, DC: Council for Early Childhood Professional Recognition, 1991. *General developmental characteristics from birth to age five are set forth in a very practical*

way, tying "what children are like" to specific sug-
gestions for "how adults can help" (pp. 40–79).
U.S. Department of Health and Human Services,
Administration of Children, Youth and Families,
Head Start Bureau, *Head Start Statistical Fact
Sheet* (Washington, DC: Head Start Bureau, 1994).

Readers should also examine various observation and screening instruments, as well as the developmental guidelines in this guidebook and in early childhood texts, to study developmental sequences for various skills.

For readers who a enjoy challenge! Do some research on the work in the 1970s, on the possible connection between perceptual-motor activities and success in reading. You will need to use your college or local library and take advantage of the interloan system, and you should also investigate the resources and articles of ERIC, the Educational Resource Information Center.

The ERIC Clearinghouse on Elementary and Early Childhood Education is at the University of Illinois at 800-583-4135. The Eric Clearinghouse on Reading is at Indiana University at 800-759-4723. ERIC can also be accessed through the Internet. ERIC can obtain abstracts or articles for you on this topic, based on the research of Bryant Cratty, Marianne Frostig, and N. Kephart, as well as more recent research.

Through college libraries or interloan, look for the book *Growth and Development: The Child and Physical Activity,* by Leonard Zaichkowsky, Linda Zaichowsky, and Thomas Martinek, published by the C. V. Mosby Company in 1980. Although the book is now out of print, it is worth the effort of a search. The authors summarize the major work of researchers who were proponents of the theory that planned perceptual motor activities are among the factors that are helpful to children in developing prereading and prewriting skills, and that these activities can also help children who have certain reading disabilities.

I have found through an ERIC database search that there is no empirical research either proving or disproving the theory that planned practice of perceptual-motor activities helps children develop reading skills. In my interviews with early childhood teachers and disabilities specialists, however, I have found ongoing support in the field for practices that support the theories of Marianne Frostig and similar researchers.

5 Daily Schedules and Lesson Plans

Introduction

In this chapter we will look at some practical information about daily schedules and lesson plans. Like blueprints, lesson plans and daily schedules are formats used to put ideas and plans on paper. In these formats, the teacher's plans and curriculum ideas are transformed into activities that children experience on a particular day. Lesson plans and daily schedules are crucial tools for the early childhood teacher.

In focusing on these tools, we will examine the purposes of the lesson plan, compare the differences between schedules and lesson plans, discuss some of the challenges of daily scheduling, and describe what comprehensive schedules and lesson plans should include. Several examples of schedules and two examples of lesson plan formats are included in this chapter.

What Is a Lesson Plan?

We need to start by examining the lesson plan itself, exploring what a lesson plan really is and what it does. One of the main purposes of a lesson plan is to help the teacher consistently to implement preplanning that reflects his or her long-range, short-range, and daily goals. For example, some daily activities in the lesson plan will probably emphasize the self-concept of children, which is a long-range and recurring theme in most early childhood programs. Other activities in the plan might relate to a short-range thematic unit that is of interest to the teacher and children. Still other lesson plan activities might relate to certain skills that are being practiced by children.

A particular literacy activity, such as playing with recycled greeting cards, could be a daily goal or objective relating to the long-range goal of developing literacy skills. Daily self-help activities could have short-range objectives such as teaching handwashing and toothbrushing, which relate to the long-range goal, or life skill, of good personal health practices.

In addition to its purpose as a tool for implementing the teacher's goals and objectives, the lesson plan is somewhat like a blueprint. Incorporated into this blueprint are reminders of all the curriculum elements that should be included every day, such as the use of art and creative media or the use of blocks and active play equipment. The lesson plan blueprint often incorporates the daily schedule so that teachers can see at a glance the consecutive order of what they have planned to happen from the beginning to the end of the day. The plan will often include staff responsibilities, or who is to do what.

The lesson plan also provides a summary of all the teacher-directed and child-initiated experiences that will take place in the learning centers of a particular setting on a particular day. Teacher-directed learning experiences will occur in large-group time, in small-group time, and with individuals during free-choice or children's activity time. Within the setting and time frames described in the lesson plan, children will engage in many types of learning activities, all of which teachers plan, offer, facilitate, or direct.

Even though only the planned learning experiences in the setting are indicated in the lesson plan, spontaneous learning excursions can and do take place in the setting during the day. These on-the-spot teaching/learning experiences, or "teachable moments," are often noted on the lesson plan after the fact by the teacher, and may become the beginning of a whole set of new teaching ideas for another day.

Additionally, the lesson plan is a written instrument. Therefore, lesson plans help provide written evidence of developmentally appropriate practices that may be implemented by teachers, and evidence of what actually occurs during each classroom day. Written lesson plans also help to document compliance with federal, state, program, and other standards.

Because lesson plans do all of these things, creating daily lesson plans consistently and well is a big order! The early childhood teacher often spends as much time working on lesson planning as on implementing the plans. What is even more frustrating is that hard work still may not result in comprehensive and consistent lesson plans that satisfy one's program supervisor, who often wants a certain result but may have little time to help the teacher achieve it.

A well-formatted lesson plan, clear in its content and as detailed as necessary, is helpful not only to the teacher but also to the teacher's supervisor, because the elements of a clearly written lesson plan will indicate all of the following:

1. Teacher-directed activities for large-group times and small-group times. (shows teacher management skills and promotes children's cognitive growth, plus attention span and socialization skills)
2. Activities in which the teacher works with individuals (shows individualized planning)
3. Ample child-initiated or free-choice time for children to engage in activities offered by the teacher, in at *least* an equal balance in duration to teacher-directed time (shows teacher planning skills and promotes children's planning, motor, cognitive, social, and self-direction skills; matches child development needs)

4. An alternating flow of both active and quiet work and play experiences (matches developmental needs)
5. Activities for outdoor time (matches developmental needs)
6. The teacher's themes and objectives connected with thematic units (shows horizontal planning)
7. The teacher's objectives for skill-focused learning activities (shows vertical planning)
8. Evidence of hands-on, concrete experiences in discovery problem solving, literacy, and with sensory experiences (matches developmental needs and priorities in early education)
9. Regularly scheduled health, nutrition, and safety education activities (matches developmental needs and early childhood priorities)
10. Evidence of activities promoting program priorities (promotes autonomy of program and its values)

Regarding item 10, in many lesson plans, written entries indicate certain program values and priorities. These might be entries concerning ecology or environmental awareness, entries demonstrating inclusion of children with disabilities, or activities indicating multicultural awareness. Sometimes the lesson plan tells us that the program or teacher puts a high priority on parent input, because a space is reserved on the lesson plan form for parent visitor or volunteer comments.

Sometimes a strong emphasis on self-concept and positive social skills is seen in the lesson plans, evidenced in entries about weighing and measuring children, or doing a group art mural, or in activities that might be titled "Our Feelings," "Somebody Is Special," "I Can Do It," "About My Family," "What a Friend Is," and "Adults Who Help Us." A great deal can be guessed about the program, the teacher, and what happens for children on a given day if the lesson plan is clear and comprehensive.

Of course, a supervisor or qualified observer could not use the lesson plan alone in making assumptions about what happens for children in a teacher's classroom. One would need to look back over many lesson plans for the current or past year to determine if what is seen in the plans is consistent. Actual observations would need to be made in the setting to determine if what is planned actually happens in practice. Further questions would need to be asked of the teacher and staff, including parent volunteers.

As a written instrument, however, the lesson plan is a type of evidence, and it is important as an indicator of the quality of early childhood teaching that is being done by the teacher. Therefore, another excellent reason to do good lesson planning is that it helps to document the quality of one's work. All of us like to get credit for the good things we do.

Before continuing our discussion of lesson plans and what details they should include, it is important to clarify the difference between a daily lesson plan and a daily schedule.

Daily Schedules

A schedule lists the times of the program day at which various events are to occur. A lesson plan does more than this; it details the specific activities that will occur within the time frames of the daily schedule. Even though the schedule tells us nothing about specific activities, it can tell us a great deal about five of the ten components that should be included in the lesson plan:

- The times and duration of teacher-directed large-group time and small-group time
- The time that individualized teaching is done
- The time and duration of free-choice or children's activity time (child-initiated)
- The balance and flow of activities
- The existence and duration of outdoor time.

The time that the teacher spends one-on-one with children, doing individualized teaching, is not always indicated clearly in writing on daily schedules, but it would be helpful to supervisors if teachers would indicate on the daily schedule that this activity occurs during free-choice or child-initiated time. Another component of the daily schedule that may or may not be indicated on the schedule in writing is the time or times of the day when teachers and children do joint planning or evaluating.

The schedule will always tell us whether or not meals are served and will sometimes provide time and duration information on routines such as toothbrushing and children's clean-up time. Look for these five elements in the five examples of daily schedules that follow.

Example 1: Half-Day Schedule, Three Hours, No Meals

8:45–9:00	Arrival and conversation
9:00–9:10	Circle; plans for activity time
9:10–10:20	Child activity time/free choice including open snack and individualizing
10:20–10:25	Clean-up and transition to group
10:25–10:35	Small-group time
10:35–10:50	Music and movement
10:50–11:10	Story time and evaluating our day
11:10–11:35	Outdoor time
11:35–11:45	Goodbyes and dismissal

Example 2: Half-Day Schedule, Four Hours, Meals Served

8:45–9:00	Arrival
9:00–9:30	Breakfast, conversation, toothbrushing

9:30–9:45   Circle; plans for activity time

9:45–11:00   Child activity time/free choice. Individualized teaching and clean-up

11:00–11:10 Small group

11:10–11:30 Outdoors or activities in gym

11:30–11:45 Music and movement; including (staggered) toileting

11:45–12:00 Story time

12:00–12:30 Lunch and conversation about our day

12:30–12:45 Dismissal

Example 3: Half-Day Schedule, Four Hours, Meals Served

8:30–9:00   Arrival/open breakfast/ conversation

9:00–9:15   Singing; planning for activity time

9:15–10:30   Child activity time/free choice and individualized teaching

10:30–10:40 Recall—evaluate our activities

10:40–11:00 Music and movement

11:00–11:10 Small group

11:10–11:30 Stretch and story

11:30–12:00 Lunch and conversation

12:00–12:30 Outdoors

12:30   Dismissal

Example 4: Half-Day Schedule, Three and a Half Hours (Meals Served and Staggered Bus Arrival)

8:30   Bus A arrives. Greeting in circle; planning for activity time. Children have simple breakfast, then read or use manipulatives.

8:45   Bus B arrives. Greeting in circle. Children eat breakfast; teachers converse with Bus B children at breakfast about plans for activity time.

9:00   Short circle; sing. Transition to activity time.

9:05–10:00   Child activity time/free choice and Individualized teaching

10:05–10:10 Clean-up

10:10–10:20 Small group

10:20–10:35 Music and movement

10:35–11:00 Outdoor time or activities in gym

11:00–11:15 Story time and fingerplays

11:10–11:20 Get ready for lunch (staggered)

11:20–11:45 Lunch and conversation about our day. Brush teeth upon finishing lunch.

11:45   Bus A leaves. Bus B children read or use manipulatives.

12:00   Bus B leaves.

Example 5: Three Hours, One Meal

8:30–9:00	Arrival/greeting. Breakfast and conversation. As children finish, brush teeth and read books.
9:00–9:20	Circle. Bend, stretch, sing as last children brush teeth. Plans for activity time and transition.
9:20–10:30	Child activity time/free choice and individualized teaching
10:35	Clean up
10:35–10:45	Small group
10:45–11:00	Music and movement
11:00–11:15	Story and conversation
11:15–11:30	Outdoors and dismissal

Although the reader has been presented with half-day schedules, full-day schedules would probably follow any of these schedules rather closely in the mornings. In the afternoons in a full-day schedule, children usually rest (some sleep; some do not) for an hour, have another outdoor time and/or activity time, then have a snack, and then read or use small-muscle manipulatives until dismissal. Often, the extra time allows for nature walks and for individual time with teachers to work on literacy skills such as children's own stories on tape or in journals.

Challenges in Scheduling

Time Management

Daily scheduling presents several types of challenges to the early childhood teacher. In this chapter, some time must be spent presenting practical solutions to those challenges. Diverse situations have purposely been presented in the five half-day examples given here to show that several factors can affect the schedule of the day, such as the number of hours, bus transportation, and meal service.

Readers can see that the number of hours in the day has the largest impact. When time is shorter and meal service is also included, as in Example 5, it is often difficult to have enough time during child-initiated activity time for individualizing, and hygiene routines must be planned and managed efficiently. Outdoor time is also shorter than in other examples; and children are dismissed from the outdoors, already dressed for dismissal.

Readers will also see the challenges that arise in the schedule when two buses arrive with children at different times, as in Example 4. Note also the changes that are made when two meals are served, as in examples 2, 3, and 4. When time is short and a healthful snack or meal must be provided, teachers may find that much time can be saved for other important things in the schedule if they offer an "open breakfast" or an "open snack" instead of having all the children and adults sit down at the same time to eat.

Example 1 shows the daily schedule of a parent cooperative center in a program that I directed. Prior to the development of the schedule shown here, parents wanted a sit-down snack time, but providing this took up fifteen minutes of the daily schedule. I wanted to add a small-group time in which children would practice skill-focused activities, but I did not want to take this time away from an already short outdoor time, and I could not take it away from free-choice or child activity time in which I did my individualized teaching. In order to get the ten minutes I wanted for small group, I had to give up a sit-down snack time and use an open snack, incorporated within free-choice time. This was a small price to pay because I felt (given my own values) that having all children end the program year with the mastery of appropriate skills was more important than having a sit-down snack.

This small change in schedule proved to be a real boon to the children in many ways. Children still had time to practice setting up, passing, serving, and cleaning up. In fact, they were able to be even more independent in these activities and in their choices of when and with whom to eat. They were still able to practice good manners and sociable language. Best of all, the daily schedule was adjusted to include small-group time. This anecdote points out the fact that the teacher's values always have an impact on the daily schedule.

In early childhood programs, concentrated learning occurs throughout the day, whether it is a three-hour or a full-day program. Much learning must occur in relatively short periods. Good teachers manage this by being innovative and by squeezing out the time they need from every opportunity. They make use of every moment, often using meal times for planning and for conversation (literacy skills), talking about health and hygiene during meals and health routines, and doing their individualized teaching during free-choice time or in other opportune moments during the day.

Balance

Another challenge of scheduling concerns the length of time for teacher-directed group times, and the flow and balance of these times during the daily schedule. First, let's talk about balance in the schedule, which means the balance between teacher-directed and child-initiated time. This has to do with the duration of time spent by children sitting and listening attentively to an adult or engaging in conversation or activities led by an adult, as compared to the time spent by children in choosing and concentrating on self-selected activities planned and/or offered by the teacher.

Basic child development knowledge tells us the need for young children to learn factual content, thinking skills, and concentration skills through active play and hands-on concrete experiences. Basic child development knowledge also tells us that young children have difficulty sitting and focusing attention on an adult for long periods, and that sitting still for short, large-group, teacher-directed times should last only about ten to fifteen minutes. Although these are well-known facts, parents (and some teachers) often want children to practice learning to sit and "concentrate" (focus attention on the adult) for much longer periods. This presents a dilemma to early childhood teachers who are doing their best to meet children's developmental needs.

Debates concerning this dilemma focus on the balance of approximately equal amounts of time for teacher-directed and child-initiated time in the daily schedule, excluding routines, which are always led by adults. Sometimes teachers need to justify or explain their rationale for this balance to parents or other adults in terms of child development.

To be successful in this endeavor, the first thing teachers might do is clarify to others their need for ample time during the day to do individualized teaching. As a practical matter, there is no other time during the program day for teachers to accomplish this task. Parents and supervisors will be able to see from the daily schedule and from observation that the teacher is free to address individual needs during free-choice time.

Teachers will also need to clarify the specific ways in which children learn the skills of concentration and attentiveness through activities occurring in the daily schedule, and be able to explain the ways children learn these skills in a manner that meets their developmental needs.

Concerned parents (or adults having difficulty with this issue) should be invited to observe children during child-planned activity time to see the intensity with which children concentrate as they are engaged in meaningful activities. Teachers should explain that as children move through the year, these concentration and attention span skills keep improving.

Next, the teacher should focus on the actual skill about which some people may be concerned—the skill of listening to an adult. It is not the *time* duration of the listening that is important, but the *skill itself.* Children are actually practicing the skill of attentive listening to adults at many times during the day. The best way for young children to practice this skill is during several short large-group times and a small-group time totaling thirty to forty-five minutes, instead of practicing it by sitting for thirty to forty-five minutes at a stretch.

Observe a group of three- to five-year-olds who have been asked to sit still for thirty minutes and listen to an adult. You will find them "losing it" after about ten minutes. They will be wiggling, lying on the floor, touching the children next to them, and paying little or no attention to the adult. In other words, children would actually be practicing *poor* concentration and attention span habits instead of good ones.

In the schedule examples presented earlier, if we add up the minutes of teacher-directed and child-initiated time, excluding the adult-guided routines and meals, we can see that in each of the examples there is an approximately equal balance of time between teacher-directed and child-initiated activities. Now let's look at the related issue of flow in the daily schedule.

Flow

Young children's learning experiences are most effective when they flow in an alternating active-to-quiet-to-active pattern throughout the program day. Incorporated into this flow of active and quiet times is the flow of indoor and outdoor activity.

An appropriate flow of activities is usually easily achieved by teachers because the order of events in the daily schedule is up to them. Care must be taken not to schedule two sit-down quiet periods back to back. Whenever this seems impossible to avoid, teachers can add a minute or two of exercise, or bending and stretching with or without music, in between two quiet, sit-down activities.

In Examples 3 and 5 of the daily schedules, this is what has been done when there are two quiet, sit down times in consecutive order. In Example 1, readers will see that music and movement occurs between small-group and story time. In all the examples, readers will see that active outdoor play follows and/or precedes a quiet activity.

Outdoor Time

Outdoor play is important in the schedule, but finding time to do it every day may be a challenge to teachers. Those with more hours in the program day find that outdoor time is easier to schedule. Sometimes teachers with short program days will cut down outdoor time to allow more time for other activities, especially in inclement weather.

Young children need time and freedom to experience fresh air and exercise outdoors with a variety of age appropriate equipment, or with the elements of the natural environment itself (snow, grass, sand or earth, small hills, curbs, and sidewalks). It is not necessary or appropriate to structure all outdoor activities.

Three- and four-year-olds are not yet ready for relay races or complex games with many rules. Teacher-directed outdoor activities that meet their developmental needs would include such activities as planting a garden, playing toss and catch, flying kites, or using a parachute. Several children could participate at one time in various guided activities, but all the children in the group would not participate at the same time.

Core Elements of the Schedule

Let's review the basic elements of the five daily schedules in this chapter. Each schedule includes all five core elements that should be found in a daily schedule; these are five of the ten elements that should also be found in a daily lesson plan.

- There are teacher-directed large- and small-group activities of appropriate lengths.

- Time for individualized teaching is designated.
- There is an approximately equal balance of child-initiated and teacher-directed time (excluding routines).
- There is an alternating pattern of active and quiet times.
- Outdoor time is scheduled each day.

Each daily schedule also includes conversations during meals, individualized teaching during child-initiated activity time, transitions, and a time for children to evaluate their day and plan for tomorrow, even though this sometimes occurs during lunch. Practical solutions to challenges in scheduling can always be achieved when teachers are motivated to work toward solutions.

It is most helpful to parents, visitors, and supervisors to see the daily schedule posted clearly in the classroom. However, planning for children sometimes changes; teachers should be sure that the posted schedule always matches what happens in actual practice. Next we need to look at the ways specific activities that occur during the daily schedule are documented—lesson plans.

Lesson Plans

The other format in which teachers' curriculum ideas find their way to paper is the lesson plan itself. As readers can see, designing a good daily schedule is half the battle. In the discussion of the daily schedule, we have already dealt with half of the ten items that were listed in the early pages of this chapter as elements that should be part of each lesson plan.

The other items that should be included in lesson plans are more qualitative than quantitative in nature; they deal more with the learning experiences themselves and how they are entered into the lesson plan than with the times they take place. These are the concrete, hands-on activities chosen by the teacher for learning experiences that have to do with horizontal planning; vertical planning; planning for early childhood education and program priorities; and planning for health, nutrition, and safety education.

Other chapters in this guidebook provide detail on incorporating all five of these elements in the daily lesson plan. The issue we need to discuss at this point is not the inclusion of these elements but the adequacy of detail in written lesson plan entries.

Quality Lesson Plans Incorporate Clear Detail

Great differences are found in the ways teachers write up these activities on their lesson plans. The quality of content, as is seen or not seen in the details given about an activity, is sometimes an issue. The range of detail in written lesson plans is diverse and encompasses a very broad spectrum. At one end are plans which offer no detail at all, and at the other are plans in which the detail is mind boggling.

Some lesson plans spell out, in many complete sentences, every one of the children's activities in terms of behavioral outcomes. "The children will each walk with alternating steps on the balance beam, then they will jump with both feet onto a carpet square. Then they will balance on one (dominant) foot for five seconds, then they will climb up and down three steps. Next they will hop (at varied skill levels) to the climber; then they will slide down the slide; last they will crawl through a cloth tunnel. They may begin the obstacle course sequence again, on the balance beam." This much detail not only is unnecessary, but if it is done in every single area of the lesson plan, it is a recipe for teacher burnout!

Instead of this overload of detail, the teacher could simply have stated, in the space on the lesson plan for "Large-Muscle Activities," what would happen in that area in order for the children to practice large motor skills. "Obstacle course" might not tell us quite enough, but "Obstacle course—climber, slide, beam, carpet squares, steps, tunnel" would give us a clear picture of what large-muscle activities would be practiced that day.

Another example of overdoing detail would be: "Easel. Large newsprint; both sides. Large brushes. Four jars tempera, both sides, in white, yellow, red and blue." Since the usual daily procedure is to use several kinds of tempera, both sides of the easel, and large brushes, it is not necessary to detail these points. (Teachers would, however, note changes such as the use of special paper or small brushes.) The lesson plan would provide adequate detail if it stated, "Easel; experiment with pastels," or "Easel; white & primary; mix pastels."

On the other hand, one should always add detail that is necessary. Teachers should not put "Book" or "Read story" on the lesson plan in the area for literacy or story time. They should list the name of the story or book, perhaps adding, "with puppet" or "children will retell." In the space on the lesson plan for music and movement the teacher would not write "Dance," but would be expected to write what kind of music, rhythm, or chants would be used. In the space on the lesson plan for sensory activities, the teacher would be expected to detail what kind of experiences would occur, such as "Pour/fill colored rice" or "Guess smells/film containers" or "Make and use silly putty."

Often, improved attention to quality and detail in lesson plans correlates with improved teacher competence. But sometimes supervisors find that teachers who do a competent and enthusiastic job in action while they are being observed with young children may have lesson plans that are vague and general. These may be those natural and enthusiastic teachers who rationalize that vague lesson planning helps them be more spontaneous.

However, when one looks at the current and past lesson plans of such teachers, the plans may provide no clear written documentation proving that the teacher does good work consistently. These might be plans that have no long- and short-range goals for children, either individually or as a group; thematic units and their objectives may be unclear. They may be plans that give no detail about the daily materials or planned activities.

Assistance in Lesson Planning

To address this problem, two things could be done. First, training could be provided to teachers in what constitutes enough detail, as was explained in the preceding examples. Such details, added to the lesson plan, would clearly show the content and quality of the activities planned. These details will tell supervisors if the teacher is presenting age-appropriate and concrete activities. The details will also show the specific activities the teacher is using to promote his or her priorities and those of the program, such as those activities promoting self-esteem skills, social skills, environmental awareness, multicultural awareness, inclusion awareness, math and science discovery skills, and literacy skills.

A rule of thumb guideline for detail can be found in an analogy about grocery shopping. I write a different kind of grocery list for myself than I do for my husband when he does the shopping! For him, I add details so that he knows the specific items I have in mind. In the same way, a guideline might be to add enough detail to the lesson plan that a substitute teacher could know what to do by reading just what you wrote. (Having a general emergency lesson plan on site for unforeseen substitute situations is, by the way, an excellent and practical idea.)

The second way to help teachers write consistently clear lesson plans has to do with the lesson plan form itself. Formats should include certain headings and spaces to remind teachers of activities that must occur. If spaces and headings are provided on the lesson plan format for "Theme," "Main Skill Objective," "Large Muscle," "Fine Motor," "Sensory," "Literacy," and so forth, it saves teachers time, energy, and paperwork, ensures that necessary entries will be made, and allows teachers to use their time and energy to fill in the details concerning activity content that are necessary. Two examples of helpful formats for lesson plans are included at the end of this chapter.

Documenting Individualized Teaching in Lesson Plans

Earlier in this chapter we discussed the need for teachers to indicate the time on the daily schedule that individualized teaching occurs. However, words listed on the daily schedule do not give enough detail to provide evidence of individualized teaching. It is important for teachers to document their individualized teaching in the lesson plan itself. Brief entries can provide written evidence of what skill or skills are practiced, and when and with whom the teacher does one-on-one teaching. Space for this kind of entry should be provided in the lesson plan format, as it is in the two examples in Figures 5-1 and 5-2 at the end of this chapter.

Placing the initials of the child or children with whom the teacher is working in the lesson plan, and briefly stating what the activity is and where or when it occurs, is all that is necessary. These details document that the teacher is transferring information that has been discovered about each child's needs through screening and observation to the lesson plan, and provides evidence that the teacher is meeting each child's needs in actual practice in the classroom.

The use of initials is not a breach of confidentiality; the teacher cares about and will spend one-on-one time with every child in the classroom at some point. All the children's initials will be seen, over time, in the lesson plans. If a teacher (or program) feels strongly that these brief notes on individualized teaching cannot be seen on a lesson plan posted on the wall or elsewhere available for reading, these notes can be put on the back of the plan.

Transitions

Although they are not usually written out in lesson plans, transitions get teachers and children from point A to point B. They are the short activities which move children smoothly from one activity to another or from one part of the schedule to the next. When teachers do not use transitions, their lesson plans or schedules may start to fall apart. Instead of moving quickly into the next learning event, teachers are wandering about gathering up children and trying to get them to a particular area of the room. Transitions might be thought of as the glue that holds the schedule and lesson plan together.

It is good practice for teachers to develop personal repertoires of a variety of transitions that work for them and that they enjoy using. In developing a repertoire, try some of each of the five basic types of transitions: musical, physical, creative, cognitive, and social.

Common musical transitions used by teachers are made-up songs telling what we are going to do next, such as "This is the way we clean our room, clean our room, . . . so we can have small-group time." Another common practice is playing quiet music during the time children who finish eating before the others go to rest on the rug to wait for the rest of the group. In this case, since children are also learning the stress-reducing skill of relaxing to music, the transition is both musical and physical.

Cognitive transitions often take the form of directions that tie in with a type of perception or memory skill, such as "If you are wearing red . . ." or "If you can recognize your name . . ." or "What do we need to do next? . . . What do we need to remember when we walk to the gym?" Other cognitive transitions might be reading or playing with lotto games while waiting for the rest of the group.

Physical transitions move children to new activities with specific movement, such as "Hop to the rug area" or "Tiptoe to the door." Most of the time, creative elements are added, such as "Tiptoe down the hall like little mice" or "Hop like a bunny," making these transition examples both creative and physical.

An example of a creative transition might be to say, "When you look like proud kings and queens getting ready to sit down to dinner, I'll know you are ready to . . ." or "Make up a silly ending to this nursery rhyme before you . . ." Teachers often combine creative and physical transitions: "Let's pretend to be butterflies as we go to the outdoor area" or "Let's make a train (form a line) and chug the train to the bathrooms."

All transitions that involve the group are social in nature, but some transitions are clearly intended to nurture pro-social skills. When teachers ask children to "find a friend to walk with," or, "Let's hold hands around the lunch table and pass on a silent hand hug or squeeze," or "Before we leave the building to go home let's do a group hug," or "Let's gather in the circle and give ourselves a hand (applause) for such a great job in cleaning up," they are reinforcing the positive social skills of the group and are also using social transitions.

Summary

In this chapter we have compared daily schedules and lesson plans and covered some of the challenges in time management, format, balance, and detail that these tools present to the teacher. We have discussed the balance of teacher-directed and child-initiated time. Examples have been provided to help the teacher make choices about the content of the lesson plan and schedule, and these should also prove helpful in improving the detail and clarity of the lesson plan for supervisors. Attention has been given to the lesson plan as a written instrument that helps to document what the teacher has planned and what happens during the program day for children.

In closing, let's review the ten core elements that should be part of every good lesson plan. The first five should be seen in brief form in the teacher's daily schedule.

1. Teacher-directed large-group and small-group times are indicated and of appropriate length. (When programs do not schedule a separate small-group time, entries show that small groups work together during child-initiated time.)
2. Individualized teaching is documented with brief details.
3. Child-initiated or free-choice time based on the teacher's plans occurs and is in balance with or predominates over teacher-directed time (excluding routines).
4. An alternating pattern of active and quiet learning activities is evident.
5. Outdoor time is scheduled.
6. Horizontal planning: Entries indicate themes and thematic learning activities (Chapter 3).

	Mon.	Tue.	Wed.	Thu.
Individualizing				
Small Group				
Transitions				
Large Group				

Week of _____
Center _____
Teacher _____

Schedule   Notes
8:45 Arrival
9:00 Breakfast
9:30 Circle
9:45 Free Choice
11:00 Small Group
11:10 Outdoors
11:30 Circle/Music
11:45 Story
12:00 Snack/Meal
12:30 Circle and Dismissal

DAILY USE:
Blocks, Paint, Sensory,
Dramatic Play, Active Play

Open-Ended Art/Sensory Media	Pretend Play/Musical Play
Discovery/Problem Solving	Literacy/Writing Center
Gross/Fine Motor	Foods/Health/Safety
Outdoor	Ecology/Environment	Antibias/Inclusion

Horizontal Theme _____

Subtheme/Unit _____

Vertical Planning Focus _____

Parent Comments/Input
(Signature and Date)

Figure 5-1 *Lesson Plan Example 1*

Teacher _____
Week of _____

	MONDAY		TUESDAY		WEDNESDAY		THURSDAY		WEEK LONG
		NOTES		NOTES		NOTES		NOTES	THEMES
8:30 Arrival/Open Breakfast and Circle									
9:00 Planning									Health/Nutrition Safety
9:15–10:30 Free Choice									
Literacy–Sensory									Anti Bias/Inclusion
Dramatic Play									Outdoors/Trips Ecology
Art Media/Fine Motor									
Large Motor									
Individualizing									Discovery/Problem Solving
10:30 Recall									
10:40 Large Group Music/Movement									
11:00 Small Group									
11:10 Large Group Stretch and Story									
11:30 Lunch									Parent Comments (Sig. and Date)
12:00 Outdoors									
12:30 Dismissal									Continued on reverse

Figure 5-2 Lesson Plan Example 2

6 Putting It Together

The Step-by-Step System for Lesson Planning

A Review of Chapters 1 through 5

In this guidebook we have referred to lesson planning using an analogy in which the early childhood teacher is an eager cook, ready to plan and write the "daily menu." Before this can be done, the teacher's ideas and activities, (just like recipes, methods, tools, and ingredients) need to be organized so that the "menu" or daily lesson plan can be more easily and quickly written. In doing this organizing, we have discussed the spontaneous, horizontal, and vertical parts of the curriculum, as well as the format of the daily schedule and daily lesson plan.

The first half of this guidebook has emphasized a system for managing and using the teacher's vertical curriculum information (skill-focused activities) in a planned and developmentally sequenced manner that provides a balance of activities in all skill areas every day. Examples of developmentally sequenced activities in five major areas—motor, perception, literacy, memory, and problem solving—were provided in seven time blocks for a nine-month program year. In these time blocks, the developmental steps for practicing skills have been emphasized, not the specific materials or strategies the teacher would enter in the lesson plan for practicing the activities.

The steps in skill sequencing and the method for organizing the activities provide a system for organizing and using the teacher's own ideas in the vertical curriculum. This is analogous to teaching someone to fish, instead of giving the person a fish, or teaching someone to cook instead of doing the cooking for him. In the first half of this guidebook, I have provided teachers with a system for managing their "methods, recipes, and ingredients" in order to write well-balanced "menus"— comprehensive lesson plans—more effectively.

Your child development knowledge and the developmental indicators in this book or others will ensure that your menu choices are developmentally appropriate. Your knowledge of your program, parents, and community will ensure that you are preparing a menu of choices that will be eagerly anticipated and appreciated.

The basic cooking methods of horizontal and vertical planning will influence your choices of recipes and ingredients for the menu or lesson plan. Your thematic activities might be thought of as your main dishes, and your skill-focused activities might be seen as other basic foods. You know the elements that always need to be included in your menu, or lesson plan, and an efficient way to put these in writing.

The menu choices that you plan, prepare, and serve will be served in the manner and order of your choice. Your horizontally and vertically planned activities will be placed on your lesson plan in the area of the setting you choose and in the order you feel is best. These menu choices will ultimately be your own creations because they will be mixed and spiced in your own individual style and will be influenced by the nature of your program.

Further spices may be added in the serving of the menu—the implementation of your lesson plan. These will be the result of your spontaneous incidental teaching in response to teachable moments generated by the interests and individual needs of the children in your group.

Now you have everything you need to do your daily lesson planning. You have the basics and you have a system. Your skill as a "chef" and your sophistication in the area of "menus" or lesson planning will continue to grow, change, and blossom.

The Ten-Step Method of Daily Lesson Planning

Getting Ready to Work

There are four preplanning steps you need to take as you get ready to do your daily lesson plan:

A. Gather what you need and find a quiet place to work. You will need your lesson plan sheet and this guidebook. You may want to copy and enlarge the tables in Appendix A to use. Otherwise you will need to use this guidebook.

B. You may also need a summary of the skill area needs of the children in your group, or your notes on the individual and/or group needs of the children in your room. (A system of managing information about individual or group skill area needs, including the use of a summary sheet, will be presented in Chapter 7 of this guidebook.) You may also wish to have other resources on child development and/or early childhood activities at hand.

C. If your group includes children with special needs or disabilities, you may want to have on hand some of your anecdotal notes and/or their individual education plans.

D. If you have not already done so, check your lesson plan form to be sure it includes or incorporates all of the core elements listed in Chapter 5. If the lesson plan form you are currently using does not leave space for something you feel you need to note, or if you wish to add an item to provide documentation for compliance with federal, state, and/or program standards, use the back of the lesson plan sheet. Now you are ready to begin the actual ten steps of creating your daily lesson plan, which follow.

Working with the Ten Steps

1. *Check your monthly calendar to see what may affect your plan.* Special program events, such as health or vision screening, may affect the daily plan, as might special visitors. Children's birthdays seen on the monthly calendar must also be noted if they will affect today's plan.

2. *Review and/or think about your own program's goals and strategies.* Every early childhood program, no matter what type or where it is, or what children it serves, has a basic philosophy through which its priorities and goals are implemented. In quality programs this philosophy is usually stated in writing, sometimes briefly, sometimes in detail. It is important for each early childhood professional student or teacher to take the responsibility of obtaining the philosophy and goals of his or her program, be it "lab school," Head Start, state-funded at-risk preschool, private- for-profit or nonprofit preschool, day care center, or cooperative preschool.

In Head Start, teachers are expected to have a thorough knowledge of the philosophy and goals of the program so that they can create effective lesson plans that mesh with the mission, philosophy and goals of Head Start.

Each Head Start program is required to have a written plan of action for each component of its services. If you are a Head Start teacher, you should have or should obtain a copy of your program's Education Component Plan. This plan will provide a comprehensive review of your program's education curriculum priorities and, better yet, provide you with specific ideas and strategies for carrying out this plan of action. It is a valuable and often overlooked tool.

If you are a student at a community college or university, you will be pursuing practicum courses or student teaching that will place you in an active role in the classroom setting. The lab school program will also have a philosophy and goals, which may or may not be in writing. As a responsible student, take action either to obtain a copy of this philosophy or to arrange an oral interview with the department head to take notes on the program's philosophy and goals.

Reviewing and understanding your program's goals and priorities will give you a mind set and direction that will help you in choosing activities for the daily lesson plan. It may also provide you with actual strategies.

3. *Review the developmental milestones of the age groups with whom you work.* In order for the activities you choose to be developmentally appropriate, be sure to scan or quickly review a developmental checklist, such as the one included in Chapter 2 of this book, providing physical, intellectual, and social-emotional indicators for the ages with whom you work.

If you have a new idea or an activity you want to try, *always* check these lists first to see if it is age appropriate. If you are using materials that accompany a screening tool as a resource for ideas, be sure you are choosing only those activities that match your children's ages and/or skill levels—activities you are sure will provide successful experiences for all children. For example, if you want your children to copy triangles, be aware that children cannot usually copy triangles successfully until they are nearly age five. It would not be a developmentally appropriate activity for three- and four-year-olds in the beginning of nine-month program year.

4. *Choose and enter the basic activities that children will always do on a daily basis.* On your lesson plan sheet, enter the basic activities that you plan every day. These are the activities that you and/or your program feel children should experience on a daily basis, such as sensory media, blocks, active play, open-ended art media, literacy, dramatic play, manipulatives, and hands-on problem solving. Most of these activities will be entered in the free-choice section of the lesson plan.

5. *Review a summary of the individual needs of your children. Choose and enter today's individualized activities.* Look at your notes on individual goals for your children, or look at a classroom summary sheet (to be discussed in Chapter 7) that lists the skill needs of all the children by group or category. Decide what individualized activities you should plan and with whom.

On your lesson plan sheet (or on the back of the sheet, if you prefer) write down an appropriate skill-focused activity and the initials of the child or children with whom you will be working one-on-one or in a small group, probably during free-choice time. An example would be "Practice tearing paper shapes—J. D. & S. M." Remember that your individualized activities might also include those for an especially gifted child.

6. *Choose and enter a variety of sequenced skill-focused activities that are developmentally appropriate for your group.* If you have already copied the tables in Appendix A for daily use, find the table for this time block of the year. If not, use the table in Appendix A of this book that would be appropriate to this time of the year. Choose and/or modify activities from each of the five skill areas that mesh with your goals for children. If you modify activities, be sure to preserve the steps of the developmental sequence for practicing the skill.

Also enter on the lesson plan any specific materials you will be using. For example, if you will be "Sorting or matching recyclables," you will want to state what kind of recyclables. Enter this activity into the lesson plan in a space that shows when and where you will do this sorting/matching. If you are "Using open-ended art media," state what kinds you are offering—for example, "easel paint/pastels," "collage/seeds and glue," "orange playdough."

Before you enter these activities on your lesson plan, note the placement for each activity as suggested in each skill area column in the table. Consider these suggestions for free choice, small group, or large group. Use these suggestions to decide when, where, with whom, and for how long you will be engaged in the activities you choose. Now enter your choices for activities on your lesson plan sheet wherever you think they will work best (small-group time, free-choice time, large-group time, or individualized time).

Place a check mark or today's date on the table next to the activities you chose for today. This will help you keep track of the activities from this particular table that you have done and not done. It will also remind you to choose activities from each of the five areas to give your lesson plan balance.

7. *Choose and enter activity ideas that mesh with your current theme or unit.* First, decide whether your children's interests and enthusiasm tell you to continue and expand on your present theme, subtheme, or unit, or to change to a new theme. Using your memories of past experiences with your theme, subtheme, or unit, as well as ideas from early childhood resource books such as those included in Appendix C, decide which activities you wish to list in today's plan. These will be activities that fit with and reinforce your theme or unit in a variety of ways and in several learning areas of the classroom.

Try to use integrated activities whenever possible, and try to address national priorities in early education (see Chapters 10 and 11). Enter the theme-related activities you have chosen on your lesson plan sheet. Your placement of theme-related activities on the lesson plan will undoubtedly indicate when, where, and for how long children will be engaged in these activities. Therefore, you will not need to write out these parameters.

8. *Choose and enter the activities required or suggested by your program that must occur regularly.* Most programs suggest that experiences in health and mental health, nutrition or foods, and safety be done and documented on a regular basis. When a program says "regularly," you should plan for an activity to occur at least one day a week. The lesson plan forms included in this book (Chapter 5) indicate spaces to note and document your planned activities in these areas.

This sort of cross-component integration is required in Head Start programs and is strongly suggested in many other preschool programs that provide comprehensive early childhood education and services. The NAEYC accreditation process suggests that programs include health, nutrition, and safety education as a regular part of curriculum planning. Therefore, the documentation of health and safety education activities on the lesson plan by teachers is important and may be necessary. Many other programs further suggest that activities in antibias/multicultural awareness and ecology or environmental awareness should also take place regularly.

Decide which, if any, of the regular or weekly activities required by your program should occur today, and enter them on your lesson plan sheet, unless they are already noted.

9. *Check anecdotal notes and individual education plans for special needs children and enter appropriate notes if necessary.* Always check your lesson plan to see if any items or activities in your setting will affect special needs children. Note changes or modifications if needed.

10. *Gather any special materials you need.* Often, you will find that you need or want a special item for the lesson plan you have just completed. Gather any such materials and have them ready to go. If the special materials you are taking require you to be at the classroom a bit earlier for setup, make the necessary arrangements.

Occasionally but regularly, take advantage of the self-assessment checklist on lesson planning and program management in Appendix B of this book to check your lesson plans for completeness and compliance with accepted standards in the field. You may wish to do this often at first if you are a new teacher.

If you follow these ten easy steps in the lesson-planning process every day, you will soon do them automatically and quickly. You will find that you are doing effective, appropriate, and comprehensive lesson plans very easily, without stress, and that you are enjoying yourself! For your convenience, these ten steps are listed again in summary form in a box at the end of this chapter.

What's Next: Preview of Chapters 7 through 11

The second half of this guidebook includes chapters on other early education elements that influence the teacher's lesson plans. For example, it is very important to remember that lesson plans will also be affected by the results of observation and screening. The information you gather about your children and how you use that information influences the entries you make on the lesson plan regarding individualized teaching. Summarizing the skill area needs of individual children and/or small groups of children will help you individualize your lesson plan and save you time. A summary sheet system to assist in this process will be shared in Chapter 7.

Returning for the moment to our analogy of the cook and the menu, your "guests," the children, will partake of the choices on your menu in the learning areas of your classroom setting. The "meal service" they will use will be your materials and equipment. The core elements of the setting, its learning centers, and materials will also affect the lesson plan. These will be discussed in Chapter 8.

Chapter 9 on "Free Choice—A Planned Activity Time" will give you tips on managing the numerous "menu choices" that could be offered during free-choice time in your lesson plan. It is in this child-initiated time that most hands-on learning occurs, as children make choices among the learning materials and engage in experiences that are often planned and guided by the teacher and staff.

In your lesson plan, you will be drawing on the thematic ideas developed in your horizontal plan, skill-focused activities, and other resources. Activity ideas emphasizing national early education priorities and integrated activities will be presented in Chapters 10 and 11 of this book.

Resources for Teachers

Whenever teachers do lesson planning, it is important to remember that some of the best resources for ideas and activities may not be written resources. The children, their parents, the children's extended families, and persons or organizations in the community are perhaps the best sources of fresh and relevant ideas.

Most preschool programs operate within the parameters of a philosophy that is communicated to teachers orally or in writing. The philosophy helps the teacher understand what program staff intend to do and how they intend to do it. If this philosophy is a written one, the program's standards of quality, goals, and strategies are often incorporated, as in Head Start's Education Component Plan. Written standards of quality for programs are usually a good resource for teaching ideas.

The teacher's own past and current experiences are another excellent source of ideas. Past work experiences, workshops and seminars, experiences at home in one's own family, and travel experiences are often seeds that bear the fruit of exciting ideas in the curriculum.

In addition, teachers may draw on college texts, professional journals, other magazines, the program's own curriculum resources or library, the local library, the ERIC (Educational Resources and Information Center) system, written community publications, government publications, and the many books available in the early childhood field. Some of these books are listed in Appendix C.

Self-Study Activity

Create two or three lesson plans by using the ten steps in this chapter. You might want to choose one of these to keep at the center as an emergency lesson plan for a substitute.

Resources for Further Reading

Read through the titles and resources listed in Appendix C. Make a list of the resources you are interested in finding, reading, or purchasing. Prioritize your list and begin your search for at least two such resources of your choice to read and study.

Summary of Steps in Practical, Effective Lesson Planning

1. Check monthly calendar and make necessary notes on plan.

2. Consider own program goals, philosophy, or education plan.

3. Review developmental milestones for the age groups in your classroom.

4. Choose and enter basic daily activities on the plan.

5. Review summary sheet of individual needs and enter choice(s) of individualized activities on today's plan.

6. Choose some skill-focused activities from each of the five major skill areas. Enter on today's plan in your small-group, large-group, or child-initiated time spaces, making modifications or adding your own details.

7. Choose and enter on the plan activities that mesh with your current theme or unit.

8. Choose and enter the activities required or suggested by your program that must occur regularly.

9. Check anecdotal notes and Individual Education Plans and enter notes in lesson plan as needed.

10. Gather any special materials you need in order to implement today's plan.

7 Individualizing the Lesson Plan

Screening and Observation

Introduction

This chapter includes a brief overview of screening and observation as methods used by early childhood teachers to assess and meet the diverse needs of young children. This overview will include the purposes of screening and observation, considerations in choosing screening tools or observation methods, and an examination of some of the kinds of observing and recording that are done by early childhood teachers.

Assessment is a term that includes both screening and observation; it is the process of using a variety of methods to observe and record what children can do and what they are likely to be able to do. Assessment through a combination of screening and observation serves several important purposes. It helps teachers plan individual instruction, communicate children's progress with parents, and find children who may have problems or who may need specialized services. In early childhood programs, assessment is most often accomplished with periodic screening and with various kinds of ongoing observations and recordkeeping. One of the biggest challenges for early childhood teachers is the task of getting the information from screening or observation tools into the lesson plan, so it can be used effectively to help children.

Several fine books on screening and observation are listed at the end of this chapter. One of the most comprehensive of these is *Assessing and Guiding Young Children's Development and Learning,* by Oralie McAfee and Deborah Leong. This book covers every aspect of assessment, including new techniques such as video recording. It also includes examples of useful forms for recording and compiling, and an excellent appendix containing developmental "red flags" for three- to five-year-olds that might signal the need for further investigation and assessment. The other resource especially recommended to readers is *Reaching Potentials: Appropriate Curriculum and Assessment for Young Children,* edited by Sue Bredekamp and Teresa Rosegrant.

In this chapter, I will not offer an in-depth discussion of assessment, but I will summarize the main elements and provide information on forms that could be used in the process of assessment and lesson planning. Our focus will be on the teacher as a competent observer, gatherer, recorder, and manager of information, and on the teacher's methods of using assessment information in working with parents and in documenting individualized teaching.

Screening

Definition and Purpose

Screening instruments usually inventory a child's abilities in areas such as functional language, reasoning, gross and fine motor skills, and self-help or personal/social development. Such screening attempts to survey a child's present abilities and potential ability to acquire new skills. This screening is based on the premise that a child's intelligence and skills are not immutable or fixed, and that intervention, planning, and individualized teaching can change and improve the child's skills and abilities.

Screening in early childhood programs is usually a limited procedure that is done when there is a concern with finding out if a child in the group has a potential problem that should be further investigated or referred for testing by a qualified diagnostician who would use broader and more comprehensive evaluation instruments. In the position statement of the National Association for the Education of Young Children, *Testing of Children: Concerns and Cautions*, NAEYC (1988) reminds readers that

> Screening tests are used to identify children who should have further individual diagnostic assessment to determine a specific problem. The results of screening tests should not be used to place children in special education programs or remove them from the classroom. Placement decisions should be made only on the basis of a complete diagnostic assessment of an individual child.

The Head Start Bureau, Administration on Children, Youth and Families, Department of Health and Human Services, has worked closely with NAEYC and other early childhood professionals to ensure that appropriate assessment procedures and follow-up are done in its programs.

Most often, general screening in an early childhood classroom is done with the entire group of young children to survey specific motor and language skills, and to check health, vision, and hearing to determine whether there are children in the group whose scores indicate that they may have a physical or health problem, a language problem, or a possible learning problem. If a problem is identified, early childhood teachers contact and work with the children's parents so that these children can be referred for further assessment, evaluation, and treatment plans done by appropriate area or community resource persons who are specialists.

IEPs and IFSPs

After such assessments, if problems are found, comprehensive efforts are made to address them by finding ongoing help for the child and family. If physical problems may affect the child's ability to learn, or if other learning deficits or disabilities are found, an individual education plan (IEP) is developed for the child by the specialists who did the testing and evaluation, in collaboration with the parents, teachers, and other pertinent staff persons. In programs serving young preschool children, this individualized plan may also be called the individual family service plan, or IFSP.

Teachers are expected to refer to these IEPs or IFSPs frequently and to develop ways to individualize their daily teaching with those children who have been assessed as having special needs or disabilities. The IEPs or IFSPs are kept in the children's file folders with their diagnostic information but should be referred to when the teacher is doing lesson planning.

Some teachers refer to copies of the IEPs or IFSPs or to their personal notes concerning these individual plans when they are writing their classroom lesson plans. The information gathered and the strategies developed on the IEP or IFSP are useful in meeting the daily needs of children with disabilities or deficits only if they find their way into the lesson plan itself. It is wise for teachers to develop consistent systems of accessing this information easily at the time they write lesson plans, even if they access it in summarized form. Later in this chapter, a summary sheet method will be presented; summary sheets are useful in addressing this challenge.

Screening for Individualized Planning

The practice of using screening instruments to find special needs in children and develop education plans to meet those needs has also led to the practice of using both screening instruments and ongoing observation to do better, more comprehensive planning for *all* children in the group or classroom.

Screening instruments can help tell the teacher which skills need to be practiced, and also help tell where each child is in the developmental sequence of learning those skills. The teacher then can use the information in long-range and daily lesson planning.

Comprehensive lesson planning that incorporates this kind of individualized teaching is encouraged in early childhood education because educators believe that individualized teaching, including a sensitivity to individual learning styles, is appropriate and effective.

Considerations in Choosing Screening Instruments

Because the use of screening instruments among early childhood programs and teachers is a common practice, here are some questions programs and decision makers should ask themselves in choosing among screening instruments.

1. Will the results of screening benefit children? Can we use the screening information, along with other information we have, to do better and more individualized job of planning for children? Will it help us find children who may need special or additional services?

2. Do these tools or instruments meet our needs? Do they meet the needs of the population we serve? Do they meet the needs, capacities, and values of our staff? Will the staff be able to use this new information, along with what they are continually learning about their children, to enhance good teaching?

3. Are the tools or instruments credible? Are they standardized, and/or are test results valid in terms of the development of the particular children we serve?

4. What information do we want? What do we want this screening or observation tool to do for us? Does it contain all the elements we need? Does it address all areas of development—social-emotional, physical, and cognitive? Will it show us children's strengths as well as needs?

5. Is it supportive of children? Can we easily administer it in appropriate, supportive ways for children? Can it be implemented as an enjoyable classroom experience that is comfortable for all the children we serve, even the youngest children, and for those of diverse backgrounds?

6. Will it help us communicate children's needs and progress to parents? Will it show parents their children's strengths and capabilities, as well as current areas of need? Will it help us to continue our work with parents as a team in an effort to help each child reach his or her full potential?

The most important point for teachers to remember about screening is that the information gained from screening tools should be easy to retrieve and use in lesson planning.

Observation

Definition

Observation is more than casual looking at children. It means gathering information about children and the program with an open mind. Observation is the basis of much of what we do in working with children. . . . Observation can:

- Provide parents, caregivers, and teachers with increased sensitivity to how children behave, think, and learn.
- Make us aware of the unique qualities of each child.
- Permit us to reflect on and compare what we see to what we have studied about growth and development.
- Help us to understand individual behavior problems and the part that adults and materials in the setting may play in these problems.
- Help us to plan activities based on children's special interests, skills and strengths.
- Provide information we can use in reporting on a child's growth and progress to parents (Betty Garlick, Michigan State University, 1980).

As an early childhood professional, you will usually be expected to do ongoing observation of all the children who are engaged in learning in your classroom. This is not a problem; if you love teaching young children, you find that observing them as they grow and learn is a fascinating part of your job.

Purpose

The purpose of observation, like one of the purposes of screening, is to gather information on individual children so that we can work more effectively with them, and can do lesson planning and teaching that is as individualized as possible. Observing with this purpose in mind does not just mean we watch children and write what we see. We need to know why we want to observe, be very attentive while we observe and record, keep our information organized, and then reflect and think about what we have learned so that we can use it in our planning and teaching.

Methods of Observation

In *Reaching Potentials,* Bredekamp and Rosegrant (1990) define and outline four basic methods of observing and recording children's behavior:

1. Narratives
   a. Diary descriptions
   b. Anecdotal records
   c. Running records
   d. Specimen descriptions
   e. Logs or journals
2. Time samplings
3. Event samplings
4. Modified child study techniques
   a. Checklists
   b. Rating scales
   c. Shadow study (in-depth case study)

Five of the most common methods of observation used by early childhood teachers are (1) anecdotal notes (a narrative method), (2) running records (a narrative method), (3) checklists (a modified child study technique), (4) logs or journals (narrative), and (5) time samplings. In today's programs, video taping (with parent permission) is increasingly being used to provide documented observations that can be reviewed by staff and discussed with parents.

Anecdotal notes are descriptive narratives, recorded after the behavior occurs, which are used to detail specific information. Running records are recorded while the behavior is occurring to document what children are doing in a certain situation. Checklists are lists on which the adult checks for specific behaviors. Time sampling is the observation of what happens in a given time period while the behavior is occurring, and is coded with tallies or symbols to determine the frequency of specific behaviors. A log or journal is a recording of brief details about each child in the group, usually made after the behavior occurs, usually describing the child's status or progress (Bredekamp & Rosegrant, 1992). All five of these methods can give the teacher or adult observer information to use in lesson planning and conferencing with parents or staff.

Some of the most useful information about children cannot be gathered in the classroom. This information about behavior occurs during the rest of the child's daily life. It can be gathered from parents, an excellent source of knowledge about their children which should not be overlooked. Most of the information teachers gather from parents is done in casual conversations, in planned interviews and conferencing, and through parent information checklists and questionnaires.

The Role of the Teacher

Because our discussion in this chapter will focus on the teacher's role as an observer, recorder, and manager of information, rather than on types of observation methods. We will examine when, where, and how teachers observe, and look at the ways screening and observation information can be used in lesson planning.

When and Where Do You Observe?

Most of the time teachers are best able to do their observing as they "float" to various learning areas during free-choice or child activity time, stopping occasionally to interact or work with children individually or in small groups.

Lead teachers will have delegated the responsibility for supervision in various learning centers among support staff and/or volunteers. As staff and volunteers remain more stationary (perhaps taking additional notes in the learning centers), the lead teacher is free to move about the room to collect observation information with anecdotal notes and/or other forms, depending on the methods or systems chosen.

How Do You Observe?

Sometimes it's not *what* you do but *how* you do it. Perhaps the most important aspect of observation is the effectiveness of the teacher in focusing on what is being observed. This may seem at first to go without saying, but many people watch without really seeing and listen without really hearing.

Inherent in the meaning of the word *observe* is a sense of calm, quiet detachment. You are not really observing children when you are constantly talking to them or employing a barrage of questions. You must be quiet to really watch and listen. You must let the children's words and actions tell you the things you want to note.

The dictionary includes the phrases "paying strict attention", and "keenly watchful" in defining the word *observant*. It includes in the definition of *observation* the phrase "the power of fixing the mind upon something." Good observing involves a fascination with what is being observed, much as new parents exhibit in observing their firstborn infant.

A. H. Maslow, writing about the ways scientists observe, reminds us that the observer should be *asking* for information, rather than telling:

> . . . if you want to know more about ducks, then you had better ask the ducks instead of telling them. So also for human children. In prescribing "what is best for them," it looks as if the best technique for finding out what is best for them is to develop techniques for getting *them* to tell us what is best for them. (Maslow, 1971).

Maslow reminds us that if we are willing to focus on children, observe them without preconceptions, and be open to what our inner eyes and ears tell us, then the children themselves, with their actions, voices, faces, and body language, will tell us what we need to know.

We have all seen teachers and other adults who are excellent observers. We sometimes call them *natural* observers, meaning that their skills are the result of some intuitive talent with which they were born. Although this predisposition may be true to some extent, I believe that the ability to observe objectively with the "unconditional regard and profound interest" that Maslow mentions in many of his books is possible for all teachers who are fascinated with what children do and how they do it.

The same kind of observation focus is seen in any person who is intensely interested in a hobby like bird watching or snorkeling. A person in this situation is so focused, and so accepting of what he or she is seeing that no distractions interfere; preconceived notions are rare or nonexistent.

The teacher, in gathering ongoing observation information, must be not only focused and interested, but also completely open to whatever may transpire. Teachers should strive to be the kind of observers of children who are able to get inside children's heads and ride silently on the wheels that are going around. We need to try not to put the words we want to hear into the mouths of children we are observing.

Here is a story that provides a humorous illustration of the preceding paragraph. In my assessment of a teacher candidate for the Child Development Associate competency-based credential a few years ago, I observed in her classroom during free-choice time. She was eager to demonstrate her use of open and extended questions, and was moving among various learning centers, interacting with children and asking questions.

She stopped near me where a little girl was intensely observing and playing with a yellow rubber duck in a dishpan of water. The teacher's plans indicated that the children had had recent science experiences with things that float and sink. The child we were observing had rummaged a knitted doll's hat from the housekeeping area, and had put the hat on the duck. This caused the duck to flop over instead of floating upright. When the child observed this, she took off the hat (which was a little big for the duck and covered his eyes) and replaced it a few times, but the duck continued to flop over, remaining only half afloat unless she held on to it.

The teacher's eyes sparkled as she asked the child, "Why do you think the duck is not floating very well?" One could almost physically hear the teacher's expectation of the child's unsaid words. She thought the child would say something about the hat making the duck too heavy to float the right way, or upright.

Well, the little girl put her hands on her hips and said emphatically to the teacher, "He is falling down because he can't see where he's going." This delightful answer, which both of us enjoyed immensely, was not the answer the teacher expected, but it was an excellent answer, indicating good thinking on the part of the child. This incident reminds us that we learn the most about children and their thought processes when we observe with open minds.

Records—How Do You Write Up What You Observe?

One of the problems some teachers have in writing up observations is a lack of skill in writing objectively. Unfortunately, inservice training on how to write objective notes is a simple but important piece of teacher training that is frequently omitted by programs that already have "too much on their table" and must attend to many other inservice priorities that may be required by their funding sources.

Simply stated, teachers should describe in writing exactly what they see and hear, and should not use subjective generalizations in their notes. For example, it is inappropriate to say, "9/17/94: X was crabby and fussy." Instead, the note should describe exactly what the child said or did: "9/17/94: Today X cried and came to me for assistance at three different times during one hour of free choice. These incidents occurred after X confronted and struggled with other children over the use of the climber, the sand toys, and a puzzle."

If the teacher's anecdotal observation includes a possible reason for the child's behavior, it should be stated as a possible reason, not a fact, unless the reason is truly based in fact: "9/17/94: During the daily casual health check at arrival time, X looked very tired; red eyes. After calling the parent, I learned that X got very little sleep last night; X is not running a fever, but lack of sleep may be the reason for this behavior." The words in your observation notes should paint a brief but objective and detailed picture of a real, living child in a real-life situation.

Observation notes that are dated, that describe objectively, and that can be clearly read when retrieved are useful in planning and teaching. Subjective, undated, and unreadable notes are not helpful.

❖❖❖❖

Early childhood program administrators and supervisors often contract with special education or mental health professionals who are required to supply periodic notes on the progress of children with special needs. These professionals should not be exempt from the requirements listed above to provide clear, objective, dated, signed, and readable observation notes.

Records—Where Do You Write Up What You Observe?

All sorts of forms for collecting observation information are used by early childhood teachers, and teachers are continually trying out or designing new ones. The most important thing to know about whatever form one is using is, "Does it work for *me*". The types of forms you use and their formats must be usable and efficient; they must work *for* you, not against you. In determining the effectiveness of your forms, you should be able to answer "yes" to the following questions:

1. Does this form help me collect the information I specifically want?
2. Does this form give me relevant information I can really put to use in planning and teaching?
3. Is it necessary to keep this form in a secure place? If so, do I have a safe place to keep it, so that a breach of confidentiality will not be an issue?
4. Do I have a system in place for easy retrieval of this information so that I can use it regularly in my planning, teaching, and my work with parents?

Summary Sheets

A summary sheet is a simple, useful tool that gives teachers information about the needs of children in the group. It is a list, on one sheet of paper, of all the needs of all the children in your classroom, compiled from the information you have collected on each child during screening and/or observation.

Teachers do not have time to look up this information in each child's folder every time they do a lesson plan. However, when a teacher has a summary sheet to look at during lesson planning time, the teacher sees the needs of all the children in his or her group at one glance! When every child's needs are listed on the summary sheet, it is much easier to keep those needs in mind when one does the lesson plan. Daily individual and small-group activities based on those needs can quickly be chosen and entered. The summary sheet helps prove that the teacher knows the needs of children in the group, and the lesson plan itself provides written evidence that children's individual needs have been met, either one-on-one or in small groups.

TRY THIS NOW You can make your own summary sheet easily, right now, on a sheet of 8½ × 11″ paper. Title the sheet "Summary of Children's Needs" or "Classroom Needs Summary Sheet." Now think of the skills with which your children need help or practice as titles or headings. Your headings might be Language, Fine Motor, Large Motor, Problem Solving, Memory, or Perception. Headings could even include Independence or Social Problem Solving. In other words, they can cover whatever skills you or your program feels are important to assess, observe, and practice. Now put these headings down on the paper; spread them out and leave space under each one for your children's names. Next list the names of children who need practice in various skills under each heading. Some children's names will appear under more than one heading because of multiple needs, and a few children may appear under only one heading, but every child's name will appear at least once.

From now on, when you want to decide which individualized activities to put into your daily lesson plan and with whom to do them, you do not have to look up information in each child's file folder. The summary sheet summarizes the basic information you need from all the file folders. By referring to the summary sheet each time you do a daily lesson plan, you will be able to choose and enter individualized activities easily and quickly. Over a period of a few weeks, you will be able to do (and to prove you did) some type of individualized teaching with every single child in the group, based on that child's needs. You will really feel proud of yourself!

When you do your actual lesson plans, you can proceed in one of two ways. Choose a child (or children) from one of the lists on your summary sheet, and plan an activity that will practice any of the skills that the child needs. Enter this individualized teaching on the lesson plan. Or choose a skill area (heading) you want to practice. Which children need this practice? Enter your practice activity and the children's initials in the space for individualization on your lesson plan form (Chapter 5, Figures 5-1 and 5-2).

There is no breach of confidentiality in placing activities and initials on your lesson plan (Chapter 5). Unless you note what you do on your lesson plan, there is no written documentation that you have actually individualized your teaching. If parents or guests wonder about the initials, explain that every child is special and that your goal is to spend one-on-one time with each and every child, to meet their individual needs. Placing the initials in your plan is a way to keep track of your time and be sure no child is missed.

Using a Summary Sheet

Here are some things you should know about using a summary sheet:

- You can use different headings than those presented in the preceding example. Many teachers use headings that indicate needs in the social-emotional and self-help areas, such as "Sharing—taking turns," or "Self-help skills," or "Helping others." Some teachers may want to use more specific headings, such as "Matching colors," or "Ordering by size," or "Dictation—words, stories."
- Children's names will appear under more than one heading if they have several low-skill areas or needs. Every child in your group will be found in at least one list, because every child has a special need for individualized help of some kind.
- You will want to design simple summary sheets because you will sometimes want to change the headings. You may find that a certain category or heading is no longer needed—for example, when all the children can take turns, or when all children can walk on the balance beam. You may find at some point in the year that you will want to add a new heading, such as "Temporal ordering—time."
- The skill needs of your children will also change. You may need to add names under a particular heading on your summary sheet, or to delete names of children who no longer need help under another heading. Periodic screening inventories or your ongoing observations and anecdotal notes on children will help you make these choices.
- Your program may do screening on all children in the middle of the year, as well as at the beginning. The summary sheet you created in the fall may require changes by January. This is why it is best to use a very simple summary sheet that you can easily redo or even discard, making changes as necessary.
- It is an excellent idea for teachers to write on the summary sheet, in small numerals, next to the child's name, the date on which the individualized practice of a skill took place. This is simply another way (in addition to writing the child's initials on your lesson plan), of documenting the dates of individualized teaching with particular children. If you place dates next to the names on the summary sheet, you will also know at a glance if you are working with some children far more often than with others.

     What teachers write in the lesson plan, combined with the record on the summary sheet and the backup information in the children's individual files, will document that they are in compliance with supervisors who request evidence of individualized planning and teaching.

- Your summary sheet will not only help you implement and document individualized teaching, but also help you in other ways. A summary sheet tells you at a glance which skill areas seem to be needed by *most* of the children in your group. Therefore, the summary sheet can help you to prioritize your choices of the skill-focused activities you want to put into your lesson plan during small-group or at other times.

Name _____ Week of _____

GAMES/SMALL GROUP

Mon. _____
Tues. _____
Wed. _____
Thurs. _____
Fri. _____

SKILLS PRACTICED

	Motor				
Motor					
Perceptual					
Memory					
Literacy					
Problem Solving					

M T W T F

SMALL MUSCLE AREA

___ Peg boards   ___ Flannelboards   ___ Sorting games
___ Puzzles   ___ Parquetry   ___ Sewing/lacing
___ Legos   ___ Water play   ___ Shapes
___ Colorforms   ___ Bristle blocks   ___ Memory games
___ Playtiles   ___ Stringing   ___ Lotto

ART AREA

___ Playdo or clay   ___ Fingerpaint   ___ Paper and glue
___ Sand/texture table ___ (Recycled) Junk   ___ with scissors
___ Easel painting   ___ Construction   ___ Other tempera painting
___ Crayons or markers ___ Collage (any)   ___ Paper with scissors

LARGE MUSCLE AREA

___ Obstacle course   ___ Using nuts and bolts   ___ Rocking boat/steps
___ Tumbling mat   ___ Using pipes and joints ___ Big hollow blocks
___ Balance beam   ___ Climber   ___ Unit blocks
___ Play with props   ___ Trucks   ___ Throwing and catching
___ Fishing with magnets ___ Creative movement   ___ Using measuring devices

DRAMATIC PLAY

___ Housekeeping
___ Dollhouse
___ With other props
___ With puppets/dolls, etc.

BOOKS

___ Alone
___ With other children
___ With adult
___ Writing center

WOODWORKING

___ Hammer and nails
___ Screwdrivers and screws
___ Saws
___ Drill

SCIENCE/MATH

___ Animals   ___ Scales   ___ Magnifying glass
___ Battery   ___ Plants   ___ Measuring
___ Count/sets/graphs   ___ Magnets   ___ Cooking

Teacher Comments:

_____
_____
_____
_____

Figure 7-1 Weekly Observation Form

An Original Observation Form

Earlier in this chapter, questions were listed to help teachers determine the effectiveness of forms. The bottom line is that any form must both accomplish its purpose and work for the teacher in a practical way. Often, teachers must take the initiative to create their own forms for observation or for compiling information. An effective method for compilation is especially important when the teacher needs to retrieve information about children to use in lesson planning and ongoing conferencing with parents.

A particularly practical form for this purpose would be one with an efficient format that could be used to compile information from several types of observation on one piece of paper. Reducing paperwork and paper files is an ongoing concern of most early childhood teachers! Sometimes the only effective way to address this problem is to design one's own form.

The example that follows is a form designed to gather and compile varied information on children for a cooperative preschool program in which I was the teacher/director. The program served twenty children, with a daily staff of one early childhood teacher/director and three assisting parents. Parent staff members rotated each day in monthly cycles. The parents and I wanted a form that collected a great deal of information, but for which very simple and objective observation-gathering methods could be used.

The form we created organized and compiled different types of observations on each child during each program day. It combined some of the elements of a checklist with four of the observation methods defined earlier in this chapter: a running record, time sampling, a log, and anecdotal notes.

Now let's look at how the form in Figure 7-1 worked in several different ways for this particular program.

Use of Figure 7-1 as a Checklist

All the learning centers of the classroom and all the key materials in each center are printed on Figure 7-1, with space to note which materials were used by the child. Thirty forms were used consecutively, one each week for each child, for the entire program year, with the exception of the two weeks before and after Christmas, and the week before and after Easter.

In the space next to each item under the learning center headings, tallies in the form of initials noted the day of the week the child interacted with or used the item or material. For example: "Computer M T Th" or "Playdough W F" would show that the child used the computer Monday, Tuesday and Thursday, and used the playdough Wednesday and Friday.

At the end of the week, the initials "M T W Th F" showed which learning centers each child used on different days of the week, what materials he or she used in these centers, and which learning centers each child avoided during that week. This use of Figure 7-1 as a checklist provided information on what every child did every day for the entire year during free-choice time. The next paragraphs will explain how this was accomplished by staff.

Use of Figure 7-1 as a Combination of Running Record and Time Sampling

Each day during free-choice time, three parent staff members supervised three general areas of the room: the art area, including sand and water; the large-muscle area, including large-muscle equipment and materials, blocks, and woodworking; and the small-muscle area, including manipulatives, literacy center, science, foods experiences, and housekeeping. (Dramatic play, literacy, science, and math sometimes surfaced in several of these areas.)

Using steno pads, the staff noted the date, the area, and the headings for the key equipment or materials available on that day in his or her area. As children came into these areas during free-choice time, the parent staff noted the child's first name under the heading of the equipment or materials the child was using.

For example, in the art area the steno page being used by the supervising adult might say "Mon. 9/17 Easel, Collage, Playdough, Sand" leaving space for children's names under each heading. Whenever possible, the parent staff person also noted on the steno page brief anecdotal observations, such as "Stayed 20 minutes" or "X played with Y entire time" or "Complex block castle."

During free-choice time, the teacher was free to "float" in all areas of the room to do individualized teaching, observing, and anecdotal notes. After class, the information on the materials and learning centers used by each child was transferred from the steno pages of the assisting staff to the child's weekly observation form (Figure 7-1).

Use of Figure 7-1 as a Log or Journal

Please note the box or grid in the upper right corner of the form, showing abbreviations for five weekdays and noting the names of the five major skill areas: (1) motor, (2) perceptual, (3) literacy, (4) memory, and (5) problem solving. The space and lines at the left margin allow room to write the name of the activity or "game" that took place during small-group time for each day of the week. The grid was used to note which skills were practiced during each of the daily small-group activities.

Each day, before the children arrived at the center, the teacher and parents discussed the small-group activity and the basic skill areas that would be practiced; the materials and activity were identical for each small group each day and were changed on a daily basis to cover all skill areas comprehensively during the week.

During small-group time, each of the four supervising adults (one teacher, three parents) took trays containing the materials that were to be used for "game time" (set up previously by the teacher and children during free-choice time) to four separate areas of the room, where they each met with four or five children from the group of twenty. A pencil and paper were included on each adult's tray in order to note brief information on each child in the group during the activity.

Adults wrote down the date, the name of the small-group activity for that day, and the names of the children in their groups. As the children played the game or practiced the skill, adults would make very brief notes next to the child's name, such as "no" (would not participate), "yes," "loved this," "10 piece puzzle," "tore a square shape," or "grouped items 5 ways." After small group, the trays were taken to the teacher's planning area, where one staff member collected the notes and put away materials while the other staff assisted the teacher with large-group music and movement.

After class, the information from each group was quickly transferred to the child's observation form, and the skills practiced were checked off on the grid. For example, if the "Game time" or small-group activity was "Crayon drawing and dictation," the grid was checked in the motor and literacy areas. If the game or small-group activity was "Eat veg. soup & discuss," the adult checked motor, perception, literacy, memory, and problem solving, because children would have eaten the soup, talked about each step they had taken in making the soup, and observed and discussed how the raw vegetables changed during cooking.

Use of Figure 7-1 as an Anecdotal Record

As the lead teacher, during the weekend, I took home the forms for each child in the group, on which all the information of the week had been compiled. During the weekend I reflected on the information on each child's form, as well as my own anecdotal notes, in order to make comments under "teacher comments" and/or on the back of the form. These comments were based on both the compilation of information on the form and my notes about individual children. When my comments had been added to the forms, they were placed into the child's confidential file or portfolio. Prior to my entering these comments, everything on the form was objective information that did not require the protection of confidentiality; complete agreement with this system had been given by parents.

Examples of teacher comments might be, "X and Y are developing a friendship you may want to support with visits at each other's homes," or " Z is avoiding the large-muscle area; we will encourage use," or "Y fascinated with goldfish and how they breathe and eat," or "X needs help with walking on balance beam; can you practice at home with homemade one or taped line on rug?" If the child seemed to be having a problem with stress or social-emotional interactions, I called the parent and shared the information immediately, instead of waiting for the monthly parent meeting at which parents reviewed the portfolios.

It did not take long to read the information and make these notes because, with our method, the form itself did most of the work. Transferring the information after each class day to the compilation form was our most time-consuming task, and this took only about fifteen minutes a day. Of course, this kind of information gathering could not have been done without the active cooperation of staff, even though the notes they took were very objective and very brief.

For teachers who do not have ample staff or volunteers to make and record daily observations in the manner described here, the form in Figure 7-1 may still be useful. Teachers might wish to use this form only for particular children about whom they desire more information, or they might wish to use it on every child regularly, but not daily. For example, a teacher might use this form to record observations on three to five children each week, rotating their choices of children for four to five weeks, until the entire group has been covered.

Use of Figure 7-1 in Portfolios

A portfolio is a way of compiling, organizing, and making sense out of various kinds of information about a child. It is not a method of assessment but a way of compiling assessment information from many avenues. A portfolio is "an organized, purposeful compilation of evidence documenting a child's development and learning over time . . . like a photograph album that brings back memories for the person involved, shows changes over time, and can introduce a new person to what has been . . . the more you study it the more you see . . . " (McAfee & Leong, 1994).

The weekly observation forms were put into the children's portfolios, along with entry forms, parent questionnaires, health screening forms, screening inventories, and periodic samples of children's drawings and dictation. Throughout the year, examples of children's cutting or tracing were added. The ongoing information compiled on the weekly observation form and in the portfolios kept me constantly aware of the individual needs of children and of the activities I would need to include in my lesson plans in order to meet those needs.

Imagine the joy of children's parents in reviewing, at monthly parent meetings, this kind of comprehensive information about their children. The weekly observation forms told them what their children had done each day at the center during that month, and what skills their children had practiced every day. Attendance at monthly parent meetings averaged over 90 percent!

By the end of the year, the portfolio contained thirty observation forms and demonstrated to parents the kinds of continuous growth their children had made all year. Portfolios were given to parents at the end of the year with the suggestion that they could, if they wished, show them to the child's next teacher. This is often an effective transition strategy.

Many of the parents who were involved with the development and use of this observation form have told me they still have and treasure their children's weekly observation sheets and portfolios, even though their children are now young adults. One parent said to me recently, "The experience of being a team teacher and observer helped me see my child in an entirely different way than I saw her at home, and that made a very positive impact on the kind of parenting I did over the following years."

Obviously, one of the greatest benefits of using the original weekly observation form in Figure 7-1 was to the staff, which in this case were all parents. Using a systematic plan for observing, and using a form that helped to compile daily observations easily, helped all the parents to become even better observers. I found that when parents observed, even though they took only brief, objective notes, they began to observe very keenly. This helped them learn more about their own children, about other children, and about how intensely children work and learn through their play. At least five of these parents, as result of this learning experience, decided to go to college and pursue degrees or endorsements in early childhood education. Observation and recording can have an impact on adults, as well as on our lesson planning for children!

This form (Figure 7-1) and the story of its use have been included in this chapter to point out how important it is for teachers to design the kinds of forms they need whenever this proves necessary, as well as to demonstrate that parents can and should be involved in the observation and recording process whenever possible.

Summary

The subject of assessment through appropriate screening and observation is one to which we cannot do justice in a guidebook of this length. Assessment is a topic that the early childhood professional must pursue more comprehensively in texts devoted entirely to this subject, such as some of the books listed at the end of this chapter.

In this chapter, we have briefly defined and described assessment, screening, and various observation methods. Guidelines have been presented to help the teacher choose screening and observation tools, and in assessing forms used in recordkeeping. We have discussed the role of the teacher as an observer, recorder, and manager of information, and stressed the importance of open attitudes and objectivity in both observing and recording.

This chapter has been included in the guidebook for several reasons: First, assessment information, when accessed and used by the teacher, has an impact on the lesson plan. Second, we need to stress the importance of the teacher's use of assessment methods to do a better and more consistently documented job of individualized teaching. Screening and observation information can only help the teacher to meet individual needs when it can be accessed in a practical way and used in the lesson plan. In addition, the lesson plan should document that individualized teaching has indeed occurred on a daily basis.

A summary sheet system was shared with readers as an example of a practical method for transferring the continually changing information we gain about children into the lesson plan. Practical tips on using summary sheets as tools for recording and using information to document individualized teaching were presented.

Another emphasis in this chapter has been observation and the importance of involving parents as team members in this process. Teachers need to know what they want to observe about children, why they want this information, and what they will do with the information. Often, to accomplish their particular observation goals, teachers need to design their own methods and forms for gathering and compiling observation information, and engage parents as assistants in getting the job done. An example of such a form and its specific uses was shared with readers, along with the impact this experience had on parent observers.

Chapter 8 will deal with another element that has great impact on the teacher's lesson planning—the early childhood setting or environment.

Self -Study Activities

1. If you are an early childhood student, you are often required to do observations of children. Find the outline of observation methods in this chapter and examine your own methods. What methods are you using? If these are narrative methods, what type are they? Ask yourself the ways you could improve your observations and make them more useful in terms of your own skills and benefits to children. If you are a teacher, ask yourself these same questions.

2. Examine the screening instruments being used in your program, and, if possible, compare them to others. Are the screening instruments your program uses to gather information beneficial in terms of the six questions presented in this chapter? If not, what do you, as a professional or student learning the profession, plan to do about your concerns? Write out a plan. To whom would you bring these concerns, and how would you do to arrange this? Would you bring your concerns to a staff meeting? How would this be put on the agenda? Outline what you would say in the meeting. If your screening instruments are appropriate, you can create a hypothetical situation in which they are not appropriate.

3. Examine the forms you are using in terms of the questions presented in this chapter. Using blank copies, try to redesign or modify a form to make it more practical and usable. Experiment with designs for combining the information on two forms into one format, on one piece of paper.

References and Resources for Further Reading

Benjamin, Ann. "Observations in Early Childhood Classrooms: Advice from the Field." *Young Children,* Vol. 49, No. 6 (1994), pp. 14–20.

Bondurant-Utz, Judith, & Luciano, Lenore B. *A Prac-* *tical Guide to Infant and Preschool Assessment in Special Education.* Boston: Allyn and Bacon, 1994.

Bredekamp, Sue & Rosegrant, Teresa, eds. *Reaching*

Potentials: Appropriate Curriculum and Assessment of Young Children, Vol. 1. Washington, DC: National Association for the Education of Young Children, 1992.

Brewer, Jo Ann. *Introduction to Early childhood Education, Preschool through Primary Grades.* Boston: Allyn and Bacon, 1995.

Betty Garlick. *Evaluating Children's Progress through Observation.* Paper presented at Michigan State University, February 1, 1980, p. 1.

Hills, Tynette W. "Assessment in Context—Teachers and Children at Work." *Young Children,* Vo. 48, No. 5 (1993), pp. 20–33.

Kamii, Constance, ed. *Achievement Testing in the Early Grades: The Games Grown Ups Play.* Washington, DC: National Association for the Education of Young Children, 1990.

A. H. Maslow, *The Further Reaches of Human Nature.* New York: Penguin Books, 1971, p. 14.

McAfee, Oralie, & Leong, Deborah. *Assessing and Guiding Young Children's Development and Learning.* Boston: Allyn and Bacon, 1994, p. 111.

Meisels, Samuel J. *Developmental Screening in Early Childhood: A Guide,* 3rd. ed. Washington, DC: National Association for the Education of Young Children, 1985, 1989.

National Association for the Education of Young Children. *Testing of Young Children: Concerns and Cautions.* Washington, DC: NAEYC, 1988, p. 2.

Vazquez-Nutall, Ena, Romero, Ivonne, & Kalesnik, Joanne. *Assessing and Screening Preschoolers: Psychological and Educational Dimensions.* Boston: Allyn and Bacon, 1992.

Another excellent resource is ERIC, the Educational Resource Information Center/Early Childhood Education Clearinghouse at the University of Illinois, 805 West Pennsylvania Avenue, Urbana, IL 61801, which provides information about current research and developments in the field of education and maintains a wide selection of materials on screening and observation.

8 Where It Happens

Basic Elements of the Setting

Introduction: Diversity of Settings

There is nearly as much diversity in early childhood settings as there is diversity in children! Classrooms are of all types . . . big and small, wide or narrow, with lots of natural light or with little, with or without exits to the outdoors, upstairs, downstairs, in schools, churches, community centers, or in their own buildings. Very few teachers say they are perfectly satisfied with their classrooms, because they are constantly striving to improve the learning setting in ways that will both help children learn, and make their own management of the setting more effective.

No matter what type of setting you find yourself in as a teacher, you can make the most of what you have in the learning environment to provide what young children need for learning. Fantastic lesson plans for young children are of no use to you if the setting works against you and not for you in implementing your plans. This chapter is intended to help you set up effective learning centers and make the most of your setting. Sometimes this is a little like "making lemons into lemonade."

We will begin with a brief discussion of the ways children learn from their environments. Then we will move on to the considerations of planning the use of space in the setting, and aspects of the learning centers themselves. Two floor plans are presented as examples at the end of this chapter (Figure 8-1 and 8-2).

Interactive Learning in the Environment

There is a consensus among early childhood educators that young children learn by doing; they learn by engaging in lively, ongoing interaction with all the materials, equipment, and persons in the learning environment. Simply stated, young children are always in a "learning mode." They want to learn, and do they learn from everything around them. When we observe young children in centers or in our daily lives, we see that what they learn depends largely on the setting or environment in which they find themselves.

In homes where parents value the outdoors and sports, children are often similarly inclined. When parents integrate the arts and music in their daily lives, children usually develop related interests in the arts and music. When parents regularly encourage their children to be involved in helping with meal preparation, cooking and baking, children usually learn a lot about how to use kitchen utensils, appliances, recipes, and various foods. In child care centers where children use age-appropriate outdoor equipment every day, children are likely to practice more large motor physical skills than children who have no access to large-muscle equipment. When early childhood programs never expose children to the traditions, art, foods, music, and books of other cultures, children are likely to have little interest in or knowledge of cultures other than their own. When children are exposed to books and varied literature every day, when they are encouraged to write or dictate their thoughts so that these can be read, and when children develop a love of storytelling, they are likely to be motivated and interested readers. Children learn from the environment around them and from adults in that environment who interact with them and facilitate their learning.

The agreement among early childhood educators concerning the importance of the environment and the hands-on learning that occurs in it has been influenced by Jean Piaget's theories of child development. Piaget was convinced that children learn through active multisensory and physical exploration of the environment, beginning in infancy. Maria Montessori, a contemporary of Piaget, emphasizes in her books *The Secret of Childhood* and *The Discovery of the Child* the importance of a prepared environment for learning, including the careful selection and introduction of materials that children use in the setting. The theories that young children are naturally motivated to learn, that they have the potential for learning in a self-correcting way, and that they learn a great deal through their senses and manipulative materials were felt to be important by both Piaget and Montessori. (Brewer, 1995; Spodek & Saracho, 1994; Elkind, 1993) In this guidebook, we will not delve deeply into the theories of Piaget or Montessori, but will concentrate instead on the classroom setting itself and on the materials in the setting that facilitate learning.

In an early childhood setting, the child assimilates new information through manipulative, concrete, and sensory experiences with the environment. The child tries to integrate the new information gained with other information he or she already has. With experience, the child becomes more and more accurate at perceiving and plugging in new information, a process that Piaget called "accommodation." When the child can take new knowledge that has been assimilated and accommodated accurately, and use this knowledge in his or her own unique way to act on or change his or her environment, teachers who are followers of Piaget's teachings would say the child is "constructing knowledge" and is learning.

Awareness of the importance of the environment as a learning place has also led to the development of more home-based and home visitor programs in early childhood education. This trend is based on the premise that the parent, the child's first and most important teacher, can nurture the child's self-esteem and skills by conceiving of the home as a learning environment and by using the many opportunities found in the home environment as learning experiences.

In center-based early childhood programs for three- to five-year-olds, the setting plays a critical role. The richer the setting in appropriate, concrete, hands-on experiences, the more learning takes place. In early childhood classrooms, the teacher and staff act as active facilitators of children's learning, offering children choices of a variety of materials that match their changing skill levels. They ask questions that stimulate children's personal responsibility and thinking skills, and provide children with ample, well-planned time to use the materials in each of the learning centers for exploring and problem solving.

Learning Centers—General Remarks

1. *Definition:* Learning centers are spaces within the early childhood setting where materials or equipment are gathered and arranged in order to promote specific types of learning skills, such as large and small motor skills, literacy skills, creative thinking skills, and math and science problem-solving skills. Learning centers are physically defined; they can be identified as separate from an adjacent area or learning center by the kinds of learning materials found within them, and by the placement of their furniture or equipment and of the low, open shelves that are often used to define their space.

2. *Size:* Learning centers do not all need to be large. Some materials need much more space than others. The reading area or writing center teachers arrange may be very small and cozy, but the large-muscle and blocks areas will need ample space. Blocks and block areas are vital aspects of learning in the early childhood setting, but room for block use and storage is sometimes difficult to arrange. Books listed at the end of this chapter and in Appendix C, as well as the floor plan examples found at the end of this chapter, will assist you in arranging your learning centers effectively in the space available to you.

3. *Arrangement:* Safety is one of the major considerations in the arrangement of learning centers in the setting. Learning centers must be arranged so that exits to the room are unobstructed and so that a safe traffic flow is inherent in the room plan. Learning centers should be placed strategically so that there are no long, straight areas, which, like hallways, invite children to run indoors. For safety and confidentiality, learning centers and the materials in them should be arranged so that they are separated from the teacher's materials, resources, and files.

Another factor in planning the arrangement of learning centers is noise level. It is generally recommended that active, noisy learning centers not be placed next to quiet learning areas such as the writing center, reading center, and science/math center. However, the dramatic play of the housekeeping area is often encouraged to overflow to the large-muscle area. There is no problem with this, as both housekeeping and active play areas are often filled with the good noises of children's language and learning.

One common problem concerning noise level is the placement and setup of the woodworking center. Many classrooms include a woodworking area because of its excellent and varied opportunities for problem solving and skill development. Some teachers provide only a stout log or stump and short roofing nails with hammers, but others provide a workbench, vise, and tools. One advantage of arranging the woodworking center in an uncarpeted area is the easy cleanup of scraps and sawdust. The disadvantage lies in the noise level that occurs when children use this equipment in an uncarpeted area.

A happy solution to this problem is to place a commercial foam-backed carpet remnant under the workbench itself, and to cover the surface of the workbench completely with another carpet remnant of the same type, using carpet glue. After all, workbenches are not built to be furniture, and their surfaces are not intended to remain smooth and unscarred. The addition of carpet on the surface and under the workbench almost completely absorbs the sound and dramatically reduces the noise level, which reduces stress in both adults and children. Similarly, recycled acoustical ceiling tiles, if made of safe materials, can be attached to bare cement block walls or to the backs of storage units to absorb noise level.

A third consideration in arrangement of learning centers is accessibility. Learning centers and the equipment in them should be accessible to all children, including those with temporary or permanent disabilities. This is certainly something to consider if teachers are planning to build a loft for the literacy or dramatic play area. Learning centers and equipment should be flexible enough in arrangement and construction to be accessible and to be modified when necessary.

Another important aspect of the arrangement of learning centers is that they be supportive of cooperative work and responsible, enjoyable play. Teachers can promote positive social interactions and cooperative work by designing learning center spaces that are suitable for small groups of various sizes, because it is in small groups that children best learn to cooperate.

Some centers can be very small, such as a quiet spot where a child or two might rest on big pillows. Other areas, such as the computer center or the writing center, could serve two or three children at a time. The reading center might serve three or four children, depending on the space available, while the housekeeping area might serve as many as four or five. The sand table used might be built for four or for six children to use cooperatively, while the block area should have plenty of space for six to build together.

The point here is that learning centers should encourage cooperative play for a wide variety of group sizes and, especially in centers for three- to five-year-olds, should include space for individuals to work and play alone, as well as near or with other children.

4. *Play slots:* Another important element of the arrangement of the setting is the number of work and play slots it offers. If you were to count up the number of spaces available in every single learning center of your classroom, including the spaces at the tables for art and table toys, and the spaces for observing at the fish aquarium or science table, you could conceptualize these spaces as your total of work/play slots. There should be at least twice as many or up to two and a half times as many work/play slots as children in a rich and effective learning setting. An ample number of play slots in the setting prevents overcrowding in any of the learning centers and provides enough interest and variety to prevent the problem of children wandering aimlessly during free-choice time.

Here's an example. If the teacher allows the use of only three or four centers or activities during free-choice time, all the children will naturally want to engage in those activities. If the activities are the climber, one easel with space for two, some crayons and paper on a table, puzzles and beads on another table, and the housekeeping area, where do you think you will find the majority of children in the group? Perhaps two or three will be in the art area and another two or three in the manipulatives area, but you are likely to see seven or eight children trying to use the climber or the housekeeping area at one time. This could lead to safety or guidance problems.

To keep children busy, happy, and learning with the materials in the setting, the teacher must make sure that many and varied interest areas are available in free choice time. The more work/play slots, the more learning occurs. As a bonus, there will also be far fewer problems in classroom management when many play slots are available.

5. *Materials:* Equipment and materials in the learning centers should be in ample supply so that children will have duplicate items to use or share easily. Storage of extra materials should be easily accessed. For example, art materials and supplies should be accessible and in the learning center where they will be used.

Storage of materials that will be rotated or brought out at different times of the year must be orderly and organized so that teachers can easily and quickly find what is needed. Since many materials and pieces of equipment in early childhood settings are rotated to promote new interest or to meet the needs of new skill levels, the challenge of finding adequate storage is often considerable. Creative solutions can often be found through staff brainstorming.

Materials within the learning centers themselves should be accessible, on low, open shelves. Children are not likely to enter or work in learning areas in which they see no materials ready to use. It is helpful if the shelves for materials are labeled with pictures and/or words so that children can be responsible in both finding and putting things away easily. This kind of labeling on shelves and storage units, often called perceptual labeling, also provides practice in perception and memory skills.

Equipment and materials in the learning centers should meet the developmental skill level needs of the children served. Because children may be of many different ages and skill levels, and because their skills change as they grow, a wide variety of materials encompassing all skill levels will be needed (developmentally appropriate materials).

Equipment and materials in learning centers should be flexible and easily adapted for special needs or purposes, as when efforts are made to include all children in all activities and learning centers. Flexible materials can be easily modified and used in more than one way. This approach is also very cost-effective.

6. *Physical definitions of learning center space:* For children to see the opportunities and plan careful choices of different learning centers in the classroom, the teacher must define the space of each learning area, and make the space inviting and attractive to children.

Learning centers can be defined with the use of different types of floor coverings and area rugs, but they are best defined with the addition of partial walls created with low, open shelves. It is important that these dividers are low so that the adult's view of the children and what they are doing in each area is not impaired. Unobstructed vision of all the areas of the setting is a management factor as well as a safety factor.

To further define learning center space, most teachers label the learning centers with simple signs or posters noting the names of the areas. These signs should be printed clearly in large letters in the kind of lettering the children will be expected to become familiar with, usually upper- and lower-case letters, with the words beginning in capital letters.

The signs might indicate "Reading Area," "Woodworking," "Blocks," or "Construction." The sign for the creative media and paint learning center should imply in its choice of wording that open-ended art media are used. Signs that state that the area is for "Art Projects" are inappropriate because they imply that the art *project* (a product) is more important than the creative *process*. A better choice is simply "Art Media" or "Creative Art Area."

It is also helpful to place posters in each of the learning center areas that explain the purposes of each area in terms of the children's learning. For example, in the art area, a poster might say, "Here is a place I learn to use my imagination, and express my ideas and feelings. I learn eye–hand coordination and fine motor skills. I learn to be responsible for materials and cleaning up. I learn the feeling of pride and self confidence." This type of poster contains very helpful information for community visitors, student teachers, and parents.

If teachers depend partially on floor coverings to define some learning centers, and if they have a choice concerning floor coverings (frequently they do not) they should consider uncarpeted areas for food service, painting, sand, and water. It is also important to try to use flat carpeting in the block areas, which will add to the structural stability of block constructions and will also cut down on the noise level.

Teachers should be aware that most three-year-olds and many four-year-olds will prefer to use puzzles and table toys on the floor, and carpeted floor space for such use should be available. It is important to use solid colors in such carpeted areas so that children's figure–ground skills will not be impaired. It is extremely frustrating for a child to look for a particular puzzle piece on a patterned carpet.

Basic Learning Centers in the Setting

In introducing this section, I want to recommend the resource book *The Creative Curriculum* by Diane Trister Dodge and Laura J. Colker. It is one of the most comprehensive books I have seen concerning the early childhood setting and its learning centers. Dodge and Colker presents a wide variety of learning center activities that meet the changing developmental needs of young children, focuses on open-ended materials and experiences so well suited to the interests and abilities of three- to five-year-olds, and emphasizes the use of child-initiated time for ample exploration of learning center materials planned by the teacher.

The use of learning centers to provide appropriate hands on learning is the heart of the early childhood curriculum. Teachers enter the activities to be offered in learning centers on the daily lesson plan. Therefore, it is important for us to review the learning centers that should be available in all classroom settings that promote quality programming. Programs in which classroom settings have restricted space should still strive to include all of the following learning centers, even if some will be small or if some equipment and space must be rotated.

1. Science and Math Discovery Learning

This center may actually be broken up into several spaces in classrooms where adequate space for a separate math/science center is not available. In this area one would find groupings of plants, small animals such as fish, guinea pigs, or snails; items from nature; pictures and books relating to current interests of children; tubbing, graphing, and counting materials; and tools for observation and measurement by children. Computers are sometimes found in this area, as well. One can easily see that some groupings of these discovery and problem-solving materials could be placed in small interest centers in various places in the setting.

In fact and in actual practice, although science and math discovery materials may be placed in one or more defined learning centers, science and math are teaching and learning opportunities that cannot be relegated to any one space. Math and science learning will occur in all of the areas of the classroom—in the sand and water center, the sensory center, the table toys area, the art area, the housekeeping area, the "cooking" area, and in other active play areas, including the outdoors.

2. Sensory Learning

This center would include a table or bins of sensory materials that are rotated for children's exploration, as well as the sand table, the water table, and clays or playdough. Usually playdough is offered in the art area. Sometimes the sand and water tables are separate pieces of equipment, and sometimes the sand or water is rotated within one table. It is always recommended that sand, water, and playdough or clay be available daily, and that other sensory materials be provided additionally in small tubs if at all possible.

Sometimes the space available in the classroom may dictate that the sand or water must be placed in a defined space or learning center. In that case, perhaps the other, rotated sensory materials might be placed in the small muscle area on a table, or even in the art area.

One solution would be to use dishtubs for water and other sensory materials and to define a space for the sand table, and use it only for sand. It is wise to divide the sand in the table with a smooth piece of wood, so that both wet and dry sand can be available to children every day. (Some children prefer to experiment by pouring and filling, and some by digging and molding.)

If the sand table is used only for sand, water can and should still be available daily. Water play can be provided in easy-to-fill plastic tubs that could be conveniently moved or set up (with big towels underneath) on a table in the small-muscle area, in the housekeeping area (to bathe dolls), or on the floor in another area. This method is not only helpful in adding to the number of work/play slots; it helps draw children into learning centers they may be avoiding, or to areas in which they do not frequently engage.

3. Housekeeping and Dramatic Play

Years ago, this area was commonly called the housekeeping "corner," but this learning center, with its traditional equipment of play furniture, play foods, utensils, dress-up clothing and mirror, need not be placed in an actual corner of the classroom. It often works out much better for teachers to define this dramatic play space in the middle of the room or in the middle of the space at one side of the classroom, leaving openings between the play furniture for "doors" through which children can enter or leave. Housekeeping play furniture is low, and if it is also sturdy, it lends itself well as dividers to define this space. The housekeeping area should also be changed at times to allow for other types of play to occur there. For example, this space makes an excellent "store," "hospital," "vet clinic," or "beauty parlor."

The teacher should also plan to set up dramatic play regularly with props stored in "prop boxes" in other learning centers such as the active play area, where large hollow blocks can be used to create the set for dramatic play scenarios such as stores, hospitals, offices, spaceships, trains, camping sites, and so on. Prop boxes can also be used to help children reenact and retell books and stories heard in the classroom, and many props can be taken outdoors for a variety of different types of dramatic play.

Most dramatic play props can easily be scrounged or collected by parents, and most parents truly enjoy this type of involvement. Prop boxes should be sturdy and labeled without stereotyping (e.g. "Post Office," not "Mailman"), and they should be stored in ways that promote rotation and frequent use.

4. Large-Muscle Learning Area

This center is often the same space used by the teacher during large-group circle times, music and movement activities, and story time. Multiple use of this space is not a problem, since the active play/large-muscle area will be used by children during free-choice time, not during teacher-directed times.

It is helpful to have clean, flat carpeting in this area for warmth, because children will be sitting on the floor some of the time. The carpet also will help control the noise level during free-choice time when children use this learning center and its equipment for climbing, obstacle courses, tumbling mats, and big blocks. Low storage units will help define this space. If flat carpeting is not available for this area, teachers often use area rugs effectively, or at least provide carpet remnant squares on which children may sit.

Ample space is ideal for this area, but teachers who have little space will find that they easily can rotate active play equipment such as climbers, balance beams, and tumbling mats on various days. Active play and equipment should be available indoors on a daily basis.

Some teachers have additional rooms in their buildings where active play equipment, including wheel toys, is kept, and children either use the additional room together as a whole group, or are rotated in small groups to this space for ten to twenty minutes of guided active play during free-choice time.

5. Blocks Learning Area

Table blocks of many types are used daily in the small-muscle or table toys area, but separate areas should be defined for the use of both large hollow blocks and unit blocks.

Because of their physical nature, it is fairly easy to store the large hollow blocks by stacking them in a low "wall" against the one of the walls of the large-muscle/active play area. Programs who use a separate room for this learning center will find that these large hollow blocks, when used as part of an obstacle course or when used with props, can be just as effectively used in another room as in one's own classroom.

If I were told that I could have only one piece of equipment or set of materials in my setting, unit blocks would be my choice. The daily and appropriate use of unit blocks teaches cooperation and social skills, creativity and dramatic play; spatial relationships; perceptual skills; and math, science, and language skills. They are the most versatile and open-ended of the nonconsumable materials in the early childhood setting, and well worth the investment of their price.

Unit blocks and space in which to construct with them must be ample and should be defined not only to create the learning center but to protect the children's constructions. The center should not be placed where traffic flow will interfere with construction. *The Block Book* by Elisabeth Hirsch (1984) suggests that the unit block area encompass at least one-fourth to one-third of the room's floor space, with proper storage on shelves that are perceptually labeled for each type of block. *The Block Book* gives readers information on all the curriculum areas that can be taught through blocks, and gives suggestions on storage, accessories, management, and guidance.

6. Small-Muscle Area

This area or learning center is defined for the use of table toys, manipulatives, and materials such as bristle blocks and puzzles, often used by children (especially three-year-olds) on the floor. The tables and the low open shelves where these materials are stored make it easy to define this area, which is often carpeted. In this area, it is important to provide a wide variety and ample supplies of materials that match the developmental skill levels of children, especially in a mixed-age group. Materials should support both success and challenge for children.

When this area doubles as the meal service and children's "cooking" or foods experience area, carpeting is often eliminated. In this case, it is sometimes possible to set aside a portion of the space for a flat, solid-colored area rug for floor play with manipulative materials; this rug can be rolled up while foods experiences were in progress, if it is in the way.

7. Foods Experiences Area

Classrooms with space large enough to supply children's foods or snack preparation areas are rare, but those lucky centers that have space to include this center place a child-sized table and chairs near the storage and sink/water supply. In most centers, a table is simply reserved for use in the small-muscle area on days when children will make playdough or silly putty, help prepare snacks, or taste foods such as fruits and vegetables.

Teachers of quality programs will want children to be involved regularly in foods and "cooking" experiences. Therefore, plans for the setting must include planning for foods experiences, even if a daily defined learning center is not available. Children learn social skills; literacy, math, science, and problem-solving skills; and nutrition concepts when the setting includes space, time, and materials for foods experiences.

8. Creative Process—Art Media Area

The learning center for creative processes with art media will include space for at least two tables and one or two easels, as well as for accessible storage of art media materials of all kinds. Clay or playdough and paint, either at the table or at the easel, should be available daily. Other table space will provide opportunities for many types of collage, fingerpaint, construction with recycled materials, drawing, cutting, and other experiences.

Equipment such as easels should be used in the manner for which it was intended. Easels were designed to be used regularly with thick, bright paints and big brushes. They were not intended to be used primarily for paper and crayons or colored chalk.

Experiences in the art area should be process-oriented and open-ended. These experiences often require children to clean up the tables or themselves, so a water supply nearby is helpful. Where one is not available in the learning center itself, teachers can use a three-shelf rolling cart to remove materials to the water supply.

9. Music and Movement

This is a learning area that usually doubles with the large-muscle/active play area, and which includes records and record player, tapes and tape player, music instruments, and accessories for movement such as paper pom-poms, scarves, and ribbons or streamers. Music and creative movement will usually take place during teacher-directed times, but children should also be encouraged to use some of the music instruments, tapes, and accessories for spontaneous play with rhythms and music during free-choice time.

Reviewers of program quality will usually check to see that music and movement materials are appropriate, accessible, and frequently used, and that they include instrumental music without words and multicultural music as well as traditional music.

10. Literacy and Library Areas

Earlier in this chapter it was mentioned that defined learning centers can be of many sizes. Sometimes the perfect small space for a quiet reading center may be adjacent to the space developed for a writing center, but this is not necessary. What is most important is that the center for reading be quiet, attractive, and comfortable. Books and picture books should be age-appropriate, should be free of bias, should often include multicultural subject matter, should be accessible, and should be properly stored so that children can see their choices. Books should be rotated and should reflect children's current interests.

Sometimes small writing centers are adjacent to or created within reading areas, but they can also be created within art areas, within small muscle areas, in computer areas, and even within science and math centers. Children will need materials such as old greeting cards, paper, envelopes, big pencils, crayons, and markers. Storage of these materials in simple baskets on low shelves is often effective.

Reviewers of program quality may look for defined spaces and materials that enhance literacy, including experience stories and children's dictation posted at children's eye level. Although settings should include a reading and a writing center, literacy, like science, is a teaching and learning web that actually takes place everywhere in an early childhood setting, and even extends to the child's home.

The computer can be a medium for literacy, even though it often has its own defined space. Children will learn to make or dictate words on the computer, and dictation from children can also be written down by adults in many other areas of the room—the art area, blocks, science, and other areas. Also, children may frequently visit the library, and books from the library, or children's own books, such as journals, may also be sent home for use in the family.

11. Construction and Woodworking

This is a learning center that takes very little space if it consists of a log set securely on a carpet remnant to be used with hammer and short roofing nails, which are brought out at the time of use. Even when a workbench is available, this center takes up little space if storage can be developed creatively for scrap wood, Styrofoam, safety goggles, and tools. Sometimes tools are stored on the wall; sometimes they are kept in a box brought out during play when woodworking is a choice that is available that day.

Workbenches should be used for the purpose for which they are intended. They should not be used as counter tops or storage units, buffet tables to serve snacks or store paper meal service, or places to dry easel paintings.

One reason workbenches are not used as much as they might be is their noise level when in use on an uncarpeted floor. Solutions to this problem were given earlier in this chapter. Woodworking is a fine activity in which children develop language, creativity, problem-solving skills, eye–hand coordination, and social skills.

12. Outdoor Area

Reviewers of program quality or standards will probably pay close attention to the outdoor space that is used. The outdoor learning area is just as important as indoor learning centers. Children should have fresh air and outdoor exercise daily unless weather conditions are prohibitive to their health and safety. The outdoor area is important not only for the development of children's physical skills and fitness, but also for many opportunities to observe and discuss the outside environment and its changes, enjoy nature, and learn more about ecology and the care of our environment.

In addition to the permanent, well-anchored, and safe equipment recommended for early childhood settings, quality programs try to provide areas for digging or for gardens, climbers that encourage dramatic play, space for homemade instruments and wind chimes, space for resting under a tree or rolling on the grass, space for riding wheel toys and using hoops and jumpropes, space for using balls and parachutes, and sometimes even space for animals. Outdoor areas should be fenced and away from hazards.

Outdoor space for inclusion of these items is sometimes hard to come by. Programs often become very creative in using parents and/or community programs to develop outdoor areas, which usually incorporate adult-made equipment and recycled materials.

Many indoor learning center materials and pieces of equipment can be taken outdoors for children's use. Children love using easels outside, as well as colored chalk, buckets of water and big paint brushes, dramatic play props, and musical instruments and tapes. Urban programs often must take all their equipment outside and back inside daily, but children are happy to help with this job. Some programs have no outdoor area because no space is available for them to develop one at a particular site. In these programs, teachers are encouraged to consider roping off safe space in a corner of a parking lot, walking to a nearby park, or taking walks in the neighborhood.

Children in rural areas often have wonderful opportunities for observing nature on outdoor walks, but urban programs have much to offer in learning opportunities for children on their walks, too. In addition to the fresh air and good exercise of walking, children often become familiar with stores or homes in their neighborhoods, greet older people on their porches, watch workers fix the street, and chat with traffic policemen or policewomen. Children in urban programs can still observe the changes in sky, weather, and plants, and will have daily opportunities to practice traffic and pedestrian safety.

13. Field Trips and Visitors

Extensions of the setting or environment are also important to children's learning. A nature walk, a trip to the grocery store, a trip to the fire station, and other field trips extend children's knowledge. Visitors coming into the center to share talents, skills, and knowledge also extend the learning environment. At the beginning of the year, in a three- to five-year-old program, trips outside the center should be kept simple and to a minimum; visitors who come into the center, sharing knowledge and things of interest to children, can take the place of many field trips early in the year.

Other Considerations in the Setting

Just as an excellent chef needs a kitchen, counter space, helpers, storage, and appliances to create the foods on the menu, the teacher needs clearly defined spaces, storage, equipment, materials, and staff in order to implement good lesson plans. Here are some other basic elements, in addition to the basic learning centers, that should be in place in the setting in order to make the most effective use of lesson plans.

1. *Light:* Just as most of us enjoy indoor rooms that have plenty of natural light supplemented with artificial light, children's learning environments also need good natural light supplemented with good artificial light. Light can be enhanced with pastel or off-white painted walls.
2. *Orderliness:* Settings should be well organized and orderly. When children see that materials are orderly, attractive and well organized, it is easier for them to make thoughtful choices and be more responsible in taking care of their environment. Clutter is distracting to both children and adults, and orderliness facilitates cleanup.
3. *Children as helpers:* Children should be encouraged, on a daily basis, to be involved in the setup and care of the setting and learning environment. Teachers use helpers in various ways; in some programs, four or five helpers are rotated on a daily or weekly basis, giving every child the opportunity over a period of time to help. Occasionally programs arrange to have every child do one small job every day. Visual cues are used to remind children of their jobs. One of the best visual cues is actual photographs of the helper jobs, with space underneath for the name of the current helper.
4. *Displays and decoration:* The most important wall coverings in an early childhood setting are displays of the children's own work and open-ended art, and photographs of children in the group, all at their own eye level. Plants of various kinds (nonpoisonous) add warmth to the room.
5. *Personal space:* There should be individualized space for each child in the group, and these spaces should be personalized. One of the best ways to individualize children's personal spaces is to label them with names and photographs. This is a great self-esteem builder. In extremely small centers with no cubbies or personal tubs, personal space can still be successfully created with personalized children's tote bags.

6. *Safety and health:* Settings for young children should be safe, and aspects of the health, sanitation, and safety of the environment should be checked by professionals. Proper heating and ventilation systems; fire exit plans; and water and sewage systems; safe, clean equipment; child-sized furniture, toilets and sinks; separate storage (inaccessible to children) of cleaning supplies and other hazardous substances; and safe entrances and exits are among the aspects that should be regularly checked to ensure children's safety and health in the setting.

7. *Required postings:* All required documents, licenses, emergency procedures, emergency telephone numbers, and fire exit plans (in both print and picture/diagram form) should be clearly posted, and emergency or first aid materials should be easy to find.

8. *Parent information:* A parent bulletin board or information area should be part of every early childhood setting, and the information there should be clear, attractive, and up to date.

9. *Social-emotional climate:* Some aspects of the early childhood setting are important but less tangible, such as the nurturing and positive attitude of adults, and their appropriate interactions with children, both in teaching and in guidance situations. Adults who model positive social interactions and praise children descriptively for following suit will find that children copy and learn positive social behaviors very quickly. Programs employ various methods of observation to monitor these aspects of the setting.

To make Head Start teachers highly aware of the important social-emotional aspects of learning settings, the On Site Program Review Instrument (OSPRI), which has been extensively used since about 1985, asks review team members to check classroom settings for indicators of a positive social-emotional climate. Such indicators are a relaxed atmosphere where children are enjoying the setting and where there is an overall sound of children and adults in dialogue, and children with children in dialogue. Adult voices should not predominate, and staff should treat parents and children with attention and respect, both verbally and nonverbally. Language, interactions, and materials should be free of stereotyping, should include multicultural materials, and should reflect antibias attitudes that build pride and self-esteem.

The OSPRI review team attempts to review, and make suggestions if necessary, concerning the positive social and emotional climate that should be evident in early childhood Head Start settings. Most of the other indicators listed in this chapter in the section titled "Other Considerations in the Setting" are also included in the OSPRI, as well as in the Center Accreditation review instrument of the National Association for the Education of Young Children. In other words, these efforts and standards are not new, and not restricted to Head Start. They are accepted as standards of quality for settings in all early childhood programs.

Summary

In this chapter we have discussed the importance of the environment and its materials for children's hands on learning. Although early childhood settings are diverse, teachers can make the most of the settings they have by considering all the aspects of the setting that affect children's learning, and by planning learning centers carefully and creatively.

We have described the learning centers and the materials in these centers that should be a part of every early childhood setting, and discussed the fact that teachers in the setting need to use methods and materials that match the changing skill levels of children. Teachers facilitate learning in the environment with ample work/play slots, with positive modeling and interactions, and with questions motivating children's thinking. Teachers also provide children with the opportunity to practice planning and problem solving as they use the learning centers and the materials in them. Two examples of floor plans for the early childhood setting are presented at the end of this chapter.

Self-Study Activities

1. Study the floor plan examples at the end of this chapter. Reread sections of the chapter concerning learning center and room arrangement that present solutions to your particular challenges or problems in the setting. Using the floor plan examples and information in the chapter as a guide, draw a floor plan of your center, with any modifications you want to try out.

2. Draw a floor plan for your own "dream center" or "ideal classroom" without looking at the list of basic learning centers to be included in the setting. Check the list when you are done with your floor plan to see if you have included all learning centers. Modify as needed.

3. Examine catalogs containing materials for the early childhood setting. Which sections of these catalogs are most relevant to the children with whom you work? Make a list of materials and equipment needed by your group.

References and Resources for Further Reading

Brewer, Jo Ann. *Introduction to Early Childhood Education: Preschool through Primary Grades.* Boston: Allyn and Bacon, 1995, pp. 38–59.

Community Development Institute, *Head Start On-Site Program Review Instrument (OSPRI).* Washington, DC: Department of Health and Human Services, Administration for Children, Youth and Families, n.d., pp. 1–18.

Dodge, Diane Trister, & Colker, Laura J. *The Creative Curriculum,* 3rd ed. Washington, DC: Teaching Strategies, 1992.

Elkind, David. *Images of the Young Child.* Washington, DC: National Association for the Education of Young Children, pp. 13–20.

Forman, George E., & Kuschner, David S. *Piaget for Teaching Children: The Child's Construction of Knowledge.* Washington, DC: National Association for the Education of Young Children, 1983.

Hirsch, Elisabeth. *The Block Book,* rev. ed. Washington, DC: National Association for the Education of Young Children, 1984.

Kritchevsky, Sybil, & Prescott, Elizabeth, with Walling, Lee. *Planning Environments for Young Children: Physical Space,* rev. ed. Washington, DC: National Association for the Education of Young Children, 1977.

McCracken, Janet Brown. *Playgrounds Safe and Sound.* Washington, DC: National Association for the Education of Young Children, 1990.

NAEYC Information Service. *Facility Design for Early Childhood Programs Resource Guide,* rev. ed. Washington, DC: National Association for the Education of Young Children, 1991.

Spodek, Bernard, & Saracho, Olivia. *Right from the Start: Teaching Children Ages Three to Eight.* Boston: Allyn and Bacon, 1994, pp. 42–46, 73–76.

Vergeront, Jeanne. *Places and Spaces for Preschool and Primary: Outdoors.* Washington, DC: National Association for the Education of Young Children, 1988.

Vergeront, Jeanne. *Places and Spaces for Preschool and Primary: Indoors.* Washington, DC: National Association for the Education of Young Children, 1987.

Figure 8-1   Floor Plan 1

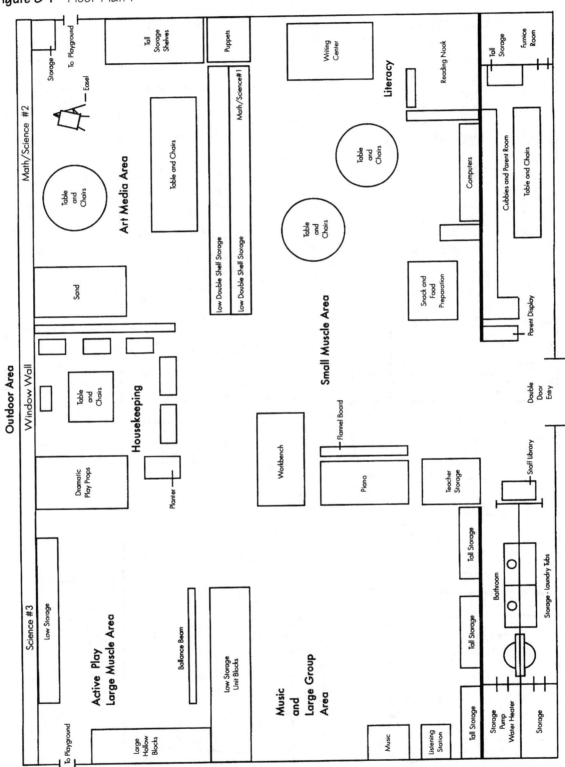

Figure 8-2 Floor Plan 2

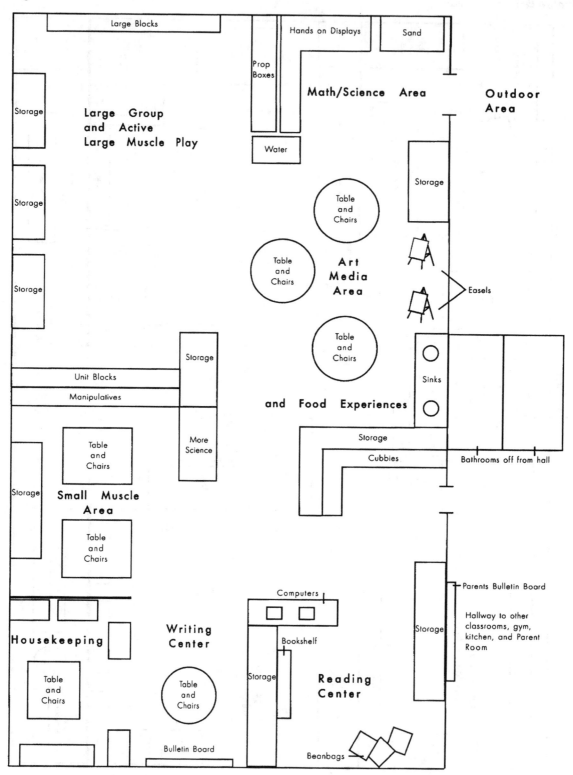

9 Free Choice

Introduction

Throughout this guidebook, the terms *free choice, child-initiated time,* and *activity time* have been used interchangeably. The reasons for this are a simple matter of semantics. Some programs also call free choice work time. All of these terms describe the time in the daily schedule or lesson plan in which children spontaneously engage in activities of their own choosing, as opposed to those activities planned by the teaching staff. The use of several terms is intended to clarify the meaning of this time of the day for different kinds of programs.

During free-choice time, children have more opportunities to engage in hands-on, concrete learning than at any other time of the day. Because this period is so important in terms of learning experiences, it is also the most challenging part of the day for teachers to plan.

When teachers understand and can clearly verbalize to others what and how children learn during free-choice time, it helps them to be more confident and more effective lesson planners. This is why we need to spend some time on a broader discussion of free-choice or child-initiated time.

Because play is an inherent part of this discussion, it would be beneficial to discuss the concept of *play* in terms of children's learning and our adult goals for their education. We should also examine specific skills children learn during free-choice time, and discuss ways for teachers to organize and manage free-choice learning activities. Effective management is to the best advantage of both the teacher and the child.

The three factors that have the greatest impact on an effective and enjoyable free-choice time (for both children and adults) are the kinds of activities that are planned, the teacher's understanding of the purpose of free-choice time, and the teacher's skills in classroom management. In dealing with the teacher's understanding of the purpose of free-choice time, we need to start with a brief review of what we know about children and how they learn.

How Children Learn

We know that young children learn all of the time, and in an integrated manner. They learn through their senses, their bodies, their curiosity, and their willingness to experiment and "find out." They learn by processing their thoughts through language as they increasingly use words to sort out and explain what they are discovering. They learn by doing. In the doing they learn many skills, including the skills of organizing and planning. In the "doing" they also integrate what they have already learned with new ways to use it; they construct new knowledge. Children learn by exploring, by trial and error, by experiencing pleasure through learning, by communicating, by imitating, and by participating fully in the learning experience.

Our Educational Goals for Children

We know how children learn. But what do we want them to learn for the long haul? As educators, what do we say about our educational goals for children? We say we want children to:

- Become lifelong learners and lovers of learning.
- Become creative and independent thinkers who can solve problems in more than one way.
- Become both planners and decision makers.
- Become able to make wise choices for their own well-being and that of others.
- Become skillful in many ways that will be necessary for success.
- Become able to be attentive and to concentrate.
- Eventually be able to put these skills to use in lifelong occupations, thereby becoming workers who contribute to the greater good of society.

Responsible Adults

If you look at this list, what we say we want children to learn, you will see that these goals are also the identifiers of responsible adults—adults who have meaningful jobs, who can make wise choices, who are thinkers, planners, leaders, and decision makers, who use their skills in many ways to benefit themselves and others, and who are always eager to keep on learning. We educators need to acknowledge that we want children to learn skills and attitudes, from early education on through high school and college, that will prepare them to be responsible, working adults.

Play and Work

If we want children to become responsible workers, we should think about what meaningful and enjoyable work means to a responsible adult. Those adults who are happiest in their work have chosen a job or career that is pleasurable mainly for the sheer satisfaction of doing it, a job that involves the use of skill and imagination, a job in which there are rules to follow, and a job in which they are actively and fully engaged.

Both parents and educators want children to become responsible adults who enjoy their work and their lives. To do this, children need to learn certain life skills. They need to learn to accept responsibility for their behavior, as well as time management skills, problem solving and decision-making skills, positive social behavior, the satisfaction of completing a task, and the enjoyment of continuous learning.

Because most high school curriculum emphasizes factual content over thinking and doing processes, children are most likely to begin learning these important skills at a much younger age. They learn them from their parents and from enjoyable activities built on their hobbies and interests in such areas as sports, clubs, family pastimes, and 4H experiences. Children learn important life and work skills from these activities, which are far more like "play" than they are "work" or "school," even though adults do not call them play experiences. Children between the ages of three and five are also learning these life and work skills, but at this age they learn them from engaging in what adults call "play."

"What exactly is play? What is the dividing line between play and work? Can an activity be both play and work at the same time?" (Hughes, 1995, 1991) In his book, Hughes says that there are a number of elements that are typical of play, and these elements can help us arrive at a definition of play.

- Play is intrinsically motivated; the desire to do it comes from within, and it is done for the sheer satisfaction of doing it.
- Play is freely chosen by the participant.
- Play is pleasurable.
- Play is nonliteral; it involves the imagination and ability of the person to create new possibilities for himself or herself.
- Play is something in which the person is fully and a actively engaged.

Usually there are rules for play, but children learn these rules willingly because of the opportunities play offers.

If you look closely at these elements in the definition of play, you will find that all of them could apply equally to the work or career of a responsible adult. You could actually substitute the word *work* for *play* in each statement. Therefore, if we want children to learn the skills that will eventually prepare them to take their roles in society and have jobs that they do well and that are meaningful to them, we would approve of all the elements of play. *Play is simply the way young children begin to learn the skills they will need as responsible, working adults.*

We know how children learn, what we want them to learn, and why we want them to learn it. Some people do not understand how young children can possibly begin learning these skills through play experiences. They may not understand that the greatest opportunities for learning these skills occurs during the free-choice or child activity time of the program day.

Free Choice—Planned Activity Time

There are very real correlations between the thought processes of children during free-choice time and the thought processes of adults as they carry out their daily business. In free-choice time, children have the chance to practice life skills and work skills that adults use every day.

As an adult, you begin each day by figuring out what you are going to do with it. You may even have planned for it the night before and made a list of the things you were going to do. Your planning will not just concern your work or your job, because many other things need to be done daily by adults, even those who work long days. You will be planning what bills to pay, what calls to make, what errands to run, whom you will spend time with, and how much time you will spend doing each thing on your list.

Your planning involves time management, prioritizing, and choice making. It involves self-discipline and self-regulation. You are the one who will accomplish the tasks you have planned; no one will be holding your hand and making your choices, telling you what to do first, or how to do it, or how long it should take.

There are certain rules you will follow in doing these tasks; these are your own rules, as well as those of society and your employer. Because of these rules, you may need to use your imagination to figure out ways to do two things at once, or adjust your schedule for the day to accommodate the rules.

There are certain parameters that will make a difference in what you do on the day you have planned. Many of these parameters are already set; they are things largely beyond your control. What car you have to use, how much money you have to spend, whether you live in a city or in the country, what the weather is like, how much traffic you need to negotiate, and how many times you get interrupted will all make a difference in how you actually get through the day you have planned.

All these things we do as adults require us to use many, many skills, most of which we take for granted. Responsible adults "get the job done." They get through each day by using real skills in planning, problem solving, and time management.

Now let's look at what we call free-choice time for children (which is not free in many ways) and illustrate how most of the daily skills and thinking processes adults use are the very same kinds of skills and thinking that children use during free-choice or activity time.

First, there are parameters and rules within children must operate, just as adults do. The amount of time they have to accomplish their plans is restricted to about one hour, and they have no control over this. The space they use and the way it is set up have already been planned and set up by adults; it is not under children's control. The physical boundaries of the learning centers, also arranged by adults, tell children some rules that do not need to be stated in words. The rules for using the space in the room may have been developed jointly with the children and the adults, but they are basically rules judged most important for safety and learning by the adults, not by children. The materials available in each learning center are also planned and made accessible to children by adults. The kinds of materials and how many are available are decided by adults. There are rules made by adults about how to use and care for materials. Whether or not an area is open or closed to children is decided by adults.

All of this is well and good, because basic child development and what we know about children tells us that children do not have the ability to set up these kinds of parameters within which to function, even though we do ask them to help in caring for the settings we adults have planned.

Just as adults are expected to take care of their personal property, not damage the property of others, and care about the environment and the community, children in early childhood settings in free-choice time are expected to do the very same things in their environment and community, the community of the preschool setting.

Children practice many other skills and learn many other things as they function during free-choice time. Here are some of the things they do and learn:

- Practice skills in planning their time, so that they can take advantage of all opportunities for learning and doing.
- Practice skills in gathering what they need in order to engage in an activity.
- Practice skills in increasing their attentiveness and concentration.
- Practice making decisions or choices appropriate to their skill levels, among those alternatives planned by adults.
- Choose with whom they will spend their time and for how long.
- Engage in learning more about their world and the people, plants, animals, and things in it.
- Engage in learning how things work and in learning new words to describe how things work, grow, or change.
- Engage in learning more about the world of adults and the roles adults play in the world.
- Engage in creative thinking and doing.
- Practice cognitive, social-emotional, and physical skills that will help them learn, and with which they will be more successful in later years. These are not only the skills of communicating, negotiating, and compromising with other people, but also specific skills in motor, perceptual, literacy, memory and problem-solving areas.

We have seen some of the skill and learning correlations between the adult world and the child's world that occur during free-choice time. This time of the program day could actually be called a planned activity time, since planning is done both by adults and by children.

Free-choice time is the medium in which children, through play, begin to learn what will be required of them as adults. Adults help them learn by setting up the right kinds of learning centers and materials for play, by creating the parameters within which children will learn, and by managing what happens during this time. Perhaps teachers help most when they believe in the worth of play and when they understand and value its purposes.

Teachers who understand the value of play know that structured, adult-directed activities such as worksheets, dittos, and workbooks are not effective in helping young children learn the skills listed here. The position paper "Play: A Necessity for All Children" of the Association for Childhood Education International (ACEI) charges teachers to take the lead in articulating the need for play in children's lives and in the early childhood curriculum.

> ACEI believes . . . that play and development through play are enhanced by carefully selected toys and equipment. Furthermore, adults have a crucial role in carefully structuring and planning the use of such materials to enable children to interact spontaneously with their learning environment. (Isenberg & Quisenberry, 1988.)

In the NAEYC pamphlet *Play Is Fundamental,* teachers are urged to allow ample time for play, keep it active, create special spaces for play, foster problem solving through play, plan for variety in play, and use the outdoors for play (McCracken, 1987). It is the competent teacher's responsibility to support these guidelines through comprehensive lesson planning. Teacher planning is part of the early childhood professional's role as a manager.

Management

Materials

As we have discussed in detail in Chapter 8, teachers or adults plan which materials and equipment will be used in the learning centers during free-choice or activity time. One of the basic management skills teachers must have is the ability to choose which materials to offer children at which times of the year, and know how many materials to offer at a time.

When teachers use a system to organize their horizontal and vertical curriculum ideas, it is easier to choose materials for each day that meet the needs of children in the group. Children who have the right kinds of materials for their developmental skills (neither too hard or too easy), and who have materials that are interesting, will be busy, happy and intensely engaged during free-choice time.

Materials need to be varied and in ample supply in order for free-choice time to be most effective. When children have to wait too long to use a material, they get wiggly and whiny. When they need to build a structure and do not have enough blocks to build it, they become frustrated. Not only will they not be able to practice construction and math skills, this situation could also lead to management or guidance problems.

If there are no interesting materials in the dramatic play area, children will not use the area to develop literacy and creative thinking skills. If there are no puzzles for three-year-olds, and only complex puzzles are available, threes will become frustrated or may not even try to practice using puzzles. If there are no books in the reading center, children will not use this area to increase literacy skills. If there are no plants and animals to observe, and no measuring tools or observation tools, children will not develop certain skills in observation, problem solving, and literacy. If there is no indoor large-muscle equipment, children will not practice their large-muscle skills.

What children will learn and practice during free-choice time is directly related to the activities and materials the teacher has planned and set up.

Play Slots

The concept of play slots in the management of the setting was discussed in Chapter 8. If a teacher finds that a three-year-old is at loose ends during free-choice time, that child might need an adult lap to sit on or a person to sit and talk with or read with for a while. A wandering four-year-old might need adult help to enter and become a part of group play.

If several children are wandering and do not seem to know what to do in free-choice time, it is a sign that not enough play slots are available to keep all children busy and engaged in learning. Another sign of an inadequate number of play slots is overcrowding in one or two areas of the setting. If eighteen children are given only five choices of activity, and if two of these are a climber or water play that are very rarely offered, almost all of the children will be on the climber or in the water, causing potential safety and management problems.

The teacher's ability to plan an ample number of play slots is an important management skill. The teacher should plan at least twice as many or up to two and a half as many play slots as children to keep all children busy and learning. Many small interest areas, for two to four children at a time, usually work best.

Balance in Stimulation

If the teacher plans to have the climber available only once a month, on that day nearly all the children will be trying to use the climber at one time. The best way to manage this is to put out the climber every day, or at least frequently, so that children will know that they can plan to use the climber at a time when it is not crowded. They will be able to make this choice because they know the climber will be available again, and often.

A similar situation can develop when teachers do not offer painting or sensory materials such as sand and water play daily. If teachers offer these materials, which are of great interest and learning potential for children, every day, give children enough time to use them, and set clear expectations for their use, teachers will not have management problems during the use of these materials.

Planning where to offer a stimulating, interesting material or activity in the setting is another management technique. For example, if teachers plan to use the climber in one area of the room during free-choice time, they should also plan at least two other very interesting materials to be offered in other areas of the room. Good choices would be water play, the use of a dry cell battery in the quiet area, fingerpainting, or a cooking experience. These additional stimulating materials will draw some children away from the climber. The more interesting the choices that are planned and available for small groups of children, the easier it is for teachers to manage children in free-choice time.

Guidance

Teachers guide children both verbally and nonverbally. Verbal guidance should be calm, clear, and firm, but soft-spoken. It should include questions that make children think about their behavior and their responsibilities, and should help children accept the consequences of their behaviors. Guidance should include clear, simple expectations and positive reminders of rules made by and for the group. Most of all, it should include praise and reinforcement that tells children the ways adults want them to behave, and what behaviors adults approve. Nonverbally, teachers have an effective impact on children's behaviors by their very presence, expression, or body language.

Other visual cues are helpful in classroom management as well. Teachers can place masking tape lines on the floor or rug to show the direction in which traffic should move. They can have children make stop signs to hang up at the entrances of restricted areas. They can use sheets or covers to tell children an area is "closed." They can have children help make taped footprints to show how many places are available (and/or limited) at the sand or water table.

Often, teachers use other types of visual cues to help children in learning to plan good use of their free-choice activity time. These might take the form of tags children hang up in the area they are currently using; only so many spaces are allotted for the tags in each learning center. Other teachers may use planning boards, where children will indicate their plans or their choices with symbols or tags.

Even though you may have excellent skills in verbal and nonverbal guidance, you can still be a victim of stress and burnout if your lesson plans for free-choice time are not carefully made. The learning setting and what is in it must work for you, not against you, and it must do a great deal of the work. You will not have time to do individualized teaching during this time (Chapter 7) if you are too busy guiding and redirecting behavior.

Planning is the key to what happens in free-choice time. Be sure you have the right materials, and enough of them; be sure you have planned interesting materials and activities in all areas of the room, along with enough play slots. If you do careful preplanning and organization, your free-choice time will look very free (and also very smooth and well run) to a casual observer. Children will all be busy, happy, and learning. You are the one who will know just how "free" it really is.

No matter how well you plan, you usually will be working with a diverse group of young children. You will need to use a variety of positive guidance and discipline techniques for effective classroom management. Here are ten guidance tips for adult managers of free-choice time:

1. Use positive modeling and have positive expectations. If you expect the worst from children, you will get it. Expect their best.
2. Use positive reinforcement and meaningful descriptive praise as often as possible. Saying "Good job" is not enough; children need to know what you like and why you like it.
3. Provide clear, simple rules and expectations, and involve children in making group rules. Remind them by asking what the rule is and why we have the rule.
4. Use both auditory and visual cues and reminders for expected behaviors.
5. Plan an age-appropriate routine that works for, not against, you to ensure that children have both active and quiet experiences and ample play spaces.
6. Plan an effective setting with a safe traffic flow and offer concrete, hands-on and sensory experiences. Sensory experiences reduce stress and tension in children (less tension, fewer problems).
7. Plan an effective use and placement of adults in the setting, and encourage their active involvement in play and learning activities.
8. Avoid wasted learning time with lines and waiting, both of which cause potential problems. Use a variety of transitions instead of lines to move children to new activities.
9. Increase a sense of "family" and responsibility to the group by praising children who help the group or each other.
10. Involve the children in praising each other for improved behavior. Peer reinforcement can work miracles.

Wise lesson planning by teachers as to the choices offered in free-choice or activity time, wise planning of the numbers of play slots offered, careful planning of the balance of stimulation throughout the setting, and good techniques in verbal and nonverbal guidance all combine to create effective and easy management of this important learning period of the day.

Summary

The main point of this chapter has been to demonstrate the value and worth of play as it relates to the life and work skills that children begin to learn in the early years. Free-choice time is the most important time of the program day for children to practice these life skills, as well as other specific skills in cognitive and psychomotor development.

What children learn during free-choice time is directly related to the teacher's planning and management skills. When teachers demonstrate good planning and management, children learn to make choices, plan their time, make learning discoveries, use their imaginations, problem-solve, practice skills, and accept responsibility for their behavior during free-choice time. The materials offered for learning, the way they are set up, and the way adults guide children during spontaneous play make the difference between an effective or ineffective free choice time.

Self-Study Activities

1. Read some of the articles or books on play in the list at the end of this chapter. Later, write up your thoughts about what you learned that will help you most in your management of free-choice time or in your discussions with others on this topic.

2. Observe free-choice time, with prior permission, in an early childhood classroom. Try to count the play slots offered, and note the particular management techniques used by the teacher and staff. Reflect on your notes later. Are there things you would have handled differently? What are they? Did you notice techniques that will be helpful to you? What are these?

References and Resources for Further Reading

Berk, Laura E. "Vygotsky's Theory: The importance of Make-Believe Play." *Young Children,* Vol. 50, No. 1 (1994), pp. 30–39.

Casey, M. Beth, & Lippman, Marjory. "Learning to Plan through Play." *Young Children,* Vol. 46, No. 4 (1991), pp. 52–61.

Christie, M. Beth, & Lippman, Marjory. "How Much Time Is Needed for Play." *Young Children,* Vol. 47, No. 3 (1992), pp. 28–32.

Elkind, David. "Work Is Hardly Child's Play." *Images of the Young Child: Collected Essays on Development and Education.* Washington, DC: National Association for the Education of Young Children, 1993, pp. 21–29.

Fein, Greta, & Rivkin, Mary, eds. *The Young Child at Play: Reviews of Research,* Vol. 4. Washington, DC: National Association for the Education of Young Children, 1986.

Ford, Sylvia A. "The Facilitator's Role in Children's Play." *Young Children,* Vol. 48, No. 6 (1993), pp. 66–73.

Henniger, Michael L. "Planning for Outdoor Play." *Young Children,* Vol. 49, No. 4 (1994), pp. 10–15.

Hughes, Fergus P. *Children, Play, and Development,* 2nd ed. Boston: Allyn and Bacon, 1995.

Isenberg, Joan, & Quisenberry, Nancy L. "Play: A Necessity for All Children." *Childhood Education,* February 1988, pp. 138–145.

Larson, Nola, Hentborne, Mary, & Plum, Barbara. *Transition Magician: Strategies for Guiding Young Children in Early Childhood Programs.* St. Paul, MN: Redleaf Press, 1994.

McCracken, Janet Brown. *Play Is Fundamental.* Pamphlet. Washington, DC: National Association for the Education of Young Children, 1987.

McKee, Judy Spitler, ed. *Play: Working Partner of Growth.* Wheaton, MD: Association for Childhood Education International, 1986.

Rogers, Cosby S., & Sawyers, Janet K. *Play in the Lives of Children.* Washington, DC: National Association for the Education of Young Children, 1988.

Sawyers, Janet K., & Rogers, Cosby S. *Helping Young Children Develop through Play: A Practical Guide for Parents, Caregivers, and Teachers.* Washington, DC: National Association for the Education of Young Children, 1988.

Schweinhart, Lawrence J. "Child-Initiated Activity: How Important Is It in Early Childhood Education?" *High Scope Resource,* Spring–Summer 1987, pp. 1, 6–10.

Schweinhart, Lawrence J. "Education for Young Children Living in Poverty: Child-Initiated Learning or Teacher-Directed Instruction." *The Elementary School Journal,* Vol. 89, No. 2 (1988), pp. 213–225.

10 Priorities in Early Childhood Lesson Planning

Introduction: National Priorities in Early Education

There is agreement among educators, researchers, and human service providers, both in our federal government and in the field, that America's children are graduating from high school with poor skills in math, science, and literacy. Our school dropout rate is high; many adults and young people cannot read. Our students rank lower than those of many other industrialized nations on their math and science achievement scores. U.S. Department of Education officials have said that, although schools have made some progress in math and science because of increased emphasis on these subjects, the findings of the National Assessment of Educational Progress (NAEP) show that U.S. students are not holding their own in reading and writing, that the progress made in the 1980s in minority student achievement has stalled, and that U.S. students are at about the same level of achievement as they were twenty years ago (*Detroit Free Press,* August 18, 1994). Educational priorities continue to be literacy, mathematics, and the sciences.

In the National Goals Report, "A Nation of Learners," the National Education Goals panel of 1993 recognizes the importance of early childhood programs to school readiness and success, and calls attention to the need for adequate health and nutrition, parent involvement, and the provision of high quality developmental early childhood programs. (National Education Goals Panel, 1993)

In the final report of the Advisory Committee on Head Start Quality and Expansion (December 1993), key issues regarding the updating of the Head Start Performance Standards included "requirements and or guidance supporting developmentally appropriate curriculum, emergent literacy, and transition of children to elementary school" . . . and "reinforcing the role of parents in the decision making process" (U.S. Department of Health and Human Services, 1993).

The Administration on Children, Youth, and Families' Head Start Bureau, working closely with its own early childhood programs and other early childhood professionals, has communicated to its programs the importance of parent involvement and the importance of planning learning activities in child and family literacy, in math/science problem solving, in environmental awareness, and in antibias or multicultural awareness. There is a consensus on these priorities in lesson planning among many other early childhood programs and professionals in the field.

These priority issues are of great concern to early childhood professionals be-cause they have an impact on our field and our planning for children. Because we work with young children in their formative early years, it is our responsibility as educators to do our best to improve child and family literacy and to increase children's interests and skills in divergent thinking and problem solving. Parents, the children's first and most important teachers, are important team members in this work. With-out the involvement of parents, we cannot hope to accomplish all that must be done. Let's take a brief look at these priority areas.

Literacy, Mathematics and Science

The most formative years for children are from birth through age eight. Many of the child's attitudes about learning, reading, and problem solving are formed within this period (White, 1975, Elkind, 1987; Bredekamp, 1992; Hamburg, 1992). Our basic child development knowledge and our ongoing observations of children tell us that the best ways to develop literacy, math, and science skills in young children are to encourage curiosity and enthusiasm, reinforce discov-ery learning and problem solving, and promote meaningful learning activities in these areas.

When young children are excited and motivated, and when they are praised for their language and their hands-on problem solving with math and science materials, their skills in these areas improve. If early childhood educators are committed to addressing national educational concerns in literacy, mathemat-ics, and the sciences, our challenge is to continue to do what we know works and to include in our lesson plans even more discovery learning activities in math, literacy, and science.

Parent Involvement

The following statements of standards for quality in programs for young chil-dren, written by the National Association of Elementary School Principals, de-fine effective parent involvement and sum up its importance:

- Open communication between parents and the school staff is basic to the success of an early childhood program and must be two way, not a situation in which educators talk and parents passively listen.
- Involvement helps parents become increasingly more effective in working with their own children and more knowledgeable about the overall operation of the school.
- Principals in cooperation with other school and community agencies provide information and ideas to parents to help them in their roles of provider, nurturer, disciplinarian, and first teacher.
- Parents must share in their children's education and progress, and in deci-sions regarding placement. Both the effectiveness and the efficiency of early

childhood programs are closely tied to mutual parent/school planning and decision making (National Association of Elementary School Principals, 1990).

Ecology and Environmental Awareness

In addition to planning and teaching priorities in literacy, math, science, and parent involvement, there is a growing concern, in our country and others, about our environment. Early childhood teachers have the opportunity to impact children's thinking about our world and its natural resources—people, plants, animals, earth, air, and water. We have both the ability and the responsibility to include ecology and environmental awareness activities in our lesson plans. In this way, we will nurture in children an awareness that taking care of our environment is important.

Antibias, Inclusion, and Multicultural Awareness

Along with caring about our world comes global awareness. Other countries in the world and the people in them are more familiar to children than in the past. Children travel with their families, people move more often, and children often find themselves in diverse communities and classrooms. Culturally relevant programming that celebrates diversity, discards stereotypes, and is inclusive of all children is both necessary and appropriate in early childhood education. Including antibias and multicultural awareness activities in our lesson plans enables children to develop awareness, respect, and appreciation of both individual and cultural differences. An appreciation of diversity and individual differences will help today's children to live and work together in a world that is becoming tomorrow's global village.

Today's teachers in quality programs will be expected to emphasize these national priorities through the learning activities of their daily and long-range lesson plans. In the rest of this chapter, we will discuss learning activities and strategies in each of these priority areas.

Literacy

The Setting

The learning setting itself plays a part in the emergence of literacy.

- The setting should promote a print-rich environment that is stimulating without being distracting, containing displays of children's words about their observations and work as well as both printed and perceptual labels for materials and storage. Labeling can be done in short sentences, if preferred, and words can be printed in both English and other languages if appropriate.

- Learning centers should be set up to encourage small-group interaction and conversations.
- The schedule should allow time for children to converse with peers and adults during meals and planned play activities.
- Dramatic play props should be used to encourage both the retelling of events and stories and the acting out of children's own dialogues in creative role play.
- Displays of children's art and work containing their own dictation should be seen at their eye level.
- The use of the computer, play telephones, tape recorders and listening stations should be observable.
- Both reading and writing learning center areas should be inviting, should contain materials appropriate to children's skill levels and current interests; and should contain children's own big books, rebus recipes and journals.

Open Questions

In their interactions with children, teachers need to ask open questions that encourage children to observe, to tell or describe, to imagine, to think of the possibilities of various answers, and to explain their reasons for their answers. Open questions are not those that have only one answer ("What is this?") the answer expected by the adult, but questions that have endless possibilities for answers.

The simplest open questions are those that ask children, "What do you think about such and such?" or, "Why do you think that happened?" or, "What are some things you could tell us about this table?" Children's answers to the open question about a table would vary, covering the table's shape, size, color, and possible uses. A more sophisticated open question about a table would be, "If you could take this table to your house, what would you do with it?" In this case, the children need to move the table mentally to a new physical environment and use their imaginations in their thinking. This level of open question opens up an entirely new set of possible answers. With three-year-olds, teachers will probably focus on "observe and tell what you think" types of questions, whereas with fours and fives, more sophisticated open questions, incorporating the child's imagination, can be used.

Open questions can be used effectively in the area of guidance. Sometimes teachers tell the children the rules, when instead they should be asking the rules. When you say, "What are you doing right now that you need to think about?" or, "What do I need you to do right now?" you are asking the children to think and to put those thoughts into words, perhaps even explaining (to the teacher's prompt "Why do we . . . ?") the reasons for the rules. Readers can see that children are apt to understand and follow group rules better when they are asked to think and tell instead of simply being told the rule by the adult.

Active Listening

Active listening is listening intently to the meaning behind a child's words and responding to them. It is a matter of reflecting back to the child's his or her own words along with the child's possible feelings underlying those words. In a manner similar to the teacher's attentive focus during observations, here the teacher is listening to the child's inner thoughts and feelings about what is being said. Teachers who are good active listeners don't interrupt children or give them the answers to questions; they wait as long as it takes for the child to say what he or she needs to say. Active listening is an excellent strategy for eliciting more language from the child; the more language, the better the chance for literacy skills to develop.

Related to active listening is the ability of the teacher to give very young children some of the words they need to describe what they are doing. The teacher can describe what is happening as a child enjoys a material or practices a skill. "You look like you are enjoying using that yellow paint. You are smiling . . . maybe yellow is a color that makes you happy." "You put one foot on that step, and the other foot on the next step . . . you are learning to be a very good climber." "Do you see the salt we put into the water? When we can't see it anymore, it has disappeared into the water. We say it has dissolved." When children hear words that describe what they are doing, and hear new descriptive words like *scrumptious* and *tantalizing aroma,* they pick up on the use of descriptive words and the literacy skill of communicating what they are doing and why to others.

Some children need this kind of adult encouragement in communicating to other children how they feel or what they need or want. Teachers sometimes need to say, " X, use words to tell Y what it is you need," or "Tell Y how you felt when she said that you could not play." Communicating our needs and feelings to others is a lifelong literacy skill, which, when used effectively, can reduce much of the stress in our lives.

Dictation and Experience Stories

The importance of writing down the child's own words about his or her art, work, math and science observations, block structures, feelings, made-up songs and stories—anything the child thinks about and

wants to relate in words—cannot be overemphasized. These pieces of dictation should be posted where the child can see and "read" and reflect on them, and examples should be placed periodically in the child's file or portfolios. Nothing seems to please a child more than having an teacher show that he or she values the child's ideas and words enough to take the time to write them down on paper.

After visitors have come to share knowledge or talents, and after outdoor walks or field trips, the children's words about the experience can also be written down on poster paper as an "experience story" or a thank-you letter.

Sometimes, when children develop rules for the room and the group, the rules they thought of and the names of the children who developed each rule can be posted as an experience story.

Other types of experience stories are "I Am Special" or "My Family Is Special" posters, including the child's own words about likes, dislikes, family members, and interests. A related kind of experience story used to promote friendships in the group is "X Is Special Because . . ." In this case, the children tell all the things they think are special about a certain child. To promote family relationships, a similar poster could be titled "What I Like Best about My Grandpa's Hands." If the child wants his or her words to be written in both English and another language, every effort should be made to do so.

Step-by-step picture or rebus recipes including the children's words in the directions are still another form of dictation or experience story. More recipes can be added as the children try new ones and can be kept in an oversized card file, in a scrapbook, or as posters. Collections of recipes could make a children's big book, and the children's words about their own parents' recipes in a collection of family recipes for the group will make delightful and original reading.

Journals

Related to dictation and experience stories are the personal journals of children, done in individual scrapbooks, in blank books, or in notebooks. Children are encouraged to write down their thoughts or feelings about the day or about

any other topics in their journals in their own ways, with their own methods of writing and spelling, as well as through dictation to an assisting adult. In this way, children can begin to write their own books on topics of their choice. Traveling journals to expand family literacy can also be developed. These blank books or scrapbooks could go home on weekends with a stuffed animal or puppet from the center, and the parents and child could write about the toy's "experiences" at their house in the journal.

Reading and Writing Centers

These centers were discussed in Chapter 8 on the early childhood setting. The space you create for reading and writing centers is not as important as what you put into these centers and how you encourage their use by children. Writing center materials can be simple and should be appropriate to children's interest and skill levels. Recycled envelopes, stickers, trading stamps, stamp pads, and greeting cards with big pencils or markers and paper will fill the bill, especially if adults praise and encourage children for using the materials frequently and for creating messages there (with or without adult help) for family members or peers.

In the reading center, books and pictures to create or reinforce interest in a thematic unit can be added to the picture books and stories for young children, which are rotated by the teacher. Books should be nonsexist and should often reflect the cultural interests of those in the group or other cultures. Sometimes puppets, flannelboard stories, photo albums of the children and their center experiences, or children's own books can be added.

Children should be encouraged to read independently or in small groups, with or without an adult during the day, as well as to hear a daily book or story in large group. If the center has few or no books of its own, funding should be developed to purchase them each year; poor-quality books in disrepair do not do much to encourage literacy. Libraries can be used regularly to supplement the center's library with books for children and families. Books and stories can be extended with props and dramatic play, with child or teacher-made flannel stories, and with tape recordings of children's own stories or conversations with each other and adults.

Dramatic Play and Props

The dramatic play areas of the classroom always abound with children's conversations. In the housekeeping area or in places where adults have helped children set up a "store," a "campsite," or a "vet clinic," teachers can hear children using their own words and many new words to describe what they are doing or pretending to do. Adding props such as magazines to a "hospital waiting room" or a "barber shop," adding part of a daily newspaper or books to the housekeeping area, adding sale or price signs in a "store," and adding recycled restaurant menus and note pads to "restaurant" play are good ways to add to a print-rich environment and enhance literacy skills.

Props can also be used to encourage children's discussions about special things that are used in their own homes and are pertinent to their own cultures, traditions, or even special disabilities or needs. Putting out several pairs of children's eyeglasses (frames only, no lenses), scavenged from out-of-date models at a store, is helpful in making a child who wears glasses feel at home. Most of the other children will love to try on or wear glasses!

Using prop boxes for dramatic play to vary the housekeeping area is a frequent strategy of teachers, but with a classroom of mixed three to fives, it may be best to set up extra dramatic play in another area so that the threes can use the "house" and its dolls and dishes to their hearts' content while older children do pretending that reflects their greater knowledge of the world and adults. Dramatic play prop boxes should be labeled clearly without stereotypes and stored accessibly for frequent use.

Teachers often use props to enhance their storytelling literacy activities, especially in circle or large group time. Some teachers keep props for characters in the stories in a special apron pocket and bring them out in their order of appearance in the story. Some teachers use mystery boxes in which an imaginary or mystery item relating to their current theme appears. During clues and prompts given by the teacher, children describe and identify the invisible item. Props can enhance stories like "Caps for Sale" and "Stone Soup," too, although the children in my own group could never be convinced that I had not made the soup entirely from the stone.

Puppets

Child-made puppets are useful as "buddies" to talk with or use in storytelling by children. Different kinds of puppets can be used to reinforce other concepts in the teacher's plans as well. A special puppet can be used to signal clean-up time; or to ask the outdoor play rules; or to ask children about taking care of their teeth, eating healthful foods, being kind to each other, or using appropriate touch. Along the same line, teacher-made or purchased persona dolls (or puppets) can be used to increase children's awareness and discussion of children who may look different than they do or who have special needs or disabilities. Excellent reading material on these strategies can be found in *Anti-Bias Curriculum* by Louise Derman Sparks.

A literacy activity related to puppets and dolls might be to let the children make "pet rocks" out of hand-sized stones, glue, and odds and ends of material, pipe cleaners, fake fur scraps, and the like. Children can make up and dictate stories about these "pets" on tape or on paper.

Blocks

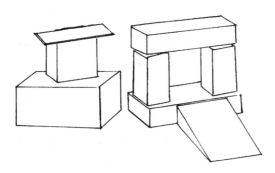

Literacy can also be enhanced in the blocks area, not only by having children name the blocks or use descriptive words to tell about block creations, but also to extend and act out a story that the children have heard or know.

The big hollow blocks and the unit blocks have different purposes (Chapter 8). Big hollow blocks are used to build a "set" in which children, as actors,

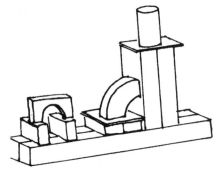

play out a role. They might be going fishing from a boat, riding on a train, or playing in an office or a fire station. If they are going fishing in a boat, be sure to include life jackets as props with the big blocks.

When they use unit blocks, children are like giants, manipulating the story emerging from the block play. Here, teachers can add small people, trucks, cars, road signs, and stone mountains and boulders. They can create a suspension bridge with tape, string, and towers, or a lighthouse surrounded by rocks and small boats. Adding these props to the use of the unit blocks enhances all sorts of language and storytelling by children.

Sharing Conversation in Groups

Early childhood teachers almost always use part of large-group circle time for the children to share in conversations. Usually these conversations are about what is going on in the children's lives, but they might also include teacher-guided discussions relating to the current themes of the lesson plans or other goals of the teacher. (health, personal safety, routine for the day, etc.)

Mealtimes are another group time in which children are encouraged to converse with each other and with adults. These sociable, relaxed conversations include what the children want to discuss (themselves and their families, their likes and dislikes, new skills, etc.), but they can also be guided discussions in which the teacher asks open-ended questions related to his or her own goals. These might include plans for the day, evaluations of the day, plans for another time, theme-related topics, and health and nutrition.

Large-group circle time for sharing conversation and increasing literacy skills is sometimes misused. It is not appropriate to the skill levels and attention span of three- to five-year-olds to sit for twenty or more minutes for "show and tell" about toys brought from home. First, it is questionable whether children really need to have show-and-tell time at all, since it is likely they will do it daily in kindergarten, and since there are so many other rich opportunities for literacy activities in the center. If show and tell is an absolute must for the teacher, there are better ways to manage it that are more appropriate for the short attention spans of threes to fives, and which will also promote their literacy and learning in more effective ways.

For example, children can do show and tell in two or three groups at the same time, guided by three adults, or they can have staggered times for "their" show-and-tell days, so that only four or five would share on any given day. To control the boredom (and sometimes the guidance problems) of toys brought from home, teachers can suggest to parents in a simple flyer or newsletter that, for example, "We are studying the color red and the concept of round. On your child's show and tell day, explore your house to find something red and round to send to talk about."

Nonverbal Communication

Teachers can help children learn about and have empathy for hard-of-hearing children, and also learn some of the elements of a new language, by using simple signing with the children. The phrases "I love you," "work," "play," "come," and "time" are easy to sign, and young children respond very well to this sort of communication. Children are great observers and users of body language. (They can always tell when adults' words do not match their real feelings.) Children can also be encouraged to discover and act out gestures that convey meaning to others without using words. They all know how to tell you without words when they like or dislike something, or "I don't know," or "Goodbye." Books without words are helpful in trying out nonverbal communication, and the book *Talking Without Words,* by Marie Hall Ets provides many good ideas.

Discovery Learning—Math and Science

Divergent Thinking

When children think of more than one way to find a solution, they are using divergent thinking skills, the same thinking skills used by scientists and mathematicians. Early childhood teachers can nurture divergent thinking and problem solving in many ways. Materials in the setting itself abound with these opportunities, and math and science activities can take place in all learning centers, as well as outdoors.

Here are some examples of divergent thinking and problem solving that could be prompted by questions. "How can we find some good ways to store our scrap wood for the workbench?" "Is there another way to use these blocks to build a ramp?" "We are out of orange tempera, but we need orange paint. Is there a way we could make some?" "We don't have a yardstick. Is there some other way we could measure how tall you are?"

Children's interactions with each other as they share materials also precipitate a need for them to negotiate and problem solve. Who would deny that negotiation is a life skill that children need to begin to learn at an early age! In the early childhood environment, all learning centers and their materials encourage this type of problem solving.

Before we look at specific examples of science and math activities, let's focus on five major learning centers where a great deal of discovery learning and problem solving takes place: the sensory center, the manipulatives center, blocks, dramatic play, and the foods experience center. Some of the problem solving in these five centers will include specific math and science activities; others will focus more on divergent thinking and discovery.

Sensory Learning

These learning centers are full of daily opportunities for discovery learning. At the sand or water table, and in exploring other textures such as recyclables, clays, and rice, children are encouraged to pour, fill, dig, mold, sort, categorize, and see likenesses and differences. They make guesses to estimate how much, or how many, and experiment to find out the answers. In this process they talk about "more" and "less"; they compare and they count. They examine intently,

with all their senses if possible, and tell what they see. These are the very things that mathematicians and scientists do. Children are practicing the same kinds of thinking, but at a concrete and sensorimotor level, not an abstract level. This is exactly where math, science, and discovery learning skills begin, which is why we want children to practice them.

It is vital that sand, water, and/or sensory materials be available to children daily, and that they be a part of daily lesson planning. Three-year-olds and young fours are particularly sensitive to learning through their senses, but all children will improve their learning skills through the daily use of open-ended, sensory materials.

Manipulatives

Anyone who has watched a child intently try to solve a puzzle or make something with manipulatives such as snap beads or bristle blocks knows that these materials promote problem-solving skills. It is important for adults to provide manipulatives every day that encourage both success and challenge. Help should be given to the child only as is really necessary to solve the problem with which he or she is working. Breaking down the skill into its smaller parts is helpful. For example, doing a puzzle has several logical steps:

- Look at the complete and intact puzzle picture first; see what it's about and what its parts and colors are.
- Turn over the puzzle, and then turn over each piece so that the colors and design show.
- Begin with the easiest parts of the picture, usually the corners.
- Watch for clues from what is remembered about the picture until all the pieces are found.

Teachers need to carefully plan, choose, and rotate the manipulatives that will be offered in this learning center to meet the skill-level needs of the children in the group. When children have created something original with a manipulative material, or successfully mastered a challenge, praise from adults and peers is important.

Blocks

The problem-solving opportunities presented by blocks have already been emphasized, but let's summarize a few of them. Blocks help children practice many skills—not only thinking skills, but also social, creative, language, memory perception, and motor skills. Blocks should be a part of every daily lesson plan. When space is a problem, big hollow blocks and unit blocks can be rotated with other equipment; table blocks can also be used to give children opportunities to practice thinking skills. With blocks, children problem solve to construct things, dealing with design and balance. They learn about shapes, sizes, space, patterns, colors; they learn the concepts of *wide, narrow, tall, light, heavy, short, long, equal, more,* and *less.* This is certainly math and science at the child's level!

Dramatic Play

In the process of dramatic play, children need to engage in the give and take of negotiation and problem solving as they figure out their roles and the scenarios of their pretending. They also problem-solve when they plan their role play, gather the materials needed, and carry out their plans.

During dramatic play, children sometimes grapple with real-life problems. Through imaginary play, which they can control, they may be able to gain a better understanding of their real-life problems and figure out ways to cope with them positively. Sometimes dramatic play simply gives children insight and understanding of the world and the roles adults play in it. Sometimes it gives them problem-solving tools for safety that may even save their lives.

Foods Experiences

There may be no better way to teach math and science skills than through children's involvement in foods preparation or meal and snacktime experiences. Not only do children estimate, measure, count, compare, sort, and discuss what they see. They also see changes in matter that occur when foods are mixed, combined, baked, or cooked. For example, they can see an egg change from liquid to solid form; they can see that some liquids, like water, can change from liquid to solid and back to liquid. Children also practice matching one to one as they set tables for meals and snacks. As a bonus, they practice literacy and social skills during foods preparation as they talk about what they are doing and take turns doing it.

Teachers who want to encourage math and science skills in children, as well as literacy, health, and nutrition, should include foods experiences in the daily lesson plan whenever possible, even if these are very simple experiences. Foods experiences should be planned at least once a week. These experiences are best implemented with small groups of children during small-group time or free-choice time.

Math Activities

Opportunities for mathematical manipulating and thinking, counting, sorting or tubbing, measuring, weighing, graphing, and learning about the concepts of time and money are available in all learning centers. However, teachers often need to note actual reminders and strategies in the lesson plan in order to take advantage of these opportunities. Some examples of math learning activities for the lesson plan have already been mentioned, but here are a few more math ideas.

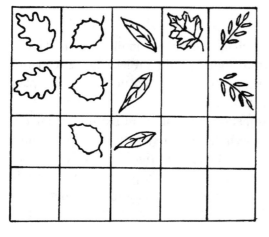

- In small group, help children notice how many of them there are. Count the body parts of one person or of two people. Count the number of shoes in the group.
- Weigh and measure children regularly, and mount this information on the wall so they can see changes in their growth.
- Graph children by size or other characteristics.
- Graph what sinks or floats.
- Graph the different kinds of crackers or cereals in a snack before eating it.
- Make a graph to show sets of two when children match pairs of sound cans.
- Use math props in dramatic play such as play money, calculators, scales, and measuring tools of all kinds.
- Sort many different recyclables—keys, bottle caps, plastic bread tags, stones, leaves, and plastic numerals.
- Graph objects from nature, such as different kinds of leaves.

Science and Nature

Science does not have to stay in a corner. Children can observe, tell, and practice learning about science concepts indoors, outdoors, and in most learning centers. Children begin to learn about physical science by using such things as balance scales, measuring tools, and dry cell batteries; they begin to learn about natural science by observing living and growing things including themselves, plants, and animals. Some science activities have already been mentioned in this chapter; many more will be found in Chapter 11.

Perhaps the most important thing teachers should remember about science with young children is to allow it to be simple. Children are excited about every small discovery, discoveries that adults often ignore or take for granted. Teachers should focus on the fact that the scientific method, at its core, simply means observing something very carefully, and telling what is seen. Sometimes an experiment might be done to see "what will happen if . . ." Again, the scientist observes and tells what is seen and why it might have happened.

Children are natural scientists; they follow these steps of the scientific method very easily. Teachers can help them to observe more carefully, help them tell more about what is seen, and experiment (safely) to see what might happen.

TRY THIS NOW   To understand how simple science can be, take some time to discover in the way that children do. Get a few friends together and find some potatoes in your kitchen. Each of you should take one potato and study it carefully. Get to know your potato well—as well as you know your best friend's face. After a few minutes, put the potatoes down and mix them up. Then, one a time, find your potato and explain to your friends how you knew it was yours. This is the kind of science we can do with young children to help them learn to observe and tell, and it is the kind of discovering that children love.

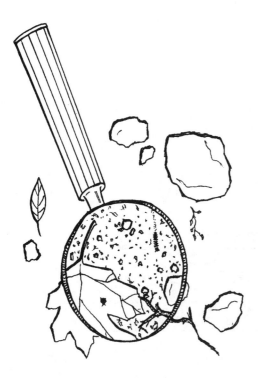

If teachers have science tables, the same old Indian corn, rocks, and magnifying glass should not stay there all year collecting dust. Science displays should be changed often, not only to encourage interest but also to mesh items with current thematic plans. If children are studying rocks, a great variety of rocks, including minerals and crystals, could be examined, as well as stone utensils of the past that were used as tools. If children are studying shells, shells and books on shells, shell buttons, and shell jewelry could also be explored.

Adults should always point out what new items are on the science table and should encourage the use of these materials with adult presence and open questions. It is an excellent idea to provide children with small flashlights and magnifying glasses for focusing on and examining the items displayed. Lighting up an item is particularly helpful in eliciting more detailed observing, comparing, and telling.

Early childhood teachers should make strong efforts to include plants and animals in the classroom so that children can observe and discuss what plants and animals need in order to live and grow. Plants and animals add warmth and life to the setting. Children can learn much from observing how animals breathe, how they eat, and what skin coverings or other adaptations (such as mouths, beaks, webbed feet, and claws) they have.

Ecology and Environmental Awareness

Early childhood teachers are, and have been for many years, the world's greatest role models for recycling items to use in teaching. Recycled materials abound in the art and sensory areas, as well as among dramatic play props and dress-ups. Sometimes, however, teachers need to remind themselves in lesson plans to talk about the fact that they are recycling things! If children are making structures or creations out of paper tubes, paper cups, and odds and ends of "junk," teachers need to point out that these things are being recycled, not only

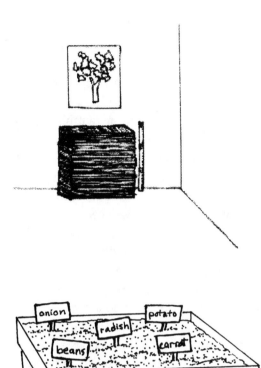

once, but again and again as children dismantle them after use and put them back in the box to use another day.

When teachers point out that old newspapers, if stacked up to a height of three feet, equal one tree, children may think more about taking care of trees or planting them. Perhaps they will go outdoors and look at trees, compare their heights, their branch patterns, and their bark, and talk about what they like about trees in their journals or on an experience poster. They maybe want to plant or "adopt" a tree to study.

Whenever possible, teachers should include activities in the horizontal plan and daily lesson plans that concern the environment and ecology. Any time children are outdoors, teachers can point out important things about caring for our environment, even if these are small but important things like controlling litter. If possible, a garden should be planted, either outdoors or inside the classroom. This can be done in a large recycled tire outside, or indoors in a toddler's recycled sandbox. Sometimes the climate or geography of a program will prohibit a growing and harvest season outdoors, but efforts to grow and harvest can be made indoors.

Antibias and Multicultural Awareness

In discussions about celebrating diversity, it is sometimes preferable to interchange the term *multicultural awareness* with the words *antibias* or *inclusion.* *Antibias* includes bias about gender, age, handicaps, and other differences as well as differences in culture or heritage. Valuing each other and cherishing both our similarities and our differences is the real issue. This is best taught when the teacher begins by centering on the children and families in the group, with both planned and spontaneous experiences.

Focusing on the phrase *multicultural awareness* can lead to too many superficial "tourist" activities like Hawaiian Luau Day, instead of simply learning to accept and value each other. Children need to learn that *different* is not *better* or *worse*—it is just *different,* and usually very interesting.

In my experience, the most competent teachers in the area of antibias or multicultural awareness are, first and foremost, aware persons. These teachers seem to have internalized attitudes of awareness and acceptance that flow from within, making the activities they plan both natural and effective. They have taken what we might call the three antibias steps of *awareness, understanding,* and *action.*

Awareness that antibias activities are important is the very first step that teachers must take; it is an inner step, taken within one's consciousness. This means that we must be aware, not only intellectually, that incorporating antibias strategies in teaching is both important and logical. We must also be *emotionally* aware that antibias activities are important. This kind of awareness leads almost automatically to the next step, understanding. This means an emotional and intellectual understanding of the impact of antibias activities and interactions on our daily lives and the lives of the children with whom we work.

When both awareness and understanding take place within the teacher, the actions taken or activities planned are very likely to be meaningful, natural, and appropriate. They may be activities that are appropriately planned or activities that are appropriately spontaneous. In either case, they will be genuine.

Awareness, understanding, and action are not always easy to achieve, but if teachers can perceive the true essence of *culture,* it helps them take these three steps more easily. Understanding what culture means, in both a larger and a more personal sense, can help teachers to feel, to model, and to teach with more of an "I'm O.K., You're O.K." attitude.

Culture in its larger sense is simply a collection of beliefs and values that a group of people hold. Knowing this, we can see that persons who live in different geographic areas, even within the same state, have different "cultures." They think differently about and hold different beliefs about the weather, traffic, tourists, and leisure activities. These are simply *different beliefs,* not better or worse beliefs. Persons in a particular field, such as early childhood education, also have a particular culture. For example, preschool teachers save everything (and I do mean everything!); they usually have cars full of "junk" that they carry about; they have numerous tote bags; and they regularly use masking tape loops.

When teachers see culture in this kind of big picture, it seems to be easier for them to understand and appreciate the culture of their own geographic area and the cultures in their own classrooms. It helps them begin teaching antibias in many small ways, often spontaneously or incidentally.

When teachers perceive and appreciate culture in this larger sense, they also understand that all the individual cultures and heritages that exist in their classrooms also exist within the broader cultures of their own locations and the culture of being "American." When this kind of awareness and understanding happens, teachers often become both more relaxed about the issues of diversity, and better able to use the opportunities for antibias teaching that are constantly available in their teaching environments.

For example, they are more apt to notice that using brown, white, and pink paint at the easel or sorting different shades of "red" potatoes will give them opportunities to talk about skin color. They are more apt to notice that labeling prop boxes as "doctor" or "mailman" is less appropriate than labeling them by a place such as "hospital" or "post office." They are more apt to be open and accepting of all their parents and more likely to treat them with unconditional regard, meeting them where they are instead of where they "should be."

When teachers feel awareness and understanding, they are more likely to look critically at what is on the walls of their rooms, at what books are in the library corner, at their block accessories, at the types of music they have, and at the dolls and props they use. Aware teachers would never plan activities or discussions of Native American traditions based on generalizations; they would know that there are hundreds of tribal nations, each with its own distinct history and tradition.

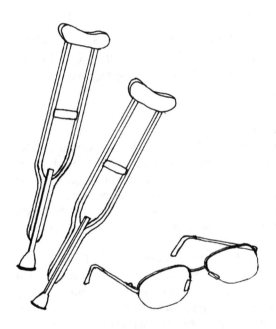

Teachers who are aware are more likely to try activities such as using Braille and sign. They are more likely to add a wheelchair or a child-sized crutch to the classroom, or a doll with a broken foot to the housekeeping area. They are more likely to get free glasses without lenses from optical suppliers and use them as props in the housekeeping area. They are teachers who include items and cooking tools from different cultures in the dramatic play housekeeping area. They are teachers who are likely to invite parents to share traditions, to try new recipes, and dance to new music.

Aware teachers, who appreciate and value diversity, know, and show by their actions, that antibias teaching is an ongoing part of the daily curriculum. They would never confine their teaching activities about Native Americans to the time of the Thanksgiving holiday, nor would they ever relegate activities valuing African-American heritage to the week of Dr. Martin Luther King's birthday. They would incorporate the contributions of Indians, African Americans, and numbers of other cultures all year long, whenever opportunities arose or could be planned. These opportunities might arise in looking at examples of art, pottery, jewelry, baskets, and other craftsmanship. Teachers might also incorporate the contributions of other cultures when they do storytelling, sing, listen to music, and talk about skilled builders, farmers, hunters, trackers, and fishermen.

The "Multicultural Principles" Information Memorandum written and distributed to all Head Start programs by the U.S. Department of Health and Human Services, Administration for Children, Youth and Families, Head Start Bureau (Head Start Bureau, 1991) provides a framework for multicultural programming. It can be obtained by writing to the Head Start Bureau and requesting *Multicultural Principles,* Information Memorandum, Log No. ACYF-IM-91-03, March 5, 1991, U.S. Department of Health and Human Services, Administration for Children, Youth, and Families.

In closing this section, and to sum up beautifully what teachers can do about bias in their classrooms, here is an excerpt from *Teaching Young Children to Resist Bias: What Teachers and Parents Can Do,* by Louise Derman Sparks, Maria Gutiérrez, and Carol Phillips (1989).*

Teaching Young Children to Resist Bias
Building self-identity and skills for social interaction are two major tasks in early childhood. Gradually, young children begin to figure out how they are the same and different from other people, and how they feel about the differences. What children learn in the preschool years greatly influences whether they will grow up to value, accept, and comfortably interact with diverse people or whether they will succumb to the biases that result in, or help to justify, unfair treatment of an individual because of her or his identity.

Research tells us that between ages 2 and 5, children become aware of gender, race, ethnicity, and disabilities. They also become sensitive to both the positive attitudes and negative biases attached to these four key aspects of identity, by their family and by society in general. Young children develop "pre-prejudice" misconceptions, discomfort, fear, and rejection of differences that may develop into real prejudice if parents and teachers do not intervene.

"Girls aren't strong." "Boys can't play house."

"You're a baby in that wheelchair, you can't walk."

"You can't play with us, only light-skinned kids can."

Many adults find it hard to accept that 2-, 3-, and 4-year-olds actually make these kind of comments. They would prefer to believe that young children are blissfully unaware of the differences between people upon which prejudice and discrimination are based. But young children not only recognize differences, they also absorb values about which differences are positive and which are not. How we as parents and teachers react to the ideas that young children express will greatly affect the feelings they will form. If we want children to like themselves and to value diversity, then we must learn how to help them resist the biases and prejudice that are still far too prevalent in our society.

How bias influences children's development
Bias based on gender, race, handicap, or social class creates serious obstacles to all young children's healthy development. When areas of experience are gender stereo-

*Used with permission of the authors and the National Association for the Education of Young Children, Washington, DC, 1989.

typed and closed to children simply because of their sex, neither boys nor girls are fully prepared to deal intellectually or emotionally with the realities and demands of everyday life. "Handicapism" severely harms children with disabilities by limiting access to the educational experiences necessary for well-rounded development. It also prevents non-disabled children from knowing and comfortably interacting with different types of people and teaches a false and anxiety-inducing sense of superiority based on their not being disabled.

Racism attacks the very sense of self for children of color. It creates serious obstacles to their obtaining the best education, health care, and employment. Racism also teaches White children a false identity of superiority and distorts their perceptions of reality. Thus they are not equipped to fairly and productively interact with more than half of the world's humanity.

The "isms" interfere as well with our ability as adults to effectively teach children about themselves and others. All of us have learned the negative values attached to gender, race, class, and handicapping conditions. And, to varying degrees, they make us uncomfortable as they affect our personal attitudes and behavior. At times, we hide such negative feelings from ourselves by denying the reality or significance of differences. We may hope to sidestep the impact of prejudice by saying "people are all the same," or teaching children it is impolite to notice or ask about differences. However, avoidance doesn't give children the information they need. By selectively ingnoring children's natural curiosity, we actually teach them that some differences are not acceptable. And by failing to attach positive value to certain specific differences, children are left to absorb the biases of society. The more that we face our own prejudiced and discriminatory attitudes toward diversity and, where necessary, change them, the better prepared we will be to foster children's growth.

What parents and teachers can do

Recognize that because we live in a racist and biased society, we must actively foster children's anti-bias development. Remember that in such an environment, we are all constantly and repeatedly exposed to messages that subtly reinforce biases. If we do nothing to counteract them, then we silently support these biases by virtue of our inaction.

Create an environment at home or at school that deliberately contrasts the prevailing biased messages of the wider society.

Provide books, dolls, toys, wall decorations (paintings, drawings, photographs), TV programs, and records that reflect diverse images that children may not likely see elsewhere in

- gender roles (including men and women in nontraditional roles)
- racial and cultural backgrounds (e.g., people of color in leadership positions)
- capabilities (people with disabilities doing activities familiar to children)
- family life styles (varieties of family composition and activities)

Show that you value diversity in the friends you choose and in the people and firms you choose for various services (e.g., doctor, dentist, car mechanic, teachers, stores). Remember that what you do is as important as what you say.

Make it a firm rule that a person's identity is never an acceptable reason for teasing or rejecting them. Immediately step in if you hear or see your child engage in such behavior. Make it clear that you disapprove, but do not make your child feel rejected. Support the child who has been hurt. Try to find out what underlies the biased behavior. If the reason is a conflict about another issue, help your child understand the real reason for the conflict and find a way to resolve it. If the underlying reason is discomfort with or fear or ignorance about the other child's differences, plan to initiate activities to help overcome negative feelings.

Initiate activities and discussions to build positive self-identity and to teach the value of differences among people. Educate yourself about common stereotypes in our society so that you can evaluate your selection of children's materials and experiences. Whenever possible, either remove those containing biased messages, or learn to use such material to teach children about the difference between "fair" and "true" images and those that are "unfair" and "untrue" and which hurt people's feelings.

Talk positively about each child's physical characteristics and cultural heritage. Tell stories about people from your ethnic group of whom you are especially proud. Include people who have stood up against bias and injustice. Encourage children to explore different kinds of materials and activities that go beyond traditional gender behaviors.

Help children learn the differences between feelings of superiority and feelings of self-esteem and pride in their heritage.

Provide opportunities for children to interact with other children who are racially/culturally different from themselves and with people who have various disabilities. If your neighborhood does not provide these opportunities, search for them in school, after-school activities, weekend programs, places of worship, and day camps. Visit museums and attend concerts and cultural events that reflect diverse heritages as well as your own.

Respectfully listen to and answer children's questions about themselves and others. Do not ignore questions, change the subject, sidestep, or admonish the child for asking a question. These responses suggest that what a child is asking is bad. However, do not *over-respond*. Answer all questions in a direct, matter-of-fact, and brief manner. Listen carefully to what children want to know *and* what they are feeling.

Teach children how to challenge biases about who they are. By the time children are 4 years old, they become aware of biases directed against aspects of their identity. This is especially true for children of color, children with disabilities, and children who don't fit stereotypic gender norms. Be sensitive to children's feelings about themselves and immediately respond when they indicate any signs of being affected by biases. Give your children tools to confront those who act biased against them.

Teach children to recognize stereotypes and caricatures of different groups. Young children can become adept at spotting "unfair" images of themselves and others if they are helped to think critically about what they see in books, movies, greeting cards, and comics and on TV.

Use accurate and fair images in contrast to stereotypic ones, and encourage children to talk about the differences. For example, at Thanksgiving time greeting cards that show animals dressed up as "Indians" and a stereotypic image of an "Indian" child with buckskins and feather headdress abound. Talk about how it is hurtful to people's feelings to show them looking like animals, or to show them portrayed inaccurately. Read good children's books to show the reality and the variety of Native American peoples. As children get older, you can also help them learn about how stereotypes are used to justify injustice, such as lower wages, poor housing and education, etc.

Let children know that unjust things can be changed. Encourage children to challenge bias, and give them skills appropriate to their age level. First set an example by your own actions. Intervene when children engage in discriminatory behavior, support your children when they challenge bias directed against themselves and others, encourage children to identify and think critically about stereotypic images, and challenge adult-biased remarks and jokes—all methods of modeling anti-bias behavior.

Involve children in taking action on issues relevant to their lives.

- Talk to a toy store manager or owner about adding more toys that reflect diversity, such as dolls, books, and puzzles.
- Ask your local stationery store to sell greeting cards that show children of color.
- Take your child to a rally about getting more funding for child care centers.

As you involve children in this type of activity, be sure to discuss the issues with them, and talk about the reasons for taking action.

Summary

Keep in mind that developing a healthy identity and understanding of others is a long-term process. While the early years lay an essential foundation, learning continues throughout childhood and into adulthood and will take many different forms. Children will change their thinking and feelings many times.

Common questions that parents and teachers ask

Q: "My child never asks questions about race, disabilities, or gender. If I raise it myself, will I introduce her to ideas she wouldn't have thought of on her own?"

A: Yes, you may, thereby expanding your child's awareness and knowledge. Your child may also have had questions for which she didn't have words or didn't feel comfortable raising until you brought up the subject. Remember that children do not learn prejudice from open, honest discussion of differences and the unfairness of bias. Rather, it is through these methods that children develop anti-bias sensitivity and behavior.

Q: "I don't feel competent to deal with these issues; I don't know enough. What if I say the wrong thing?"

A: Silence "speaks" louder than we realize, sending messages that are counter to the development of anti-bias attitudes. It is far better to respond, even if, upon hindsight, you wish you had handled the incident differently. You can always go back to your child and say, "Yesterday, when you asked me about why Susie uses a wheelchair, I didn't give you enough of an answer. I've thought about your question some more, and today I want to tell you. . . ." If you really do not have the information to answer a question, you can say, "That's a good question, but I don't know the answer right now. Let me think about it a little and I will tell you later." Or, "Let's go find some books to help us answer your question." Then be sure to follow through.

Examine your own feelings about the subject raised by your child's questions or behaviors. Feelings of incompetence often come from discomfort rather than a lack of knowledge. Talk over your feelings with a sympathetic family member or friend in order to be better prepared the next time.

Q: "I don't want my children to know about prejudice and discrimination until they have to. Won't it upset them to know about injustices?"

A: It is natural to want to protect our children from painful subjects and situations. Moreover, adults may mask their own pain by choosing not to address issues of bias with their children. Avoiding issues that may be painful doesn't help children. Being unprepared to deal effectively with life's realities only leaves them more vulnerable and exposed to hurt. Silence about children's misconceptions and discriminatory behavior gives them permission to inflict pain on others. It is alright for children to sometimes feel sad or upset as long as they know that you are there to comfort and support them.

"Why is that girl in a wheelchair?"

Inappropriate

"Shh, it's not nice to ask." (admonishing)

"I'll tell you another time." (sidestepping)

Acting as if you didn't hear the question. (avoiding)

Appropriate

"She is using a wheelchair because her legs are not strong enough to walk. The wheelchair helps her move around."

"Why is Jamal's skin so dark?"

Inappropriate

"His skin color doesn't matter. We are all the same underneath."

   This response denies the child's question, changing the subject to one of similarity when the child is asking about a difference.

Appropriate

"Jamal's skin is dark brown because his mom and dad have dark brown skin."   This is enough for 2- or 3-year-olds. As children get older, you can add an explanation of melanin:

   "We all have a special chemical in our skin called *melanin.* If you have a lot of melanin, your skin is dark. If you have only a little, your skin is light. How much melanin you have in your skin depends on how much your parents have in theirs."

"Why am I called Black? I'm brown!"

Inappropriate

"You are *too* Black!"

   This response is not enough. It doesn't address the child's confusion between actual skin color and the name of the racial and/or ethnic group.

Appropriate

"You're right; your skin color *is* brown. We use the name *Black* to mean the group of people of whom our family is a part. Black people can have different skin colors. We are all one people because our great-great-grandparents once came from a place called Africa. That's why many people call themselves *Afro-Americans.*"

"Will the brown wash off in the tub?"

This is a fairly common question because children are influenced by the racist equation of dirtiness and dark skin in our society.

Inappropriate

Taking this as an example of "kids say the darndest things" and treating it as not serious.

Appropriate

"The color of José's skin will never wash off. When he takes a bath the dirt on his skin washes off, just like when you take a bath. Whether we have light or dark skin, we all get dirty but our skin stays the same color after we wash it. Our skin is clean after we wash, no matter what color it is."

"Why does Miyoko speak funny?"

Inappropriate

"Miyoko can't help how she speaks. Let's not say anything about it."

   This response implies agreement with the child's comment that Miyoko's speech is unacceptable, while also telling the child to "not notice," and be polite.

Appropriate

"Miyoko doesn't speak funny, she speaks *differently* than you do. She speaks Japanese because that's what her mom and dad speak. You speak English like your mom and dad.

It is okay to ask questions about what Miyoko is saying, but it is *not* okay to say that her speech sounds funny because that can hurt her feelings."

"Why do I have to try out that dumb wheelchair? . . ."

. . . asks Julio who refuses to sit in a child-sized wheelchair in the children's museum.

Inappropriate

"It is not dumb. All the children are trying it and I want you to."

This response does not help uncover the feelings underlying Julio's resistance and demands that he do something that is clearly uncomfortable for him.

Appropriate

Putting his arm around Julio, his dad gently asks, "Why is it dumb?" Julio: "It will hurt my feet, just like Maria's feet." Dad: "Maria can't walk because she was born with a condition called cerebral palsy. The wheelchair helps her move around. Nothing will happen to your legs if you try sitting and moving around in the wheelchair. It's okay if you don't want to, but if you do try it you'll find out that your legs will still be fine."

Children can learn to become anti-biased!

We can all take heart from examples such as the following examples of 4- and 5-year-olds challenging racism: Kiyoshi (age 4½) sees a stereotypic "Indian warrior" figure in the toy store. "That toy hurts Indians' feelings," he points out to his grandmother.

Casey (age 5) and another White friend, Tommy, are playing. Casey calls two other boys to join them. "You can't play with them, they're Black," Tommy says to him. Casey replies, "That's not right. Black and White kids should play together. My Dad tells me civil rights stories."

After hearing the story of Rosa Parks and the Montgomery bus boycott, Tiffany (age 5½), whose skin is light brown, ponders whether she would have had to sit in the back of the bus. Finally, she firmly asserts, "I'm Black, and anyway all this is stupid. I would just get off the bus and tell them to keep their old bus."

Kiyoshi, Casey, and Tiffany are learning to think critically and to speak up when they believe something is unfair. They are becoming "empowered": gaining the confidence and skills that will enable them to resist and challenge bias and to participate in the creation of a more just society.

Parent Involvement

Parents, . . . the primary care givers and teachers of children, are partners with professionals whether or not they are accepted as such. Their interaction with their children makes them a part of the system. The home and school are entwined. It rests . . . on the schools to develop or to strengthen a positive relationship with parents . . . to ensure the continuity and developmental environment that children so desperately need (Berger, 1991).

Early childhood educators have known for many years that working as partners with parents is important. A study of parent involvement in four federal programs—Follow Through, Title I, Title VII, and the Emergency School Aid Act—found that parent involvement helps children try harder and do better in school, and provides more continuity in children's education (1991).

Encouraging a high degree of family enthusiasm for their children's public schools and child care centers is one of the best ways in which teachers can attempt to build children's self esteem and can reduce discipline problems and can boost children's regard for themselves as learners. When a member of a child's family takes part in his school life in a positive manner, even briefly and infrequently, the child's self esteem seems to soar. (Greenberg, 1989)

At no time in history has parenting been more difficult, nor our work with parents more challenging. Families come to early childhood teachers for information, support, and confidence. They look to us for knowledge and new skills that can improve the quality of their lives. They want to nurture their children's skills and self-concept, but often they have greater needs for self-esteem and confidence than do their children. One of the most important things we can do as early childhood teachers is to praise parents for each and every effort they make to be involved in their children's educations. This means we welcome them in our centers, introduce them to the group proudly, thank them for whatever help they give us, write them as many short, positive notes about their children as possible, and talk to them whenever we can, whether in person or by telephone. All of these things make parents feel important and needed, and all of them can help parents stay involved.

We know there are benefits to children when their parents are involved, but there are also benefits for the parents themselves.

- They can grow in confidence, inner strength, and skills.
- They can see themselves as the child's first and most important teacher.
- They can better understand their children and their children's total development.
- They can begin to see ways the home can be an environment for learning, as well as the school.
- They can become better able to nurture children's physical health and well being, as well as social-emotional and intellectual skills.
- They can become better advocates for their own children and others.
- They can improve family bonding and communication, which may help prevent problems with children in later years.
- They can learn that learning can be fun and that enjoying learning together reduces stress and builds lifelong relationships with their children.

When parents benefit in these ways, the children do too, and this can result in long-range benefits to our nation: improved family literacy, improved family fitness and health, improved problem-solving skills, and improved family communication that can prevent youth and teen problems.

All this may look good on paper, but even when parents know these general benefits to themselves and their children, they may not buy in to regular, ongoing parent involvement. For some, just surviving each day is all they can handle. Others are working several jobs and have little time or energy to observe or help out in school, or talk to the teacher about the child. There are a few important ways to help motivate parents, even tired and busy ones, to become more involved in their children's learning.

- Teachers who accept parents as they are and respect their interests, family values, and life-styles
- Teachers who have positive, open attitudes, and who spend as much or more time listening than talking
- Teachers who share with parents simple, enjoyable learning activities they can do at home
- Teachers who can explain exactly what their children are learning, how they are learning it, and how this learning will help them in later years

Parents will also buy in much more often when they know how their participation will help them and their children. One way teachers can communicate this is to explain to parents exactly what their children are learning as they "play" and exactly how they are learning it. To help accomplish this task, the time blocks shared with teachers in this guidebook can also be shared with parents.

Good communication with parents is the job of both early childhood teachers and their programs. Two-way communication with parents, which encourages their input and ideas, is one of the major strategies of teachers and programs in showing parents exactly how their participation helps them and their children.

Two-way written communication consists of efforts such as the following:

- Parent newsletters, including parents' own news
- Displays and bulletin boards for sharing information
- Portfolios of children's work with parent comment sheets
- Journals, scrapbooks, and albums that are joint efforts
- Notes and letters between home and school
- Parent suggestion boxes or newsletter columns

Two-way verbal communication examples are:

- Telephone calls
- Informal conversations
- Conferences and home visits
- Parent meetings
- Social events
- Parent orientations and open houses
- Parent volunteers in the classroom, and/or volunteering in ways that help the teacher and the children

In my experience, when parents volunteer in the classroom, even infrequently, they learn more about their children and what their children are learning than in any other way. Teachers who have many parent volunteers and parent visitors are teachers who make parents feel welcome and needed, and who involve their volunteers in meaningful jobs as part of the teaching staff. They are teachers who encourage parents to sing, tell, or read stories, assist and encourage children during free-choice or activity time, help with journals and dictation, help observe and take notes, and lead small-group learning experiences.

Some early childhood programs are asked to provide written evidence or documentation of parent input to the curriculum, parent involvement, and parent volunteer time. In Chapter 5, a simple strategy for documenting parent input, right on the lesson plan itself, was shared with readers. Here are other ways to document parent involvement:

- Written notes and minutes of parent classroom meetings, and parent board and council or committee meetings
- Parent input to long-range plans in curriculum. When these plans are annually reviewed or revised, parents should be represented, and their names as well as those of other review committee members should be on a cover sheet for the plans, along with signatures and dates of the review
- Parent evaluations of the program, at least annually
- Parent interest surveys
- Parent volunteer sign-in sheets
- Home visit forms that show what occurred and was discussed during the visit (such as the child's progress in all areas of development), joint plans for the next home visit, and the teaching and learning ideas left with the parent for use in the home. Dated signatures for the teacher and parent should be included.

Summary

This chapter has explored five priority areas in early education, and has provided readers with comprehensive teaching strategies for literacy, problem solving, math and science activities, antibias or multicultural strategies, and activities for teaching children about ecology and the environment. It has also provided strategies in encouraging parent involvement.

In addressing these priority areas, the early childhood teacher has a both a wonderful opportunity and a challenging responsibility. The early childhood field has traditionally worked to improve the quality of life for children and families. These efforts must be both continued and improved in order for an impact to be made. Early childhood teachers, working with young children in their formative years and with their families, have the best chance to address national priorities in ways that can make positive changes in our country's future.

More ideas for activities that could be used in lesson planning will be shared with you in the next chapter on integrated learning activities, as well as ways to organize these ideas and get them down on paper in your lesson plans.

Self-Study Activities

1. Choose two priority areas in this chapter about which you want to learn more. In the periodical section of your library, look up and read articles on these topics. Many excellent articles on these subjects can be found in two of the major professional journals of the early childhood field, *Young Children*, the journal of the National Association for the Education of Young Children (NAEYC) and *Childhood Education*, the journal of the Association for Childhood Education International.

2. Go back in this chapter to the priority area or areas that are most important to you as a student or teacher. List the activities in these areas that gave you new ideas for teaching. Now list those activities that fit your horizontal or thematic planning, and list those that are skill-focused ideas that fit in with your vertical planning. Try to add them to your long-range horizontal plan or to your monthly skill-focused goals.

References and Resources for Further Reading

The suggested reading listed here emphasizes articles concerning early education priority areas published in professional periodicals. Further resource books suggested as reading in early childhood education priority areas will be found listed in Appendix C under the headings "Literacy," "Discovery and Problem Solving," "Ecology/Environment and the Outdoors," "Celebrating Diversity," and "Parent Involvement." Choose and read several books from Appendix C that are new to you or of interest to you.

Associated Press. *Detroit Free Press,* August 18, 1994, p. 4A.

Advisory Committee on Head Start Quality and Expansion. *Creating a 21st Century Head Start: Final Report.* Washington, DC: U.S. Department of Health and Human Services, December 1993, p. 31.

Billman, Jane. "The Native American Curriculum: Attempting Alternatives to Tepees and Headbands," *Young Children* Vol. 47, No. 6 (1992), pp. 22–25.

Berger, Eugenia Hepworth. *Parents as Partners in Education: The School and Home Working Together.* New York: Macmillan, 1991, pp. vi, 3.

Bredekamp, Sue. *Developmentally Appropriate Practices for Programs Serving Children Birth through Age 8,* expanded ed. Washington, DC: National Association for the Education of Young Children, 1992, p. 66.

Brock, Dana R., & Dodd, Elizabeth L. "A Family Lending Library: Promoting Early Literacy Development." *Young Children,* Vol. 49, No. 3 (1994), pp. 16–21.

Bundy, Blakely F. "Fostering Communication between Parents and Preschools." *Young Children,* Vol. 46, No. 2 (1991), pp. 12–17.

Cartwright, Sally. "Learning With Large Blocks." *Young Children,* Vol. 45, No. 3 (1990), pp. 38–41.

Cosgrove, Maryellen Smith. "Cooking in the Classroom: The Doorway to Nutrution." *Young Children,* Vol. 46, No. 3 (1991), pp. 43–46.

Crosser, Sandra. "Making the Most of Water Play." *Young Children,* Vol. 49, No. 5 (1994), pp. 28–32.

Dighe, Judith. "Children and the Earth." *Young Children,* Vol. 48, No. 3 (1993), pp. 48–63.

Edwards, Linda C., & Nabors, Martha L. "The Creative Arts Process: What It Is and What It Is Not." *Young Children,* Vol. 48, No. 3 (1993), pp. 77–81.

Edwards, Linda H. "Kid's Eye View of Reading: Kindergartners Talk about Learning How to Read." *Childhood Education,* Vol. 70, No. 3 (1994), pp. 137–141.

Elkind, David. *Miseducation: Preschoolers at Risk.* New York: Knopf, 1987.

Elster, Charles A. " 'I Guess They Do Listen': Young Children's Emergent Readings after Adult Read-Alouds." *Young Children,* Vol. 49, No. 3 (1994), pp. 27–31.

Galen, Harlene. "Increasing Parental Involvement in Elementary School: The Nitty-Gritty of One Successful Program." *Young Children,* Vol. 46, No. 2 (1991), pp. 18–22.

Goldhaber, Jeanne. "If We Call It Science, Then Can We Let the Children Play?" *Childhood Education,* Vol. 71, No. 1 (1994), pp. 24–27.

Greenberg, Polly. "Ideas That Work with Young Children: Teaching about Native Americans? or Teaching About People, Including Native Americans." *Young Children,* Vol. 47, No. 6 (1992), pp. 27–30.

Greenberg, Polly. "Ideas That Work with Young Children: How and Why to Teach All Aspects of Preschool and Kindergarten Math, Part 2." Young Children, Vol. 49, No. 2 (1994), pp. 12–18, 88.

Greenberg, Polly. "Parents as Partners in Young Children's Development and Education: A New American Fad? Why Does it Matter?" *Young Children,* May 1989. Washington, DC: National Association for the Education of Young Children, 1989, pp. 61–62.

Hamburg, D. *A Decent Start: Promoting Healthy Child Development in the First Three Years of Life.* New York: Carnegie Corporation of New York, 1992.

Head Start Bureau, Administration on Children, Youth and Families. *Multicultural Principles for Head Start Programs.* Washington, DC: U.S. Department of Health and Human Services, March 1991, pp. 4–6, 20–21.

Henniger, Michael. "Enriching the Outdoor Play Experience." *Childhood Education,* Vol. 70, No. 2 (1994), pp. 87–90.

James, Alfred. "Will It Hurt 'Shade'? Adopting a Tree." *Childhood Education,* Vol. 68, No. 5 (1992), p. 262.

Karmozyn, Patricia, Scalise, Barbara, & Trostle, Susan. "A Better Earth: Let It Begin with Me." *Childhood Education,* Vol. 69, No. 4 (1993), pp. 225–229.

Kasting, Arlene. "Respect, Responsibility and Reciprocity: The 3 Rs of Parent Involvement." *Childhood Education,* Vol. 70, No. 3 (1994), pp. 146–150.

Mills, Heidi. "Teaching Math Concepts in a K–1 Class Doesn't Have to Be Like Pulling Teeth . . . But Maybe It Should Be!" *Young Children,* Vol. 48, No. 2 (1993), pp. 17–20.

National Association for the Education of Young Children. "Enriching Classroom Diversity with Books for Children, In-Depth Discussion of Them, and Story-Extension Activities." *Young Children,* Vol. 48, No. 3 (1993), pp. 10–12.

National Association for the Education of Young Children. "Educate Yourself about Diverse Groups in Our Country by Reading." *Young Children,* Vol. 48, No. 3 (1993), pp. 13–16.

National Association of Elementary School Principals. *Early Childhood Education and the Elementary School Principal: Standards for Quality Programs.* Alexandria, VA: NAESP, 1990, pp. 48–51.

National Education Goals Panel. *A Nation of Learners.* National Education Goals Report. Washington, DC: U.S. Department of Education, 1993.

Perry, Gail, and Rivkin, Mary. "Teachers and Science." *Young Children,* Vol. 47, No. 4 (1992), pp. 9–16.

Rivkin, Mary, ed. "Science Is a Way of Life." *Young Children,* Vol. 47, No. 4 (1992), pp. 4–8.

Sparks, Louise Derman, Gutiérrez, Maria, and Phillips, Carol. *Teaching Young Children to Resist Bias: What Teachers and Parents Can Do.* Washington, DC: National Association for the Education of Young Children, 1989.

York, Stacey. *Roots and Wings.* St. Paul, MN: Redleaf Press, 1991.

11 Integrated Activities

Introduction: Integrated Learning

In addition to the five priorities in early childhood education discussed in Chapter 10, there is an additional objective: the implementation of integrated activities. One of the best ways to provide appropriate, meaningful learning experiences to children is to put integrated learning activities into our lesson plans. This chapter tells why we should do this and how we will do it. After examples of ideas for integrated activities are presented, we will review how these ideas are actually put into the lesson plan by the teacher.

The most meaningful learning experiences for young children are those we call integrated learning activities. Integrated activities combine learning experiences that are related in content and purpose; they incorporate several curriculum areas. Integrated activities may occur in various areas of the setting and may integrate or unite several or many parts of the curriculum. To *integrate* means, literally, "to form into a whole, incorporate into a larger unit. consolidate, blend, homogenize, or commingle." We may know what *integrate* means, but we need to stop and think about why integrated activities are so important in teaching young children.

Children do not learn neatly, one item at a time, with bits and pieces of their beings. Education for young children cannot easily be neatly boxed and called forth when it is convenient for the teacher, or when the bell rings that says it is now time for such-and-such subject. Children are always learning and always open to learning, not just when adults would like them to be learning. Children learn, with all systems on "go," to the best of their individual capacities, in every waking moment.

Children learn with their bodies and senses, their memories, their perceptual skills, and their thinking skills. They learn with their feelings and emotions. None of these capacities are ever turned off during the learning process. Children learn in relation to their environment, which is not just the classroom setting but includes their families, their homes, the outdoors, the neighborhood, and the community that is their world.

Children are whole human beings, and they learn as integrated, whole people, with all parts simultaneously engaged in the process. Children also learn in unique combinations of their own learning styles—verbal, spatial, physical, and social. Some learn better in some of these modes than in other modes. Some children learn better visually than through auditory means; some need tactile experiences to reinforce what they learn from seeing and hearing. If children learn through an integrated process, it follows that the most meaningful learning experiences we can provide are those that are integrated.

Simple Integrated Activities and Webs

In Chapter 3 of this guidebook, we talked about teaching and learning webs as a way to illustrate the teacher's plans to use an activity to integrate several curriculum areas, adding more parts to the learning web as new interests emerge from the children. Most of these activities will be entered on the lesson plan during free-choice or activity time, but some may occur in large group or small group as well. Integrated activities are often a combination of both horizontal and vertical planning.

In this chapter, we will examine what I will call simple and complex integrated activities, or simple and complex learning webs. A simple web is one in which only one experience or one material in the classroom is used to integrate various curriculum areas. Readers will quickly think of many early childhood materials that have this flexibility, such as unit blocks and water play. We will look at three such examples before going on to present other, more complex examples of integrated activities or learning webs. What follows are three examples of simple integrated activities or webs concerning playdough, dramatic play, and bean bags.

Playdough

When children play with playdough or other clays such as silly putty, they generally use this kind of open-ended medium in the art area to make their own creations. Creativity and creative thinking are primary curriculum elements that are integrated when children use playdough. Another is the easily observable practice of small motor and manipulative skills. If we take our imaginations a bit further, we know that children often mix colors of playdough to create new colors. This integrates discovery learning and cause-and-effect thinking skills.

If children are encouraged to talk about how the playdough feels and smells, and the things they are doing to it, they are practicing both sensory perception and literacy. If the adult writes down what they say they can do with playdough on a poster or large paper, literacy skills will be expanded to dictation that includes words like *twist, poke, pinch, stretch, pound, press,* and others. If the adult takes a print with the playdough of some object or texture in the room, and asks children to guess where the print came from, they will be practicing both thinking and memory skills.

In addition, when children make balls or "snakes" out of playdough, they are beginning to experience conservation skills, even though usually they do not yet fully understand this concept. When they place big, small, and medium balls or snakes on the table in order by size, they are practicing another thinking skill, that of ordering or seriation.

If children help make the playdough during free-choice time, they will be practicing many math and science skills, as well as literacy, safety, and motor skills. They will estimate, pour, count, measure, observe the ingredients and describe them, and tell what happens to them in cooking, learning about cause and effect.

TRY THIS NOW Draw this learning web on a piece of scrap paper or notebook paper. Make playdough the central focus point, and add all the curriculum areas it covers. Although playdough is a simple material, it integrates a great many areas of curriculum, forming a web that looks something like the many petals of a flower or starburst.

Dramatic Play

Dramatic play and role play are excellent learning activities, which also lend themselves to integration with many curriculum areas, as we have seen in other chapters. Most of the time, it is recommended that adults facilitate but not become highly involved or directive in dramatic play. Occasionally, however, a teacher may want to review several curriculum areas at the same time by incorporating them into a pretend situation.

Picture a teacher who has chosen a child or two to help him or her with "pretending" for the audience of the whole group, or imagine the teacher in this scenario working one-on-one with a child in free-choice time. The teacher wants to reinforce concepts in health and safety and has chosen some dramatic play props for playing "office" in order to do this. The teacher has shown the child a tote bag or briefcase containing items such as paper, envelopes, a calculator, and a telephone. The teacher and child or children choose a space in the room for the location of the "office" and pretending.

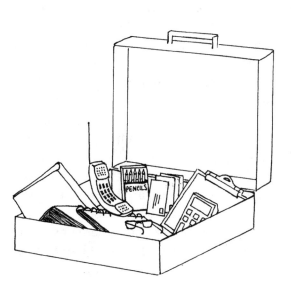

Next, the teacher might ask, "When you start your day at the office, you don't wake up there, do you? Where do we really wake up?" When the child explains waking up at home in a bed, the teacher and child can go to a different area of the room to pretend "waking up," stretching, doing a few knee bends, or bending to touch their toes.

"What is the next thing you do when you wake up? Do you get dressed first, or eat breakfast?" The child and teacher can pretend to look outside to check the weather, decide what clothes to wear, pretend to dress, then go into the real or pretend bathroom to pretend to wash faces and hands with soap (telling why). Next they would go to another area to pretend eating breakfast.

At the pretend breakfast, the teacher could ask what foods we should eat for breakfast and what would be good to drink. The child can choose what breakfast should be and can talk about other good breakfast foods and why we need to eat breakfast. After the pretend meal, the teacher could ask, "What do we always try to do after we eat?" and lead the child to decide to brush his or her teeth. Usually the child and teacher would return to the "bathroom" area and pretend to brush (gently, round and round, way in back too); then look in the mirror to see our clean teeth; and then, perhaps, brush, pick, or pretend to braid our hair.

Now it may be time to go to the office. Who shall we say goodbye to and hug? Do they have the office phone number? Where is the car and the car keys? The child and teacher can now use two chairs, side by side, for a car, unless the child chooses to travel to work in some other manner. In the car, the teacher should give the keys to the child, who will drive the car, and should ask, "What is the first thing we always have to do before we start?" Usually the child will know that we must put on our seat belts first. Perhaps the child will check the mirror and the gas when starting the car. Maybe the car should be warmed up.

During the drive, the teacher could say, "Oh, I see a red sign up ahead with white letters . . . it is a circle . . . no it is an octagon shape. What does that mean?" The child will say it is a stop sign, and the teacher can ask what we should do. When we stop, we have to look both ways (more pretending). Next, the teacher should "see" a traffic light and ask the child what to do if the light is red, green, or yellow. (Be prepared for any answer!)

A few moments later, the teacher might say he or she sees some litter along the road. What can we do? What does the child think about this? Later, the teacher can say they have arrived at the office. The child parks the car, they get out, lock the car, and go into the "office," where the child begins to examine and use the contents of the briefcase.

During the seven or eight minutes of this dramatic play episode, the teacher will have integrated and reinforced many health and fitness concepts (sleep, exercise, appropriate outerwear, handwashing, toothbrushing, grooming, and hygiene) as well as good nutrition.In addition, the child has acted out and internalized many safety concepts. The adult and child were also engaged in conversation throughout the scenario, some of which focused on the environment. The simple learning web would look like Figure 11-1.

Dramatic play is a wonderful vehicle for integrating safety and health concepts, not only in this scenario, but in many others, such as playing "camping," or going to the "beach" or the "river." In the housekeeping area, potholders, bar soap, infant seats with safety belts, and emergency and baby sitter numbers by the play telephone can be useful props that integrate safety education. Math or counting can usually be incorporated into dramatic play in some manner, as can cause-and-effect concepts.

Figure 11-1   Learning Web for Dramatic Play

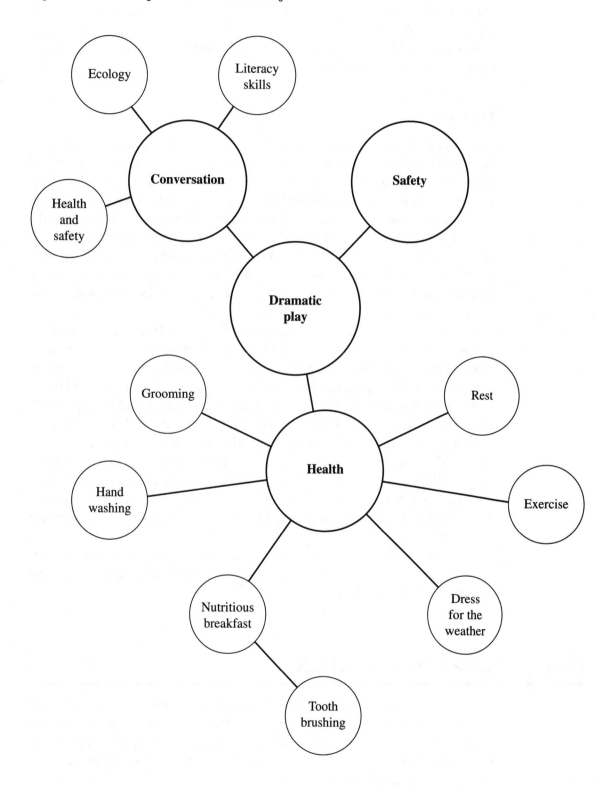

Literacy abounds in dramatic play of any kind, and dictation or experience stories can be written about pretend excursions as well as real field trips. Field trips always extend the environment and enrich children's learning experiences. They also provide opportunities to act out a field trip and what was learned there after the trip, in the classroom.

Bean Bags

Sometimes simple classroom materials lend themselves to opportunities for integration, if we will use our own divergent thinking skills to use them in new ways. Bean bags are usually square or rectangular and are made from scrap material. Why not try making them in other shapes and of other materials? Why not make some of these shapes big and some of them small? Why not make them in different colors and with different textures—real or fake fur, velvet, burlap, scrap leather, and so on? At the same time, why not stuff them with something other than beans or rice? Small bags could be stuffed with many fragrant things, including potpourri, fragrant dried grasses, cinnamon sticks, cloves, or cotton scented with peppermint extract.

With bean bags like this, the teacher is offering a multisensory learning experience and an opportunity to describe and talk about colors, sizes, shapes, smells, and textures. In addition, the bags can be used in many ways to promote motor development, practice the use of prepositions, and name body parts.

A few shapes could be made on the floor or carpet with masking tape. Children could use these as targets and toss bags of particular shapes, colors, or sizes into them. They could put the bean bags on their heads and walk around the circle or stand next to the square on the floor, or even jump into a shape. They could hop, run, or gallop with the bean bag on their heads, inside their elbows, or under their chins. They could walk with a bean bag between their knees. Many areas of curriculum can be integrated when we use old materials in new ways.

If we were to draw a simple teaching and learning web describing the integration of learning experiences around the simple focal point of bean bags, the web would look like Figure 11-2.

Complex Integrated Activities and Webs

Now let's turn our attention to more complex integrated activities and more complex learning webs. The first two examples in this part of the chapter, an apple and old newspapers, will be presented first as simple webs. Then we will see what a more complex web would look like if children's emergent interests were expanded in the teacher's lesson plans.

Figure 11-2   Learning Web for Bean Bags

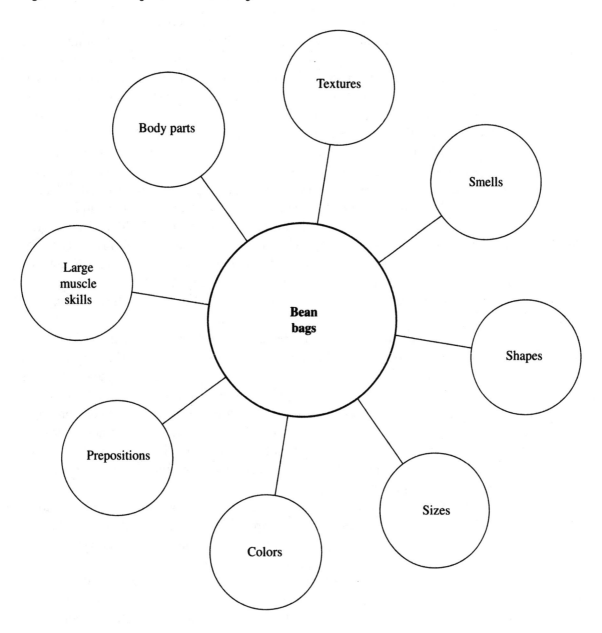

An Apple Snack

Teachers know that activities with foods or snacks cover and unite many parts of the curriculum, but sometimes they simply take this learning for granted and don't capitalize on the opportunity to expand the integration of this simple activity to its fullest extent. Most teachers do comment and ask open questions as children prepare a snack, so that children will practice skills in nutrition, math, (measuring, estimating, counting), science (changes, cause and effect), colors, shapes, and the names of foods and ingredients.

Let's look at the example of preparing just one apple for a group of four people (one adult and three four-year-olds) in a small-group situation. First, the teacher should ask the children what they need to do (always) before they handle foods. Expanding on the children's answers, as the teacher and children wash their hands with soap and water, the teacher might ask children why we wash our hands before we "cook." When teachers ask about health rules and routines, instead of tell, children need to think and to explain the reasons, which gives them more practice in both thinking and language skills. In this example, the children are learning and practicing a health concept as well as thinking and telling.

Next the teacher might show the children the apple, ask them to describe it (size, shape, color, bumpy or smooth, smell, stem or no stem), and ask about other apples they have seen, and if their colors were different or the same as this one. The teacher's use of open questions could expand the children's language, memory, and literacy skills. Have the children ever seen or climbed an apple tree? Were there flowers on the tree and bees buzzing, or bare branches, or were there apples on the tree? What time of the year would that be? Next the children should and wash and dry the apple, and talk about why we need to do this. (Apples are sprayed with pesticides.)

Then the teacher should ask the children what they think should be done. Here are four people, and only one apple. The children will suggest that the apple be cut up, which gives the teacher the opportunity to discuss ways we use such tools as knives safely, and only when an adult is present.

Here, the teacher should take time to show children how the knife is made, helping them observe the handle, and both the sharp and dull sides of the knife. The teacher should help the child cut the apple in half, holding the apple and placing one hand over the child's for the necessary pressure and for safety. When round objects are cut, they wobble, and adults should help with the first cut so that the next cuts, if any, can be made with the flat side of the fruit or vegetable down on the cutting board. If parents are observing, the teacher may want to comment that showing a child the parts of the knife and how to use it safely can be a good problem prevention technique.

At this point, the teacher again has a chance to ask the children what to do when there are four people and only two pieces. Have the children count the people and the pieces. They will say that the apple must again be cut, and can figure out the best way to do so. If children have not directed that there be two more cuts, the teacher will repeat the question and problem-solving process until there are four (let's count them) pieces of apple, all of the same size. It is interesting for children to see at this point that all four pieces can be put back together and held to form the whole apple again. They have just had a concrete, meaningful experience in using fractions.

Other things should have been going on simultaneously during this entire cutting process. As the apple is cut, the children can describe the inside of the apple, how it is wet, how good it smells, and how the inside differs from the outside. Do the children notice and comment that, even when apples have different colors outside, the color inside is the same? (Just like people!)

When the apple is cut, seeds will be observed, and children can describe them, count them, and decide whether or not to save them to put on the science table, plant them, or use them in a collage or in other ways. The core of the apple can be examined, and children can decide if the core should be discarded, given to one of the classroom pets, or put into the compost pile outside.

When all the work is completed, children can pass and serve themselves the pieces of apple, perhaps using "Please" and "Thank you." When they eat the apple (chewing it well and talking about why this is safer than gobbling), they can describe (when their mouths are not full) the apple's taste and how the taste compares with other apple foods (pie, apple butter, apple sauce, apple juice). They can discuss their preferences and what they know about the ways these other apple foods are made, or special times when they eat them. Children should be encouraged to lead and expand the conversation in any direction, and to enjoy a relaxed, sociable snack time. If they use the apple pieces with a dip, a whole new avenue of thought and language can be developed.

Of course, some teachers may also want to show children that apples can be cut another way, to see the "star" inside. If apples are in abundance at this time, this snack experience might lead to conversations about apples or other fruits, including planning a trip to an orchard, or plans to sort and graph apples or to make applesauce.

The whole process of using an apple snack as a simple integrated experience or simple learning web takes about fifteen minutes, depending on the children and their spontaneous verbalization. In that fifteen minutes a teacher would have combined, united, and *integrated* the following parts of the curriculum: safety, health, nutrition, memory, language, perception, motor skills, sensory learning, problem-solving skills, antibias, environmental awareness, and social skills. All the national priority areas of literacy, math, science, antibias and environmental awareness would have been covered. More specifically, children experienced integrated learning about colors, shapes, smells, textures, counting, fractions, comparing, apples, tools, and focused observation (science). There is much more to having an apple as a snack than one would suspect!

A simple web, starting from the interest point of the apple snack itself and integrating it with all the curriculum areas mentioned above, could be drawn as in Figure 11-3. But a more complex web could describe the ways that the emerging interests of the children could lead the teacher to build on and expand the teaching and learning web, adding and integrating many, other related topics into the curriculum. At some point, the apple web might even look like Figure 11-4.

This and other simple foods experiences are excellent home visitor activities. The home visitor can easily involve the parent or have the parent lead the activity throughout the process. The activity takes very little time but includes all the elements that home visitors are encouraged or required to cover on a home visit. All the examples presented in this chapter could be suitable for either the classroom teacher or the home visitor.

Figure 11-3   Learning Web for a One-Apple Snack

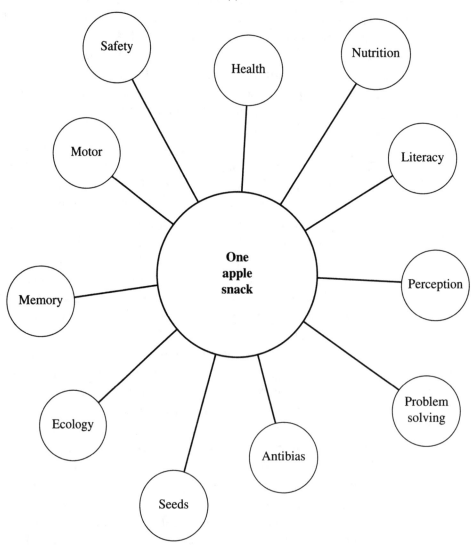

Figure 11-4   An Expanded Learning Web for a One-Apple Snack

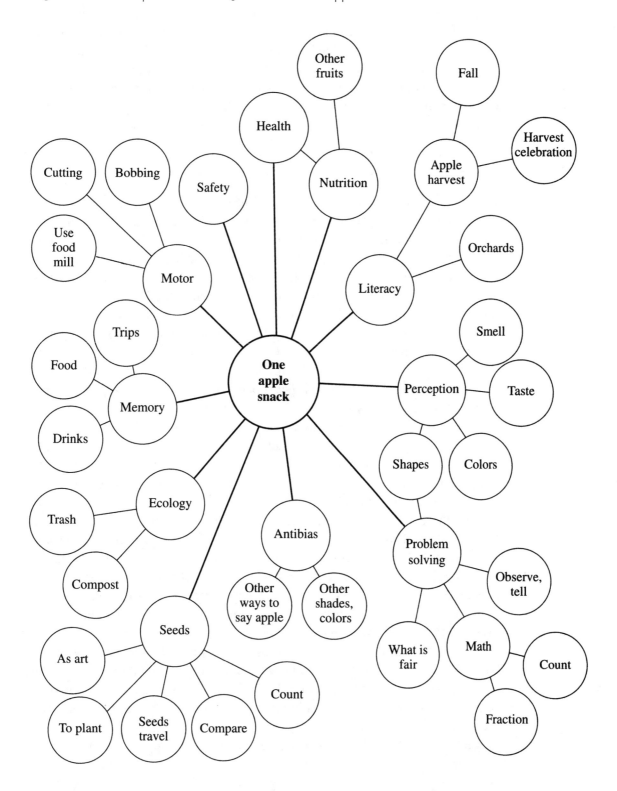

Integrated learning, as in the apple example, can be done with almost any simple food or snack. But when foods experiences become too complicated, it is harder for the teacher to integrate curriculum areas effectively, because the focus is on the food, not on the learning experience. Early childhood educators need to remember that the primary purpose of snacks and foods experiences is health and nutrition, and the secondary purpose is the incorporation of other curriculum areas. We are not in the business of teaching children to create fancy appetizers, and there is more to be seen in a healthful snacks than "ants on a log."

Newspapers

Old newspapers are easy to obtain and can be used to integrate such curriculum areas as large and small motor skills, literacy, creativity, the use of prepositions, the naming of shapes and body parts, recycling concepts, safety concepts, cause and effect, and dramatic play. If there is enough space inside the center, or outside on a pleasant, calm day, the teacher and staff could do the following activities with several small groups of children, simultaneously. But the first time these ideas are introduced, and most of the time thereafter, the teacher would choose seven or eight children to be involved during large group and would repeat the activity to be sure all children would have a turn.

Start by putting sections of old newspaper, folded once, on the floor in a circle, just as you would place carpet squares on the floor as sit-upons. "Who would like to come play this game?" It is wonderful to include parents in this game when they are visiting in the classroom. "What are some things we could do with this paper?" The teacher could start by leading the choices to walk around the paper, stand next to it, jump over it, hop around it, or sit under it. This would be followed by putting your toe on the paper, your knee, your elbow, your nose, or your chin.

After this active movement incorporating prepositions and body part names, the teacher and children could sit on the floor and talk about some of the many ways we use old paper. Children may say or may be led to tell how paper is used to train puppies, clean fish, or start campfires. They will talk about how people read papers, color on them, put them on the easel, or protect the floor with them when the walls of a house are being painted. They could talk about taking paper to the recycling center.

The teacher could ask children to close their eyes and then tear or crumple paper, and then ask what the sound was, and ask them to point to the direction of the sound source. The teacher could go on to say that it is lots of fun to tear paper, too, and everyone could enjoy tearing strips of paper or even shapes like rectangles, squares, or circles.

With the addition of an old sheet, the teacher, parents, and children could crumple paper balls and toss them into the sheet, which has become a pretend skillet in which to make popcorn. They could pretend to add the oil and turn on the heat, taking time to comment on never cooking or using the stove at home unless a grown-up is helping. When everyone grabs the edges of the sheet, the

pretend popcorn can sizzle and get hotter and hotter until it pops . . . all over the area, of course . . . as children and adults use hands and arms to shake the sheet.

Young children need to be brought down to a calmer state after all this excitement. The teacher can ask each of them to gather up the crumpled paper balls in small piles in front of themselves. Now the group can pretend that the popcorn has changed into snow, and talk about snowball safety. ("What do we do with snow;?" "Where are safe places to throw snow?" "Why?") The group should also discuss icicle safety. Big icicles fascinate children, but they can be deadly.

After this brief quiet period, have the group divide into two teams, and have a grand and glorious, safe snowball fight. This is great exercise and fun. The teacher can declare the contest a draw and bring out an old, clean empty pillowcase. "Let's make a big, giant snowball by putting all the small ones inside the pillowcase."

Children will happily clean up the crumpled paper and can then play toss and catch with this giant stuffed ball. Even two- or three-year-olds, who might normally be unable to catch a big ball, will successfully catch a stuffed, lightweight, squishy pillow. Pillows feel familiar and safe. This ending circle game employs active movement but is structured so that it brings children down to a calm state after the excitement of the snowball fight.

The children will notice that their hands are dirty. Help them think about and discover where the newsprint ink on their hands came from, and take time to wash hands with soap and water. As they return to the group or circle, a discussion could occur about how paper is made from the wood pulp of trees. Children might be interested in knowing that three feet of stacked old newspapers equal one tree.

As you see, old newspaper, in a time frame of about fifteen to twenty minutes, can give teachers the opportunity to integrate and incorporate many curriculum areas and to expand the learning web to new areas. A complex web about newspapers, adding many more potential curriculum areas could look more like Figure 11-5.

Figure 11-5 A Complex Web about Newspapers

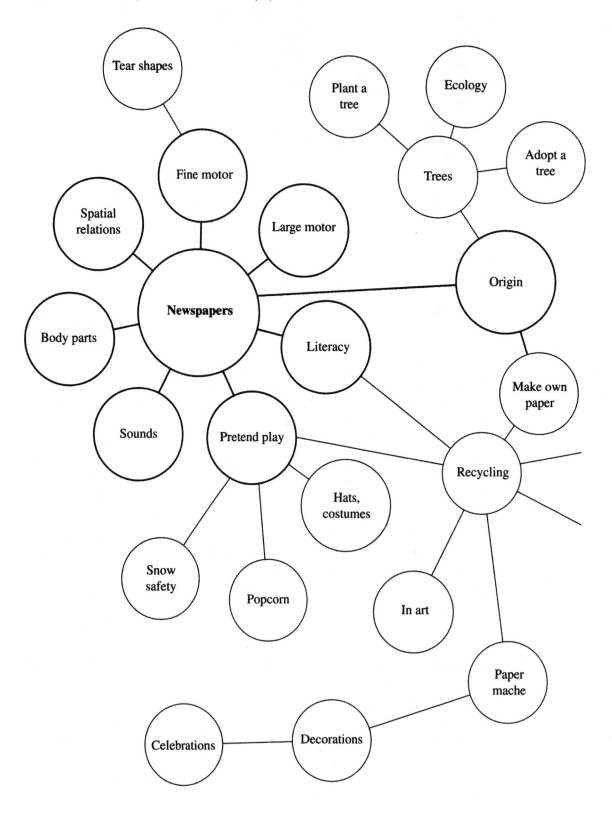

Earth

Earth and water provide excellent opportunities for planning integrated activities. In Chapter 3, a narrative example of a simple integrated activity on soil or earth was presented, followed by an illustration of what would happen if more interests emerged and more curriculum areas were covered (see Chapter 3, Figure 3-1, an illustration of a complex learning web about soil).

TRY THIS NOW   On scrap or notebook paper, make or trace a rough copy of that complex web. Now let's explore ways the web could change and grow, depending on your emerging interests and those of your children.

Suppose your children have already gone outside to collect and sort different kinds of soil, examined it carefully, talked about it, smelled it, weighed and measured it, and tried to dissolve it in water, while telling what happens at each step. They have already practiced many skills in literacy, mathematics, and science.

To expand on the "experiments" part of the web and to do an activity relating to ecology and the environment, children might do an experiment to see what happens when you fill a large glass jar with moist earth and put different items into the jar, between the dirt and the glass, so that you can see what happens over time. Try some of these items: a piece of Styrofoam, an aluminum ring from a flip-top can, a cigarette filter, a small piece of bread, a small piece of carrot or other vegetable, a piece of an apple core, and a piece of a leaf that has fallen from a tree.

When children watch the jar for a few weeks, they will see that the bread, vegetable, fruit, and leaf all disappear into the earth, but the other items do not. This is an excellent way for children to become aware of the use of compost, the need to stop or control littering, and the purpose of sanitary landfills. Your web has grown from experiments to the use of earth as compost, and from compost to new areas of learning, landfills and litter.

In your rough drawing, look at the area of the original web that grew from "soil" to "different kinds," then to "topsoil," and then to "plants." Here is a way to extend the "plants" part of the web to a new area, "terrariums."

Children might want to use some of the topsoil for plants to make a terrarium for the classroom and put small plants or animals inside it to observe. Some teachers find they can keep small hermit crabs, lizards, or toads successfully in terrariums, and in some classrooms I have seen small snakes, and even a tarantula spider, in a terrarium. Most often, mealworms are used to feed snakes, toads, and lizards. Some of these animals try to hibernate during part of the year.

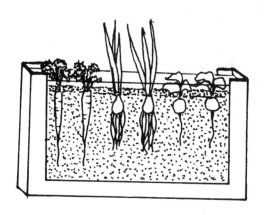

Look again at the "plants" part of your sketch of the soil web. Children might add to the "plants" part of the web by doing experiments with seeds or bulbs and tubers planted in soil, and examine or compare the roots that grew from the seeds, bulbs, and tubers. They might want to know more about crops planted in topsoil. Now the plants part of the web would have grown new curriculum connections to seeds, bulbs, tubers, and crops. Children may notice that some plants grow in sand. If you plan activities about this, you will be adding a new connection to the "sand" part of the web.

Look back at the original focus of the web, soil itself. Here is another way to extend the learning web and its illustration. Most children are interested in tracks. First of all, they do a lot of "tracking in," and adults comment on this. In addition, finding tracks outside is exciting for children. Both animal and human tracks can often be found outside in earth or in snow.

Children can look at tracks with their eyes or with magnifying glasses, talk about and compare them, try to figure out what person or animal made them and why. Where was the person or animal going? Children can look at the bottoms of their own shoes and compare the different kinds of tracks made by their shoes or boots. With careful supervision, they can look at vehicle tracks and compare differences in those of cars, trucks, or the school bus.

Now you see that you have been able to add a new part to the web. It has grown from soil to tracks, and from tracks it has grown to include human tracks, animal tracks, and vehicle tracks. This is an especially good curriculum activity in areas of the country where trackers have long been considered as important people.

Let's think about one more way this web could change and grow. All children will be interested in the fact that some animals live underground, in the dirt. If they want to learn more about what animals live in soil or make their homes in it, the illustration of your web would grow from the center, soil itself, to a new connection, "animals." From "animals," many more new connections could be added. For example, children could study worms or ants, and the teacher could purchase or create an ant farm for the classroom. Children might want to learn about moles or other animals that live underground.

Water

TRY THIS NOW   Water, one of the basic necessities of life, is another good medium for many types of integrated activities. Use some scrap paper to design a rough sketch of a learning web containing some of your ideas for learning activities about water. Your ideas might include any on the following list and many more. Some of your ideas will change, depending on the interests of your group.

- Water for drinking and cooking
- Water for cleaning
- Water for plants and animals
- Water for enjoyment and relaxation
- Water for experiments with sounds and music, dissolving, blowing bubbles, floating and sinking, estimating, weighing, boiling, freezing, melting, and painting
- Animals and plants that live in water
- Jobs—people who work with water
- Transportation on the water
- Water safety
- Conservation and water pollution

Transferring Web Information into Horizontal and Vertical Plans

This is a good time to mention that drawings of teaching and learning webs are excellent brainstorming and preplanning devices. But you can see that the ideas in your webs will still need to find their way to the paper of a long-range plan, monthly plans, and your daily plan. The systems in this guidebook for organizing horizontal and vertical plans can help you accomplish this.

Look at the web about earth to see which parts of it are designed to give children a greater body of knowledge, or factual content. These are the parts that fit your horizontal plan. The parts of the web that give children practice in actual skills fit your vertical curriculum plan. For example, in the web you drew about soil or earth, here are the parts of the web that fit into your long-range horizontal plan:

- Children learn facts about different kinds of earth
- They learn different uses for soil
- They learn about animals that live in the earth

- They learn that they can do experiments with soil
- They learn that they can plant things in soil

But when children actually *do* the experiments, or *do* the planting, or *do* the telling and dictating about what they observe, they are practicing skills. All of the problem-solving skills they practice will be related to skills in their planning, their process thinking, and their science and mathematics skills. Their "telling" will be a literacy skill. These are the parts of the web that fit your vertical planning:

- Create pots from clay and compare different pottery (motor, creative problem solving, and literacy).
- Make a terrarium for small plants and animals to observe (motor, problem solving, literacy).
- Plant seeds, bulbs, and tubers to observe (motor, problem solving, literacy).
- Do experience posters about uses for gravel (motor, problem solving, literacy).
- Make sand paintings (motor, creative problem solving).
- Observe and graph changes and comparisons of roots growing from seeds, tubers, and bulbs (literacy, problem solving).
- Do experiments to see what plants can grow in sand (literacy and problem solving).
- Try to dissolve earth or sand (literacy and problem solving).
- Examine earth; discuss and compare (problem solving and literacy).
- Weigh and measure earth (problem solving, motor).
- Do compost experiments (literacy, problem solving).

Transferring Web Information into the Lesson Plan

Now you can see that what is drawn on your web about earth or soil can be sorted into the horizontal and vertical parts of your curriculum. You can put the horizontal parts into your long-range plan and put the vertical parts into your monthly and daily lesson plans.

Let's use another example to take this management process to the next step. Suppose you have decided to use water as the basis for many integrated activities, and you have drawn your initial planning in a rough sketch of a learning web about water. You already know what parts of that web are content-focused (horizontal) and what parts are skill-focused (vertical). You have already planned for activities in your web that promote children's self-esteem, activities that support their abilities to work with others, and activities that promote their awareness about our world and the living things in it.

Now you need to put your entries into daily lesson plans. You need to decide whether they fit best in "large group," "free choice or planned activity time," "small group," or maybe even "outdoor" time or "meal and snack" time. Some may even fit into the lesson plan format in "ecology/environment" or "health and nutrition." Let's take examples of some of the specific integrated activities you have planned about water, and see some of the ways they could be entered in a daily lesson plan.

Large Group

- Show a large see-through container or pitcher of water to the group, and or pass small paper cups of water to drink. Ask children to tell you what they observe or know about water and its uses. Write an experience chart or poster listing their comments as they talk (*horizontal curriculum:* facts about water, *vertical curriculum:* memory and literacy).
- Show pictures of water in many forms to the group and let them comment. Do an experience poster listing what they say about different forms of water, such as lakes, oceans, rivers, falls, and ponds (*horizontal:* facts about forms of water; *vertical:* memory and literacy).
- Show globes, maps, and pictures of our world, explaining that the earth has more water than land and that lands are surrounded by water (*horizontal:* facts about water and our earth; *vertical:* literacy and memory).

If it were the beginning of the year with a group of threes and fours, these activities could also be done in small group, and might elicit more language in small groups than large. Notice that these activities follow the sequence of showing a concrete example of actual water, then pictures of water, and then more abstract illustrations of water.

Small Group—Skill Practice

- Use small cups of water, a small paper plate, and eye droppers to let children learn how to use the eye droppers. Ask them to drip and count the drops they make on the plate. At another time, paint or food coloring can be added to the water (*horizontal:* facts about water; *vertical:* motor, literacy, problem solving).
- Use water with small cups, individual straws, and several pieces of paper towel at each place. Let children blow bubbles in plain water; ask how to make more bubbles that last longer. Add liquid soap and blow bubbles to see the difference. At another time, add small drops of food color to the

surface of the bubbles to see geometric patterns formed at the base of each connection. Try different colors to see what happens. Capture and save paper towel designs with a plain paper "print" (*horizontal:* facts about water, water bubbles, and colors with water; *vertical:* motor, problem solving, perception, literacy, and creativity).

- Let children see and discuss how musical sounds can be made with water in glasses, and compare the sounds made in glasses filled in differing amounts. Make music. (*horizontal:* facts about water; *vertical:* motor, literacy, problem solving, and creativity).
- Have children experiment by dissolving salt in water, and discuss and compare the results. Try other substances as well (*horizontal:* facts about water and dissolving. *vertical:* motor, problem solving, literacy).
- Let children talk about and make their own drawings of some things that live in the water; write their dictation next to the drawings (*horizontal:* facts about life in the water; *vertical:* motor, perceptual, literacy, memory, creativity).

If further discussion included facts and problem solving on clean water or water pollution, this could also be entered in the ecology section of the lesson plan format.

- Talk about what happens when there is no rain for gardens and crops. What do we do about this? Follow up in free choice with experiment comparing a marigold plant that is watered with one that is not (*horizontal:* facts about plants and water; *vertical:* literacy, memory, and problem solving).

This is sometimes appropriate for large-group time, and if discussion and problem solving were included, it could be entered in the ecology section of the lesson plan form.

- Talk about the ways animals drink and how these are different from ours. Discuss where animals go to drink water. What happens if the water is dried up or dirty? What could we do? (*horizontal:* facts about animals and water; *vertical:* literacy, memory, problem solving).

This is sometimes appropriate for large-group time and could also fit under ecology in the lesson plan format.

- Talk about and draw things that could "go" or float on top of the water or underwater. Add dictation to drawings (*horizontal:* facts about water; *vertical:* literacy, motor, memory, creativity).

This is sometimes appropriate for large group, in which dictation could be done as a group poster. Follow up with free-choice group art mural and dramatic play.

- During small-group snack or meal, let children pour and serve themselves water in addition to whole milk or juice. Talk about the ways water is good for you (*horizontal:* facts about water and health; *vertical:* motor, memory, literacy).

If discussion includes health, this can also be entered in the health and nutrition part of the lesson plan.

- During foods experiences at meals and snacks, possibly prepared ahead during free-choice/activity time, let children make drinks from water and powdered mixes, discuss what happens when water is added, and compare these drinks (*horizontal:* facts about water; *vertical:* motor, literacy, perceptual, problem solving).

If discussion includes comparisons of the nutritional values of drinks, this can also be listed in the nutrition and health part of the lesson plan.

- During health routines such as handwashing, talk about dirt, germs, and why we use soap. You can also talk about skin color and that we can wash off dirt, but skin color in each of us is different (even in all Caucasian children) and does not come off. Skin color is uniquely ours and comes naturally from our parents (*horizontal:* facts about water and soap; *vertical:* motor, literacy, perception, memory).

This can also be entered on the lesson plan format under health and, if discussion of skin color was included, under antibias or multicultural awareness in the lesson plan.

Free Choice—Planned Activity Time

- In the foods experiences area during children's activity time, let children help make foods from mixes and water. Some can be mix and eat activities; some can be mix and cook or bake activities. Talk about changes that occurred and make comparisons. Try instant versus cooked pudding and compare the taste and the preparation time (*horizontal:* facts about water and foods; *vertical:* motor, literacy, perceptual, memory, problem solving).

If nutrition was discussed, this can also be listed in the health part of the lesson plan format.

- Let children help prepare vegetable soup to eat the same day or the next. Talk about the tastes and how cooking in water changes the taste, smell, and look of the vegetables. Talk about the changes that occurred during cooking, and recall the steps in the process of making the soup *horizontal:* facts about water and foods; *vertical:* motor, perceptual, literacy, memory, problem solving).

Nutrition will be discussed, so this can also be entered in the health and nutrition part of the lesson plan format.

* Have children help wash and dry chairs and tables or dolls and housekeeping dishes with small buckets or tubs of soapy water, small brushes and towels. Put towels under the tubs or buckets for splashes. Talk about why we keep things clean (*horizontal:* facts about water and soap in controlling dirt or germs; *vertical:* motor, perceptual, literacy, memory, problem solving).

This can also be entered in the health part of the lesson plan format.

* Have children estimate and discover how many cups of water at the water table can fill a large container or small bucket. Discuss "more" and "less," as well as counting the cups as they are poured (*horizontal:* facts about water and mass; *vertical:* motor, perception, literacy, problem solving).

Depending on the skill levels in the group, try similar guessing, discovery, and cause-and-effect experiments with water wheels, basters, and siphons (same skills).

* Freeze some water in ice cubes and set them out to be observed and discussed as they melt. Snow, if available, can also be used is this way. Graphs can be made to compare the speed at which snow and ice melt in the classroom, or even in different areas of the building. A variation is to make ice and compare the time it takes to freeze outside in cold weather versus inside in the refrigerator (*horizontal:* facts about water and changes from liquid to solid; *vertical:* motor, perceptual, literacy, problem solving).
* Do sink-and-float activities at the water table or in tubs. Have children experiment, observe, tell, and graph what happens. See what happens when a toy boat is filled with heavy, small pebbles. Another variation is to use real clay and experiment to discover and compare how clay balls sink, but clay pancakes float (*horizontal:* facts about water and buoyancy; *vertical:* motor, literacy, memory, problem solving).
* Put a variety of objects found underwater, such as pebbles and shells, into the water table. Add toy boats if desired. Notice how rocks, shells and pebbles look different when wet or dry. Discuss (*horizontal:* facts about water; *vertical:* motor, memory, literacy, perceptual, problem solving).
* In a dramatic play area add "fishing" props, either for fishing from boats or

docks, or for ice fishing. Include props such as appropriate clothing and life jackets, and discuss safety. On another day, try "beach" props, including empty sun block lotions, sunglasses, hats, life preservers, and sandals. Consider snorkeling props and paper underwater creatures (*horizontal:* facts about water; *vertical:* motor, literacy, memory, problem solving, creativity).

This is also a health and safety activity.

- Do follow-up activities from group discussions. For example, do experiments with watering versus not watering a plant, or do a group art mural of things that live in the water. Sand could be glued to the bottom of blue/green paper, and children's own designs of colored or painted fish, creatures, and plants can be cut out and pasted to the mural (*horizontal:* facts about marine life; *vertical:* motor, perceptual, memory, literacy, problem solving, creativity).
- In the sandbox or sand table, create an island surrounded by water. See pictures and maps of islands for comparison and discussion (*horizontal:* facts about water and land; *vertical:* motor, literacy, memory, problem solving, creativity).

This learning can be extended to discussions of what is in the water around islands, what foods island dwellers often eat, and what sorts of art and jewelry they make. If learning about island cultures is included, this can be entered in the antibias/multicultural awareness section of the lesson plan format.

Outdoor Time

- Have children collect and measure rain water in a bucket or rain barrel. Tell, dictate, and/or graph observations (*horizontal:* facts about water; *vertical:* motor, perceptual, memory, literacy, problem solving).
- With safe supervision, get samples of water from a nearby pond, stream, or beach. Observe, compare, and discuss. Is the water clean or polluted? Fresh or salty? (*horizontal:* facts about water; *vertical:* motor, perception, literacy, problem solving).

If the discussion includes clean water and pollution, this can also be entered in the ecology part of the lesson plan format.

- If there is snow, consider spraying it with pink or red tempera mixed with water, from big spray bottles, as in the Dr. Seuss story *The Cat in the Hat Returns* (*horizontal:* facts about water and paint; *vertical:* motor, literacy, perceptual, memory). Children can also have opportunities to help mix tempera powder paint with water for use in the art area.
- Where ice is available, "adopt" an icicle to observe and study (even photograph) from a *safe* distance. Watch changes in the growth of the icicle. Dis-

cuss and graph (*horizontal:* facts about water and its changes from liquid to solid; *vertical:* literacy, problem solving, perception, memory).

This is also a safety activity.

- See what happens in cold climates when soapy water bubbles are blown outdoors in below freezing conditions (*horizontal:* facts about water and temperatures; *vertical:* motor, literacy, problem solving).
- With small buckets of water, wet the pavement or side walk and draw on it with colored chalk. Find out and note how long the pavement takes to dry or the water to evaporate. Another variation is to use wallpaper or big brushes and plain water in small buckets to "paint" the sidewalk, or the side of the building; watch the change caused by evaporation (*horizontal:* facts about water and evaporation; *vertical:* motor, literacy, perception, problem solving, creativity).

Now you can see how to take ideas from your preplanning web, sort them into vertical and horizontal planning, and organize them for inclusion in your daily lesson plans.

Summary

In this chapter, we have talked about integrated activities as a logical and meaningful way to teach young children, who are always learning and who learn in an integrated manner. We have looked at both simple and complex integrated activities and seen examples of these, including dramatic play, beanbags, playdough, apples, newspapers, soil, and water. The teacher's mental planning for integrated activities can be drawn as teaching and learning webs, and these webs, whether they are simple or complex, can continually change, depending on the emerging interests of children.

Pictures of learning webs are wonderful aids in thinking and planning. They open your mind to the many possibilities for children's emergent interests in the curriculum. In addition, when you look at a complex web, you can see that it includes activities that are both knowledge-based and skill-based, or *horizontal* and *vertical.* However, a teacher would not be carrying around a batch of pictures of learning webs to use as a year long horizontal plan. *These webs are a planning device, not a yearly plan!*

To do daily lesson planning, you will still need a system to put your ideas on paper in a long-range horizontal plan for the year. An outline format, such as seen in Chapter 3, makes it easy for you to adjust to emerging curriculum interests. To do good daily lesson plans, you will also need a system to manage your skill-focused ideas. Be sure you are planning a balance of all skill areas, and that you are meeting the needs of each child in your group. The system presented in Chapters 4 and 6 and Appendix A should give you such a system.

Using integrated activities, supporting children's emergent curriculum interests, and facilitating children's learning by implementing hands-on activities in the classroom are some of the most exciting and challenging aspects of teaching young children. Teachers of young children need to be flexible, creative, full of energy, able to think on their feet, and able to do several things at a time. This is a demanding, but exhilarating and fulfilling career. If this is what teaching means to you, there is no better choice than to teach young children.

Self-Study Activities

1. Go back over some of your old lesson plans and find two materials or experiences that you expanded, during one day in the classroom, to integrate other areas of the curriculum. Now draw the two simple learning webs that would illustrate your teaching. Are there ways you could have added to your webs?

2. Review old lesson plans or your horizontal long-range plan of themes for the year. Could some of these theme activities have been expanded to integrate other emergent interests of the children? What could you have done to encourage this? Draw complex webs for two such thematic units, imagining and including other topics that might have emerged and been integrated.

3. Draw a learning web about one of your own personal interests or hobbies. Might other interests emerge that could be added?

Resources for Suggested Reading

Appendix C will provide suggested books, including many ideas for integrating various parts of the curriculum with thematic content and with learning skills. However, the books suggested here are those most relevant to this chapter.

Brewer, Jo Ann. *Introduction to Early Childhood Education, Preschool through Primary Grades.* Boston: Allyn and Bacon, 1995.

Fortson, Laura Rogers, & Reiff, Judith C. *Early Childhood Curriculum: Open Structures for Integrative Learning.* Boston: Allyn and Bacon, 1995.

Jones, Elizabeth, & Nimmo, John. *Emergent Curriculum.* Washington, DC: National Association for the Education of Young Children, 1994.

Trostle, Susan L., & Yawkey, Thomas D. *Integrated Learning Activities for Young Children.* Boston: Allyn and Bacon, 1990.

APPENDIX A
Skill-Focused Activities

I hope that readers will copy and enlarge, if necessary, the seven tables or time blocks in Appendix A for daily use in writing lesson plans. With this appendix as a guide, it will be possible to plan developmentally sequenced, skill-focused activities for various times of the program day in different areas of the setting from the beginning to the end of the program year.

The format of each of the seven time blocks in this appendix will also remind teachers to offer experiences consistently in all five skill areas (motor, perceptual, literacy, memory, and problem solving).

It is important to remember that this appendix has been developed to present a *system* of organizing and using information. This includes the information in this guidebook as well as all other information that teachers bring to the experience of lesson planning. The activity examples should serve as a springboard for your own skill-focused activity objectives.

MOTOR

Large Group
Body Movement:
Copy and/or create to music, songs,
    chants, rhymes.
Act out prepositions.

Free Choice
Using Blocks:
Use unit and large hollow blocks.
Stack, lay, carry, build.
Active Play Inside/Outside
Use all types of locomotion, including
    wheel toys.
Follow line or path with body or toy.
Practice climbing and rolling.
Jump with both feet.
Toss, catch, and pass with big, soft
    beanbags, or paper-stuffed pillow-
    case.
Use hammer with pegs or *soft* wood
    or Styrofoam.

Clays and Playdough/Sand and Water:
Use freely; fill, pour, float, sink, mold
    and dig.

Dressing and Undressing:
Practice with outer wear, dress-up,
    and zipper/button toys.

Art Media:
Use crayons, markers, chalk, paper.
Use easel paint and fingerpaint.
Paint at tables.
Use varied collage materials.

Manipulatives, Table Toys, Floor Toys:
Use large, easy puzzles.
Use large pegs/pegboards.
Use large lego blocks.
String large beads.
Use stack and nest toys.
Use shape box toys.
Use snap and bristle blocks.

Small Group
Games:
Follow object with eyes.
Tear paper at random.
Use tongs and pinch clothespins.
Trace simple templates with fingers;
    free form, one line.
Practice pouring water.
Practice any manipulatives.

Meals and Snacks:
Pour, pass, serve, spread.
Clean up, brush teeth.

PERCEPTUAL

Large Group
Music and Circle:
Use instruments.
Recognize body parts.
Listen to sounds and identify some.
Notice what we are wearing.

Free Choice
Blocks:
Use all types.
Handle and match types.

Exploring with Senses:
Use clays, playdough, water, sand,
    earth.
Explore and match textures.
Handle and match recycled items.
Handle collage items.
Match familiar objects.
Use various paints.
Compare colors used in art media.
Notice smells, tastes.

*Manipulatives, Table Toys, Floor
    Toys:*
Use simple, large puzzles/parquetry.
Use face–body parts activities.
Match textures.
Match familiar silhouette shapes.

Cleanup:
Use pictures and perceptual labels.
Recognize sound cues.

Small Group
Games:
Compare sounds; high, low, loud,
    soft.
Tell direction of sound source.*
Compare ourselves regarding sizes,
    hair, eyes.
Guess a hidden object by touch
    alone.
Match some primary colors.
Compare objects; big, small, like,
    unlike. Match like objects.
Examine/match circles and ovals.
Identify simple sounds.*
Recognize familiar shape silhouettes.

Meals and Snacks:
Perceive colors, textures, tastes,
    smells and temperatures.

LITERACY

Large Group
Literature:
Hear stories and books.
Do fingerplays and rhymes.
Do songs and chants.
See flannelboard stories.
Use/talk with puppets.

Conversations:
About work and play choices.
About plans and routines.
On simple rules for safety.
About friends and names.
On things that make us happy or sad.

Body Language:
Move to music.
Imitate animals and nature.
Act out prepositions with music, rug
    squares.

Free Choice
Talk/Listen/Do:
Use books and pictures.
Use people's names.
Name items and equipment.
Talk about healthful ways.
Use friendly words.
Use, talk about safe ways and rules.
Play with puppets.
Talk about art and creations.
Use picture recipe to make playdough.
Use tape recorder.
Use listen station.
Use play telephones.
Examine computer.

Dramatic Play:
Converse spontaneously.
Use materials creatively.

Writing Center:
Do creative "writing" and communi-
    cating.

Small Group
Games:
Discuss "me," my home and family.
Start a "me" book.
Discuss pictures about feelings.
Discuss work and play choices.
Use puppets together.
Discuss health and safety.*
Read a picture book.*
Discuss visitors/helpers.*
Discuss outdoor walks.*

Meals and Snacks:
Discuss and name foods. Tell
    preferences.

MEMORY

Large Group
Learning Together:
Copy adult modeling.
Imitate in simple games of "Do What I
    Do."
Hear and talk about stories.
Sing songs in unison and call and
    response.
Enjoy and learn fingerplays.
Try counting by rote up to 5 in songs,
    rhymes, birthdays.
Learn daily schedule, routines, limits.
See picture sequence of daily
    schedule.
Use names of friends in songs, rhymes
    and games.
See own name in print.

Free Choice
All Area Learning:
Learn names of areas, materials and
    equipment.
Learn how we use materials and
    equipment.
Learn names of friends.
Learn limits, expectations and routines
    with practice and helpful visual
    cues.
Learn helpers' jobs with practice and
    helpful visual cues.
Use healthful habits at snacks and
    meals, when toileting, and in
    cleaning to prevent spread of
    germs.
Use safety habits with materials,
    movements, fire drills.

Cleanup:
Learn adult cue to start.
Learn where things go.

Small Group
Games:
Talk about fire and tornado drills.
See sequenced pictures of the daily
    schedule.
Recall today and what I liked best.
Repeat own and each other's names in
    rhythmic chant.
Remember summer and family fun.*
Recall one or two objects when these
    are removed from a group and
    hidden.
Guess names of areas from adult
    clues.
Sometimes recognize own printed
    name.
Recall some friend's names.

Meals and Snacks:
Learn the routine.
Copy positive social language.

PROBLEM SOLVING

Large Group
Conversations:
On work/play choices from day's
    options.
On the schedule of the day.
About nature, the weather, and its
    changes.
About our body parts and their use.
    (demonstrate)
On what makes us feel happy or sad.

Free Choice
Blocks:
Stack, lay, connect.
Compare different structures.

All Area Learning:
Begin to know areas and materials by
    use.
Make work/play choices.
Begin to plan the use of time.
Ask questions and use senses to gain
    information.
Negotiate turns with materials.
Explain wants and needs with words.
Match, sort, and tub materials.
Manipulate materials.
Examine computer.
Observe properties of sand, water,
    paint, playdough/clays.
Observe changes resulting in mixing
    colors.
Make playdough; measure, mix; see
    changes.

Dramatic Play:
Choose items for role play and
    pretend.
Plan and carry out play.

Science and Math:
Observe and handle nature items.
Observe our plants and animals.
Measure and weigh ourselves.
Estimate in pouring and filling.

Small Group
Games:
Discuss play choices and plan one
    choice for next time.
Tub and sort items.
Count own body parts.
Count heads and noses of those in
    group.
Blow bubbles with individual cups/
    straws; observe.

Meals and Snacks:
Set table with one-to-one match.
Help prepare snack when possible.
Problem-solve when using utensils.
Estimate in pouring, filling.

MOTOR

Large Group
Body Movement:
Copy and/or create to music, songs,
 chants, rhymes.
Act out prepositions.

Free Choice
Using Blocks:
Use unit and large blocks freely.

Active Play Inside/Outside:
Use varied locomotion, including
 wheel toys.
Follow line with body or toy.
Try balance beam, FLAT.
Use steps/rocking boat.
Use indoor climber.
Use mats to jump and roll.
Balance on one foot; try to hop.
Toss/catch large, light items.
Jump over a low rope; rake, jump in
 leaves.
Use hammer and soft materials or
 pegs.

Clays and Playdough/Sand and Water:
Use freely; add variety.
Pour, fill, float, sink, dig, mold.

Dressing and Undressing:
Outer wear, dress-up, and zipper/
 button toys.

Art Media:
Use crayons, markers, paper, and
 scissors.
Do varied painting, fingerpaint, and
 collages.
Try spray painting.
Try dripped-glue designs.
Try hole punch designs.
Try rubbings from nature.

Manipulatives, Table Toys, Floor Toys:
Use all appropriate manipulatives
 freely.

Small Group
Games:
Tear paper with purpose.
Use simple templates with curves; one
 line.
Fold paper; either one or two folds.
Learn about eye dropper painting.
String paper tubes, big pastas, or
 cereals.
Snip or fringe with scissors.
Practice any manipulatives.

Meals and Snacks:
Pour, pass, serve, and spread.
Carry, clean up, brush teeth.

PERCEPTUAL

Large Group
Music and Circle:
Use instruments.
Match sounds of like instruments.
Identify other sounds.
Compare ourselves; sizes and other
 characteristics.
Guess hidden objects by touch alone.
Notice what we wear.

Free Choice
Blocks:
Use all types.
Handle, match, and find types.

Exploring with Senses:
Use clays, playdough, water, sand,
 mud.
Match textures and recycled items.
Mix and match paints.
Do more smelling and tasting.
Sort items found in nature such as
 leaves, stones, seeds.
Use some musical instruments in play.

Manipulatives, Table Toys, Floor Toys:
Use materials fully.
Use blocks, flannel pieces, beads,
 pegs, and parquetry to create own
 patterns.

Clean Up:
Use perceptual labels.
Recognize sound cues.

Small Group
Games:
Match primary colors, unnamed.
Hum together; match a pitch.
Recognize a voice.
Identify familiar sounds on tape.
Match familiar shapes.
Match simple objects to their pictures.
Reproduce easy three-part patterns
 with model in view using cubes,
 beads, or other objects.
Find or match circles, ovals, squares.
Guess objects by touch.*
Match big and small objects.

Meals and Snacks:
Perceive and discuss tastes, smells,
 textures, colors.
Perceive that some foods have shapes.

LITERACY

Large Group
Literature:
Hear stories and books.
Do fingerplays and rhymes.
Do songs and chants.
Use flannelboard and puppets.

Conversations:
About choices and plans.
On rules for our room and group.
About feelings and fears.
About friends and names.
About new toys and equipment.

Body Language:
Move to music.
Use gestures and imitations.
Try signing a simple word or phrase.
Add to actions with prepositions.

Free Choice
Talk/Listen/Do:
Use books/pictures.
Use names of people and materials.
Use and talk about healthful ways.
Use friendly words.
Use and talk about safe ways/rules.
Use puppets and flannelboard.
Answer open questions.
Do artwork dictation.
Try new recipe cards.
Use the computer.
Tape record/listen.
Use play telephones.

Dramatic Play:
Use new props and materials.
Converse spontaneously.

Writing Center:
Create original communication.
Try new materials.

Small Group
Games:
Continue "me" book as a personal
 journal.
Discuss foods, health, safety.*
Discuss feelings of self and others.
Discuss visitors, trips, and walks.*
Discuss our plants and animals.
Begin simple dictation or experience
 stories.

Meals and Snacks
Discuss and describe food. Talk with
 peers and adults.

MEMORY

Large Group
Remembering Together:
Copy adult modeling.
Imitate in simple games of "Do What I
 Do."
Hear stories and songs.
Do fingerplays/rhymes.
Know what comes next in schedule.
Try rote counting to 5 in non-
 stereotyped songs, rhymes.
See and discuss pictured sequence of
 routines such as fire drills, meals/
 toothbrushing.
See visual cues for limits/rules and
 helper jobs.
Know many names of friends and
 adults.
Recognize and name familiar sounds.
See own name in print (name tag,
 creations).
Remember summer or past events.
Remember fun times with friends/
 family.
Recall name of a person hidden when
 adult gives clues.
Repeat simple oral or clapped rhythm.

Free Choice
All Area Learning:
Know names of areas, equipment, and
 materials.
Know how to use these appropriately.
Use names of friends.
Know rules and expectations.
Remember helpers' jobs; use visual
 cues.
Practice health habits.
Practice safety habits.

Cleanup:
Remember light or sound cues.
Know where things go.

Small Groups
Games:
Recall two things I did today.
See, match own name in print.
Remember walks, trips, visitors.*
Recall two or three objects removed
 and hidden.
Recall/do one or two tasks while
 seated.
Find one primary color when named.
Find circles and ovals.
Repeat a simple clapped or oral
 rhythm.

Meals and Snacks:
Remember the routine.
Use positive social language.
Begin to talk about food groups.
Talk about foods for healthy teeth.

PROBLEM SOLVING

Large Group
Conversations:
About work and play choices.
About the daily schedule.
About weather changes and how these
 tell us seasonal changes.
On rules developed by the group.
On "last time" or "next time."
On body parts and their use.
About ways we can relax.

Free Choice
Blocks:
Stack/lay, connect, enclose.
See parts of whole.
Compare differences in structures.

All Area Learning:
Know areas by use.
Make work/play choices.
Ask questions and use senses to gain
 information.
Negotiate wants, needs, and turns with
 words.
See step-by-step process in use of
 media and manipulatives.
Begin to see parts of whole in puzzles,
 designs.
Match, sort, and tub materials.
Use computer.
Try new multisensory media; colors,
 clays.

Dramatic Play:
Plan and carry out play.
Do safety and health habit role play.

Science and Math:
Notice and handle new items; count
 some.
Observe/tell about nature and our
 plants and animals.
See changes mixing, cooking and
 grinding.
Use the balance scale and measuring
 tools.

Small Group
Games:
Use minilight and a magnifier to
 examine nature items found.
Blow bubbles with individual cups/
 straws; add drops of food color;
 observe and tell.
Sort nature items in two ways.
Graph selves by size or in other ways.
Guess, find out what floats or sinks in
 cup of water.
Match three or four items one to one.

Meals and Snacks:
Continue to help in set up and
 preparation.
See changes in foods experiences.

MOTOR

Large Group
Body Movement:
Copy and/or create to music, songs, chants, rhymes.
Act out prepositions.
Try simple pantomime.

Free Choice
Using Blocks:
Use all types.
Use accessories.

Active Play Inside/Outside:
Use varied locomotion; roll, jump, dig in snow if available.
Use jumpropes, hoops.
se balance beam *raised*.
Use rotated indoor active equipment daily.
Follow simple four-part obstacle course; beam, jump, steps, mat.
Balance on one foot; try to hop.
Toss and catch big, soft ball.
Hammer; try vise and short coping saw with Styrofoam or *soft* wood.

Clays and Playdough/Water and Sand:
Add variety; accessories.
Pour/fill, sink/float, dig.
Wash our dolls and chairs.

Dressing and Undressing:
Outer wear, boots, dress-up, and zipper/ button toys.

Art Media:
Use variety of *open-ended* art media daily.
Try new colors and materials.
Try stamp printing.
Try simple paper chains.

Manipulatives, Table Toys, Floor Toys:
Use all appropriate materials.
Add smaller legos, beads, and pegs.

Small Group
Games:
Use short Phillips screwdriver/screws in ceiling tile.
Cut paper apart at random or folded once.
Trace ovals or circles.
Tear simple or random paper shapes.
String smaller beads.
Use easy lacing materials.
Try three-dimensional constructions with tape and recycled items.

Meals and Snacks:
Pour, pass, serve, clean up, brush teeth.
Help prepare foods whenever possible.

PERCEPTUAL

Large Group
Music and Circle:
Use instruments and identify their sounds.
Compare and guess objects by touch.
Notice what we wear.
Talk about circles we see in room.
Perceive gestures as words.

Free Choice
Blocks:
Use all types.
Handle, match and find types.
Name some shapes.

Exploring with Senses:
Try new variety in clays and playdough.
Make play do prints by pressing against objects.
Try new variety in sand and water.
Examine earth from outdoors.
Examine snow indoors if available.
Look at animal, bird tracks in snow or earth.
Observe/compare tracks of our boots.
Sort and match textures, nature items, recyclables.
Mix paint; try brown with pink and white for pastels.
Enjoy taste and smell experiences.
Use instruments in choice time.

Manipulatives, Table Toys, Floor Toys:
Use all appropriate items.

Cleanup:
Use perceptual labels.
Recognize sound or light cues.

Small Group
Games:
Match like pictures in simple lotto games.
Continue reproducing simple patterns with pegs, flannel pieces, beads, and table blocks when model is seen; try four-part pattern if appropriate.
Do easy sound-matching games with film containers or cans.
Match familiar shapes and big and small shapes.
Match primary colors and one or two secondary colors.
See differences in items like our shoes.*
Find and/or match circles, ovals, squares, triangles.

Meals and Snacks:
Perceive tastes, smells, textures, colors, shapes.
Perceive "not full enough" and "too full".

LITERACY

Large Group
Literature:
Hear new, varied literature.
Try stories without words.
Try experience stories and a Big Book.

Conversations:
About choices and plans.
About adjusting rules made by the group.
About feelings and family.
About family traditions.
About friendships.
About new materials.
About health and safety.

Body Language:
Represent ideas with music
Imitate animals and nature.
Sign "I love you."
Safety and health role play.

Free Choice
Talk/Listen/Do:
Use books/pictures.
Use and talk about healthy ways.
Use friendly words.
Use and talk about safe ways and rules.
Use puppets and flannelboard.
Dictation; art and constructions.
Dictation; science area observations.
Add new recipe cards.
Use computer.
Tape record and listen.
Use play telephones.

Dramatic Play:
Use "house" as a shop or restaurant.
Pretend "company" is coming.

Writing Center:
Use varied, recycled greeting cards.
Use other materials freely.

Small Group
Games:
Continue personal journal.
Discuss family traditions for special days.*
Discuss health and safety.*
Discuss special days and "company."*
Read a book together.
Answer open, what-if questions.
Discuss things I can do alone, or for others.

Meals and Snacks:
Discuss foods, some food groups, and simple nutrition.
Discuss foods for "special days" with peers and adults.

MEMORY

Large Group
Remembering Together:
Copy adult modeling.
Play simple games of "Do What I Do."
Participate in stories, songs, fingerplays, rhymes.
Count by rote up to 8 in songs, rhymes.
Try to count to 3 in another language.
Know what comes next in the schedule.
Know and state our group rules.
Know friends' and adult helpers' names.
Recognize own name in print.
Remember family fun and special days.
Remember special class events and visitors.
Repeat sounds and simple rhythms.
Act out familiar story or rhyme.

Free Choice
All Area Learning:
Use names of things, friends, areas.
Know rules and expectations.
Know and do helpers' jobs.
Practice health habits.
Practice safety habits.
Pretend restaurant, "company," and shopping.

Cleanup:
Remember cues and know where things go.

Small Group
Games:
Remember two or three things I did today.*
Find circles, ovals and squares when named.
Talk about summer, fall, past winters.*
Answer questions about a short story just heard.
Remember our walks and trips.*
Remember family traditions and/or special foods served.
Recall three objects or shapes removed and hidden.
Recall and do two tasks.
Furnish words omitted in familiar song or rhyme.*
Repeat a silly word or phrase.

Meals and Snacks:
Remember routine and positive language.
Remember some food groups; see food pyramid.
Remember foods we like or dislike.

PROBLEM SOLVING

Large Groups
Conversations:
About work and play choices.
About weather and seasonal changes.
About the names *fall* and *winter.*
On what we do when a parent is "too busy."
About the holidays.
See pictures or symbols of the three most current holidays.
Discuss and help to sequence the holidays represented.
Represent ideas in creative movement.

Free Choice
Blocks:
Sort/compare, see parts, connect, enclose.
Begin to bridge and repeat simple patterns.
Begin to use accessories.

All Area Learning:
Make work and play choices.
Ask questions and begin to discover answers.
Negotiate turns, wants and needs with words.
Match, sort, and tub materials.
Experiment with manipulatives and constructions.
Use computer.
Use multisensory media fully; try new varieties.

Dramatic Play:
Plan and carry out play.
Do safety and health role play.
Try new roles and ideas with new props.

Science and Math:
Observe nature and our plants and animals.
Observe and handle new items; count some.
Use new or different tools for measuring.
Use scales and magnifier.

Small Group
Games:
Repeat water experiments.
Arrange three items by size.
See snow or ice melt.
Sort objects two or three ways.
Give adult one to three items.
Discuss how to be safe when we go shopping.*
Discuss ways to feel better when sad.*
Graph holiday cookie cutter shapes.

Meals and Snacks:
Continue past experiences.
Try some different types of holiday foods.

MOTOR

Large Group
Body Movement:
Copy and/or create to varied music and rhythms.
Try side-to-side moves.
Use pantomime to represent ideas, feelings, or nature's changes.

Free Choice
Using Blocks:
Use all types and use accessories.

Active Play Inside/Outside:
Use varied locomotion; include snow equipment if appropriate.
Use balance beam *raised.*
Use mats to tumble.
Use jumpropes and hoops.
Use varied four- or five-part obstacle courses.
Balance on each foot.
Hop; try to gallop.
Toss and catch; toss into target.
Use hammer, saw, vise, Phillips screws.
Add recycled embellishments to constructions.

Clays and Playdough/Sand and Water:
Add new variety, tools, and accessories.

Dressing and Undressing:
Practice with outerwear, dress-up, shoes/boots.

Art Media:
Use *open-ended* art media freely.
Experiment with new colors/tools.
Try string painting.
Do more stamp prints.
Tear and cut varied papers.

Manipulatives, Table Toys, Floor Toys:
Use all appropriate items; rotate as needed.

Small Group
Games:
Trace circles, ovals, free forms, and hearts.
Cut paper folded twice.
Tear simple paper shapes.
String small beads.
Use lacing materials.
Practice tying one simple knot with shoelace or yarn.
Cut paper apart on one thick, straight line.
Do three-dimensional constructions with tape and recyclables.
Draw own picture with marker or crayon.

Meals and Snacks:
Carry, pour, fill, pass, serve, spread, clean up.
Help prepare foods; wash vegetables; pare a carrot.

PERCEPTUAL

Large Group
Music and Circle:
Use instruments and guess their sounds.
Guess objects by touch.
Guess a visible object or a person from visual clues given.
Hear a special sound amid background noise.

Free Choice
Blocks:
Handle, match, and find all types.
Perceive shapes and other attributes.
See patterns created or repeated.

Exploring with Senses:
Experiment with new variety in clay, playdough, sand, water, and textures; include snow.
Observe and compare tracks in snow or earth.
Experiment with paint and painting tools.
Continue to handle, sort, and match.
Make playdough prints; guess where from.
Continue taste, smell, and foods experiences.

Manipulatives; Table Toys; Floor Toys:
Use all appropriate items freely.
Use more complex parquetry designs.
Use more complex puzzles.
Use simple picture lotto cards.

Cleanup:
Use perceptual labels.
Respond to sound and light cues.

Small Group
Games:
Use easy picture and symbol lotto.
Try reproducing simple five-part patterns with model seen.
Match or find circles, ovals, hearts, squares.
Match big, small, medium.
Use sound-matching cans.
Match three primary and three secondary colors.
Guess a person's voice.*
Guess where texture or object prints on playdough were made.
Practice puzzle or parquetry skills.
Perceive interesting similarities and differences among us.

Meals and Snacks:
Perceive and describe tastes, colors, textures, shapes.
Observe a food and guess the method of cooking it.
Sort and match cereal or cracker snacks.

LITERACY

Large Group
Literature:
Hear new and varied literature.
Help tell story to group.
Do experience stories and use Big Books together.
Use sequenced pictures of day's schedule, seasons, and holidays to tell about.

Conversations:
About play choices and plans.
On getting along with friends and family.
About the events of our holidays.
About ways we learn with our senses and our questions.
About staying healthy and healthy foods.
About ways we stay safe in bad weather.
About visual cues/pictures of our group rules.

Body Language:
Represent ideas and feelings in movement.
Act out a story or rhyme.
Try more words in sign.

Free Choice
Talk/Listen/Do:
Use friendly, safe, and healthy ways.
Converse with peers and adults.
Use puppets and flannelboard.
Continue dictation in art/science and/or other areas.
Try dictation about block and other three-dimensional constructions.
Use and add new recipe cards.
Use computer and telephones.
Tape record and listen.

Dramatic Play:
Add new prop boxes and props.
Pretend vet, hospital, and other safety/ health role play.
Pretend bus, office, stores.

Writing Center:
Use all materials, including old greeting cards.

Small Group
Games:
Answer "What if . . ." and "What do you think?" questions.
Discuss/plan what to buy at store to make vegetable soup.
Continue personal journal.
Start a traveling journal that rotates among families.
Sequence simple story cards.
Write a thank-you letter using picture and dictation.
Talk about learning with our senses and questions.
Describe what I like about another person.

Meals and Snacks:
Converse sociably with peers and adults on foods/topics.

MEMORY

Large Group
Remembering Together:
Copy adult modeling.
Help tell stories/rhymes.
Sing favorite songs.
Count by rote to 10 in songs and rhymes.
Count to 5 in another language.
Recall our group rules with the help of pictures/visual cues.
Recall sequence of day using pictures of schedule.
Play and sing name games.
Recognize own name in print.
Talk about holiday fun, trips, and company.
Repeat sounds and easy clapping rhythms.

Free Choice
All Area Learning:
Know names of friends, areas, materials.
Know expectations for behaviors.
Do helpers' jobs; help set up room.
Practice health habits.
Practice safety habits.
Pretend with new props in new areas.
Use flannelboard to tell familiar story.
Use simple sequence cards.

Cleanup:
Remember the cues.
Know where things go.

Small Group
Games:
Talk about the holidays.*
Find and/or match circles, ovals, squares, and hearts.
Tell three things I did today.
Recall three shapes when seen, then hidden.
Recall and do two or three tasks.
Recall holiday traditions and special foods served.
Furnish words omitted in a familiar rhyme.
Sequence pictures or symbols of the past three holidays.
Repeat silly words or phrases.
See and talk about photos taken of the group.

Meals and Snacks:
Remember positive language.
Talk about some food groups.
Recall having this food before.
Talk about what is in vegetable soup.
Talk about how to cook soup at school.

PROBLEM SOLVING

Large Group
Conversations:
About work and play choices.
About weather and seasonal changes and their effects on us.
About the sequence of summer, fall, winter; use pictures.
See and discuss school days and at-home days; record them on a blank calendar with symbols (school bus and house).
Represent ideas in creative movement.
Plan how to cook vegetable soup.

Free Choice
Blocks:
Cooperate; use accessories.
Repeat simple patterns.

All Area Learning:
Make work/play choices in all areas.
Ask questions; try to find answers.
Answer open questions.
Negotiate with words.
Reweigh and remeasure ourselves.
Regraph ourselves and see changes.
Work on a group art mural.
Count things and people.
Experiment with art, multisensory media, and manipulatives.
Tell about cause and effect in using materials and media.
Try new tools with sand, water and paint.

Dramatic Play:
Plan and carry out new ideas, roles, and use of props.

Science and Math:
Observe nature, plants, and animals, and notice changes.
Observe and handle new items; count and sort some. Use tools and methods for observing or recording.

Small Group
Games:
Order three items by size; give adult three items.
Introduce use of magnets.
Count the eyes, ears, noses, feet of two people.
Use food color or crepe paper to see color changes in water.
Discuss something red and round from home.
Prepare vegetables for soup; observe, describe.

Meals and Snacks:
Graph a cereal snack; count, discuss *more, less, most.*
Eat soup; discuss preparation and changes that occurred.

MOTOR

Large Group
Body Movement:
Copy and/or create to varied music.
Represent ideas/feelings/nature in
    movement.
Act out prepositions; move "sideways."

Free Choice
Using Blocks:
Use all types with accessories.
Build sets for dramatic play w/big blocks.

Active Play Inside/Outside:
Use varied locomotion.
Do parachute play.
Use balance beam *raised;* carry object.
Use jump ropes and hoops.
Use mats; tumbling, obstacle courses.
Varied four- or five-part obstacle
    courses, sometimes with slide.
Practice hopping, galloping.
Toss/catch; try using target.
Use all woodworking tools; embellish/
    paint creations as option.

Clays and Playdough/Sand and Water:
Add new variety, such as small hosing,
    wheels, syphons.

Dressing and Undressing
Continue practice, including shoes/boots.
Help peers with these tasks.

Art Media:
Use *open-ended* art media freely.
Experiment with new methods, materials.
Work on an art mural with others.

Manipulatives, Table Toys, Floor Toys:
Use appropriate items; and try more
    complexity.
Work cooperatively with some materials.

Small Group
Games:
Trace circles/ovals, hearts, free forms;
    try triangle.
Tie a knot on top of one knot.
String small beads, cereals, pastas.
Cut thin paper folded three times at
    random.
Cut folded paper on thick, simple curve;
    create heart.
Tear paper shapes including heart shapes.
Cut paper on one thick line with several
    curves.
Use new lacing materials.
Draw picture with marker or crayon.
Do three-dimensional constructions
    (tape and recyclables).

Meals and Snacks:
Continue prior experiences; help in food
    preparation.

PERCEPTUAL

Large Group
Music and Circle:
Use and guess instruments by sound.
Hear two sounds amid background
    noise.
Guess visible object or person from
    clues.
Guess visible shapes in room from clues.

Free Choice
Blocks:
Handle, match, find, label, and describe.
Describe patterns in constructions.
Use descriptors; tall, short, narrow, wide.
Work cooperatively to build.

Exploring with Senses:
Experiment with new varieties of media.
Experiment with playdough prints.
Experiment with painting; observe
    changes.
Taste and smell experiences; match
    sweet/sour.
Observe changes mixing, cooking,
    chilling foods.
Observe/compare tracks in snow, mud
    or earth.

Manipulatives; Table Toys; Floor Toys:
Use all appropriate items fully.
Use more complex puzzles and
    parquetry.
Use symbol and picture lotto cards.
Use matching sound can games.
Sort and find pictures of a given subject.

Cleanup:
Use perceptual and printed labels.
Respond to sound and light cues.

Small Group
Games:
Use picture and symbol lotto.
Match and/or find varied shapes,
    including square, triangle.
Reproduce five part patterns with
    pegs/beads; model seen.
Match real objects to symbols for
    numerals one, two, and three.
Match and/or group big, small, medium
    items.
Sort recyclables in three or more ways.
Guess a voice, match a hummed pitch.*
Match or find primary and secondary
    colors.
Observe likenesses and differences
    among us.

Meals and Snacks:
Discuss changes in foods after
    preparation.
Describe tastes, textures, colors, shapes.
Graph a snack by shapes or size;
    compare.

LITERACY

Large Group
Literature:
Hear/help tell varied literature.
Experience stories based on interests, events.
Use more Big Books.
Hear entries from traveling family journal.
Hear dictation recorded about plants, animals.

Conversations:
About work and play choices.
About staying healthy.
About friends and helpers.
About how adults teach us about our world.
About helpers like ranger, garbage collector, snow plower.
About trips that teach us new things.
Plan for a field trip and how we travel there.

Body Language:
Act out simple story or rhyme.
Represent ideas, feelings in movement.
Sign the words *time, work, play.*

Free Choice
Talk/Listen/Do:
Converse. Ask questions; answer open questions.
Use and talk about safe, friendly, and healthful ways.
Use puppets and flannelboard.
Continue dictation in art, science, blocks.
Dictate words to accompany art mural.
Use computer and telephones.
Tape record and listen.
Use recipe cards and add new ones.

Dramatic Play:
Try new role play, new props, new areas.
Continue safety/health role play.
Pretend places: fire station, office, hospital, store.

Writing Center:
Use all materials, including recycled greeting cards,
Write valentines or notes to peers and/or family.

Small Group
Games:
Continue personal journal; hear some entries.
Continue traveling journal; hear some entries.
Discuss ways adults help us learn about our world.
Dictation: What I like best about a family member.
Write thank you with picture to adults after field trip.
Answer "what if" or "what do you think" questions.
Make up a new ending to a familiar story.

Meals and Snacks:
Converse sociably with peers/adults.

MEMORY

Large Group
Remembering Together:
Copy adult modeling.
Help tell stories, rhymes, fingerplays.
Sing familiar songs and chants.
Count by rote to 10 in songs and rhymes.
Count up to 5 in another language.
Recall/discuss adult visit or field trip.
Repeat chanted or clapped rhythms.
Correct familiar rhyme that adult says "incorrectly."
Tell the end of a familiar story.
Talk about names for school days and at home days.

Free Choice
All Area Learning:
Know names of friends, areas, materials.
Name shapes of many blocks.
Know expectations for behavior.
Observe/discuss past events seen in photos.
Do helpers' jobs; help set up the room.
Practice health and safety habits.
Pretend in new ways with new props.
Recall and act out a past field trip.
Recall and act out other places we know.
Use simple sequence cards in play.
Use flannelboard to tell familiar stories.

Cleanup:
Remember the cues.
Know where things go.

Small Group
Games:
Tell how we used our senses to do something today.
Recall four objects or shapes when seen, then hidden.
Use picture sequence games.
Find circles, ovals, squares, hearts, triangles.
Use the names of colors.
Recall methods that keep us healthy or safe.
Recall what we like about a peer and dictate to make ". . . is special" poster.
Repeat several days until all children have posters.
Repeat a silly sentence.
Practice repeating home address.
Reproduce three- or four-part pattern; model hidden.
Recall "Who helps us when . . . ?" memory game.

Meals and Snacks:
Recall foods we have most or least often.
Recall healthy foods and food groups.
Recall how we made something to eat.

PROBLEM SOLVING

Large Group
Conversations:
On work/play choices.
On weather changes and their effects on us.
On sequence of holidays and approaching holiday.
Represent approaching holiday or trips with symbols on blank calendar with the school and at-home days.
Represent the *names* for school and at-home days on calendar.
Represent ideas and feelings in movement.
Plan a field trip together; discuss all aspects.

Free Choice
Blocks:
Cooperate in building related structures.
Explain uses of parts of a structure.
Build/represent a place where adults help us.

All Area Learning:
Make work and play choices.
Use time effectively; work/play in all areas.
Ask questions and discover answers.
Experiment with computer.
Explain reasons for wants and needs.
Explain reasons for group rules.
Work on group art mural.
Count things and people.
Experiment with multisensory media and manipulatives.
Observe/tell about cause and effect during play.
Estimate/guess "what will happen" during play.

Dramatic Play:
Plan and carry out new ideas with roles, props.
Recreate a place where adults help us.

Science:
Experiment with new items and observation tools.
Make simple graphs of experiment results.

Small Group
Games:
Sort recyclable items in three or more ways.
Use recyclables to make sets of one to four; give adult four items.
Discuss something brought from home that is made of wood.
Count the eyes, ears, noses, or feet of three people.
Graph various physical characteristics among group.
Order hearts by size, smallest to largest.
Play lotto games: What's missing or does not belong.

Meals and Snacks:
Continue prior experiences and graph more snacks.
Discuss our thoughts about our own "cooking".

MOTOR

Large Group
Body Movement:
Copy/create to varied music and rhythms.
Represent ideas, feelings, nature in
    movement.
Use prepositions combining movement
    with an object.
Practice ways to relax.

Free Choice
Using Blocks:
Cooperate, using all blocks and
    accessories.
Build "sets" for dramatic play w/big
    hollow blocks.

Active Play Inside/Outside:
Use varied locomotion, including
    galloping.
Use jumpropes, hoops, wheel toys,
    parachute.
Fly a kite or blow and chase bubbles
    outside.
Walk on balance beam raised higher
    but securely at one end.
Use balance beam raised securely at both
    ends.
Use mats and tunnel in varied obstacle
    courses.
Practice hopping, sliding, and galloping.
Catch a large bounced ball.
Toss and catch; toss into target.
Try brace and bit in woodworking with
    adult help.
Continue use of other woodworking tools.

Clays and Playdough/Sand and Water:
Continue to experiment with new media.
Dig earth to prepare it for planting.

Dressing and Undressing:
Continue practice; help peers with these
    tasks.

Art Media:
Use *open-ended* art media fully.
Experiment with pastel paints and new
    materials.
Work on an art mural with others.

Manipulatives, Table Toys, Floor Toys:
Use appropriate but more complex
    materials.
Make some simple musical instruments.

Small Group
Games:
Trace circles, hearts, triangles, free forms.
Trace/cut out large paper ovals, circles.
Cut on one thick line that has several
    curves.
Try cutting a line with a few zig zags.
Tie one knot with a shoelace doubled
    into two loops.
Use yarn needle and yarn to sew at
    random on burlap.
Repeat prior small motor experiences
    desired.
Do three-dimensional constructions
    with tape and recyclables.

Meals and Snacks:
Repeat prior experiences. Wash our
    chairs/tables.

PERCEPTUAL

Large Group
Music and Circle:
Use our own homemade instruments.
Hear two special sounds amidst
    background noise.
Guess visible object, person, or shapes
    from clues.

Free Choice
Blocks:
Handle, find, label, describe
    constructions.
Use descriptors: wide, narrow, tall, short,
    heavy.

Exploring with Senses:
Experiment with new varieties of media.
Taste/smell experiences; match salty,
    sweet, sour.
Perceive changes, cause/effect during
    cooking.
Cook eggs, see change from liquid to
    solid.
Perceive shoots, growth of new grass
    and plants.
Recognize last name when printed some
    of the time.

Manipulatives; Table Toys; Floor Toys:
Use all appropriate items fully.
Sort/group pictures of given subject.
Use puzzles and parquetry; simple to
    complex.
Use symbol and picture lotto cards/games.
Match/find sets of items with numerals
    1 to 5.
Use matching sound cans; find identical
    pairs.

Cleanup:
Use perceptual and printed labels.
Respond to sound and light cues.

Small Group
Games:
Use picture and symbol lotto games.
Examine/sort small potatoes to see
    differences.
Match and/or find varied shapes.
Reproduce five-part patterns of items;
    model seen.
Group items by size.
Group recyclables in three or more ways.
Match identical pairs of sounds in
    containers.
Match and find colors.
Use number lotto games.
Find numeral 1, 2, or 3 when adult
    shows corresponding set.
See/discuss a "map" or floor plan of
    classroom.
Connect three to five dots when start and
    direction are shown.

Meals and Snacks:
Perceive/describe textures, colors, shapes.
Graph a snack by shapes or size.
Help prepare foods.

LITERACY

Large Group
Literature:
Hear/tell varied forms of literature.
Experience stories based on interests, events.
Use Big Books; make new ones from own stories/journals.

Conversations:
About work and play choices.
About staying safe and healthy.
About friends and helpers.
About trips and walks that we take or plan.
About things I can do with pride.
About things I want to learn to do.
About seasonal changes in the weather and effects on us.

Body Language:
Act out simple stories or rhymes.
Represent ideas, feelings, nature in movement.
Talk without words; gestures or sign.

Free Choice
Talk/Listen/Do:
Converse with peers and adults.
Answer open questions posed by adults.
Use, talk about safe, friendly, and healthful ways.
Continue dictation in art, blocks, science.
Use flannelboard and puppets.
Use computer and telephones.
Practice calling 911 and telling my address on phone.
Use tape recorder and listening station.
Use recipe cards; add more.

Dramatic Play:
Continue safety/health role play.
Continue new props; try "space," airplane, ship, train.

Writing Center:
Use many materials for communication; including invented ones.

Small Group
Games:
Continue personal journal; share some entries.
Continue traveling journal; share some entries.
Talk about things that happen in this new season.*
Talk about things I can do, things I want to learn to do.*
Do thank-you letters to adult helpers or places visited.
Make up our own group story.
Answer "What if . . . ?" or "What do you think?" questions.
Play rhyming games including real and silly words.*
Discuss something green brought from home.
Make a poster of a web; show a theme and units.

Meals and Snacks:
Continue prior experiences.

MEMORY

Large Group
Remembering Together:
Copy adult modeling.
Help do stories, rhymes, fingerplays, songs/chants.
Count to 10 by rote in nonstereotyped chants, rhymes.
Count in another language.
Try other words in another language.
Recall/discuss walks and changes seen outdoors.
Recall/discuss visits or field trips.
Practice remembering names of the days of the week.
Furnish the correct ending to a familiar story.
Correct words in rhyme that the adult says incorrectly.

Free Choice
All Area Learning:
Use names of friends, helpers, materials, areas.
Name the shapes of many blocks.
Know expectations for behavior.
Observe/discuss past events seen in photos.
Do helpers' jobs; help set up the room.
Practice health and safety habits.
Pretend with new props; reenact field trips.
Use sequence games and cards.
Use the names of colors.
Use flannelboard to tell stories/rhymes.

Cleanup:
Remember the cues.
Know where things go.

Small Group
Games:
Tell some senses used today in work and play.
Recall four or more items when seen, then hidden.
Find circles, ovals, squares, triangles, rectangles.
Recall sequence of past holidays and approaching holiday.*
Discuss past family vacations and trips.*
Correct funny, incorrect endings to rhymes by adult.*
Reproduce three-part pattern when seen, then hidden.
Practice saying my home address.
Remember ways we stay safe and healthy.*
Remember what plants need to be healthy.
Remember what seeds need to sprout.
Recall/do three tasks that include movement.
Try to remember parents' first and last names.
Repeat sequence of three silly words or five numerals.

Meals and Snacks:
Remember positive social language.
Recall healthy foods and food groups.
Recall how we prepared a food.

PROBLEM SOLVING

Large Group
Conversations:
About work and play choices.
On weather/seasonal changes and effects on us.
Add words to blank calendar that represent days of week.
Plan for coming trip or event; discuss all aspects.
Talk about yesterday, last time, next time, and tomorrow.
Observe/discuss our growth; discuss things we need for growing.
Represent ideas, feelings, and "growing" in movement.

Free Choice
Blocks:
Cooperate in building; use accessories.
Describe/explain construction; use descriptive words.

All Area Learning:
Use time effectively to work/play in all areas.
Ask questions, find answers; answer open questions.
Use words to negotiate, compromise, and explain.
Work together on group projects.
Note cause/effect in experiments.
Plant a garden; start plants from seeds or cuttings.
Note cause and effect in plant/seed experiments.
Count things and people; estimate quantities in play.
Guess "what might happen."

Dramatic Play:
Plan and carry out new ideas with props.

Science:
Experiment with new items, tools, and methods.
Experiment with seeds and plants.
Experiment with earth; see what disappears or remains over time in jar of earth. See whether earth dissolves.
Discover what plants/seeds need in order to grow.

Small Group
Games:
Sort items/recyclables in three or more ways.
Use items to make sets of 1 to 4; give adult 4.
Make sets; match them to numerals 1 to 5.
Introduce dry cell battery.
Experiment with battery and switch.
Dictate to make list of reasons we like plants.*
Read and discuss an appropriate book on the environment.*
Order items by size: biggest, smallest, middle-sized.
Match one to one up to seven or more.
Play "what does not belong," "what comes next."

Meals and Snacks:
Continue prior experiences.
Help in food preparation.

MOTOR

Large Group
Body Movement:
Copy/create to varied music and rhythms.
Represent ideas, feelings, nature in movement.
Use prepositions combining body movement and object.
Practice ways to relax.

Free Choice
Using Blocks:
Use all types and accessories; work cooperatively.
Build "sets" for dramatic play with big blocks.

Active Play Inside/Outside:
Varied locomotion; gallop, duck walk, try to skip.
Jump ropes, hoops, wheel toys, parachute.
Balance beam; carry an object; turn around and return.
Walk on balance beam set on its narrow edge.
Use multipart obstacle courses; varied equipment.
Toss and catch; use targets.
Catch large bounced ball; bounce ball to peer.
Bat a ball with plastic "big bat."
Fly a kite; blow and chase bubbles outside.
Dig and weed in garden or digging area.
Use available woodworking tools; paint if desired.

Clays and Playdough/Sand and Water:
Use new and old varieties, tools, and methods.

Dressing and Undressing:
Practice self-help and help peers as well.

Art Media:
Use *open-ended* art media indoors and outside.
Use old and new methods, materials, tools and colors.

Manipulatives, Table Toys; Floor Toys
Use all appropriate materials; work cooperatively.
Cut out magazine pictures if desired.
Design with yarn needles/yarn on appropriate backing.
Work with small beads.

Small Group
Games:
Begin to print letters in name if interested.
Tie bow by making one knot; then make a second, top knot with the two looped shoelaces.
Draw picture with crayons or markers.
Cut paper on one thick zig-zag line.
Trace and cut large circles, triangles, or squares.
Tear large paper circles and squares.
Copy a circle or oval and an X or cross.

Meals and Snacks:
Continue all prior experiences.

PERCEPTUAL

Large Group
Music and Circle:
Continue to use music instruments.
Guess visible persons, objects, shapes from clues.
Begin to recognize first and last name in print.
Begin to know left and right sides of body.

Free Choice
Blocks:
Find and label blocks; describe constructions.
Use descriptive words; discuss repeated patterns.

Exploring with Senses:
Experiment with old favorites and new media.
Continue foods, taste and smell experiences.
Continue to perceive changes and cause/effect.
Make and use universal visual symbols in play.
Perceive changes/growth of plants, animals, and selves.
Perceive changes in nature outdoors.

Manipulatives; Table Toys; Floor Toys:
Use all appropriate items fully.
Sort and group pictures of a given subject.
Use puzzles and parquetry simple to complex.
Use symbol and picture lotto cards/games.
Group sets of items matching numerals up to 10.
Use matching sound cans; find pairs.

Cleanup:
Use perceptual and printed word labels.
Respond to light and sound cues.

Small Group
Games:
Observe/compare differences in visiting animal babies.
Find/name circles, squares, triangles, and rectangles.
Use more complex picture and symbol lotto cards.
Reproduce five or more part patterns with model seen.
Group items; name them by size, shape, and color.
Group sets of items that match numerals 1 to 7.
Connect three to eight dots when start and direction are shown.
Match and name letters in own first name.
Examine simple map, adult-drawn, of a walk we took.
Examine/discuss other shapes; diamonds, stars, octagons.
Discuss something brought from home that is flat.

Meals and Snacks:
Perceive/describe textures, colors, shapes of foods.
Perceive/describe attributes of dishes, bowls, and cups.

LITERACY

Large Group
Literature:
Hear/help tell varied forms of literature.
See, hear, tell own experience stories and made up stories
Put stories in print and on tape.

Conversations:
About work and play choices.
About staying safe and healthy.
About friendships and helpers.
About trips and walks we plan to take.
About weather/seasonal changes and effects on us.
About things I can do for myself and for others.
About ways plants and animals help us.
About the ways we can help plants and animals.
About things we love about family or caregivers.

Body Language:
Act out simple stories or rhymes.
Represent ideas, feelings, nature in movement.

Free Choice
Talk/Listen/Do:
Converse and ask questions of peers and adults.
Talk about ways we find our own answers.
Answer open questions that require the use of imagination.
Use safe, friendly, healthy ways; explain reasons.
Continue dictation; include comments about trips.
Continue use of literacy materials, including computer.

Dramatic Play:
Continue safety/health role play; pretend picnics, 911, campfires, swimming, fishing, boating.
Continue to use props; re-create places visited.
Incorporate water and camping safety in play.

Writing Center:
Use all materials for creative communication.
Encourage "invented" spelling and writing.

Small Group
Games:
Continue personal and traveling journals.
Talk about ways we can take better care of plants and animals in our world; dictate to make ongoing list over several days.
Talk about the animals we have seen; homes, ways they get food, and "clothes" or coverings.
Discuss something from home that you use to help animals.
Write a special note to mother, grandmother, or caregiver.
Do group or individual thank-you letters with drawings.

Meals and Snacks:
Continue prior experiences and conversations.

MEMORY

Large Group
Remembering Together:
Copy adult modeling.
Help tell stories, rhymes, fingerplays, songs/chants.
Count rote to 10 or more in nonstereotyped songs/chants.
Count in another language.
Practice other words in another language; hello, goodbye, please, thank you.
Recall/discuss past events; see their symbols on calendar.
Name days of the week and see their names on the calendar.
Remember past seasons and holidays and help sequence them.

Free Choice
All Area Learning:
Use names of friends, helpers, materials, areas.
Name shapes of blocks and equipment in setting.
Know expectations for behavior.
Use the names of colors in play.
Observe/discuss past events seen in photos.
Do helpers' jobs; help set up the room.
Practice health and safety habits.
Pretend/act out past experiences with props.
Use flannelboard stories and other sequence games.

Cleanup:
Remember the cues.
Know where things go.

Small Group
Games:
Tell some things I did today and who I did them with.
Recall four or more shapes seen, then hidden.
Find and label circles, squares, triangles, rectangles, etc.
Reproduce four or more part pattern when seen, then hidden.
Practice saying my home address and parents' names.
Correct funny, incorrect ways adult says my address.
Practice saying my telephone number.
Recall and do three tasks that require movement.
Recognize and name numerals 1 to 7 or higher.
Remember some things we have learned about animals.*
Remember summer and the things we do on vacation.*

Meals and Snacks:
Remember positive social language.
Recall healthful foods and food groups.
Recall foods we have prepared or cooked.

PROBLEM SOLVING

Large Group
Conversations:
About work and play choices.
On weather/seasonal changes and their effects on us.
About the symbols on our calendar.
About a way to show numbers for the days in a month; see these numbers placed on the calendar for the first time.
Talk about today, yesterday, and tomorrow and see them on our calendar.
Talk about how we have grown since school started.
Talk about plans for an event or trip.

Free Choice
Blocks:
Cooperate in building; describe/explain constructions.

All Area Learning:
Use time effectively to work in all areas.
Ask questions/find answers; answer open questions.
Use words to negotiate, compromise, and explain.
Work together on group projects of interest.
Note cause and effect in experiments.
Harvest plants from garden; use in food experience.
Count things and people and estimate quantities.
Guess "what might happen" in play.
Reweigh and remeasure ourselves; graph results.
Use computer.

Dramatic Play:
Carry out new ideas with new and old props.
Pretend going to new school and riding the bus.

Science:
Experiment with dry cell battery, switch and minilight.
Experiment with new and old materials in all areas.
Use words, graphs, and dictation to record observations.

Small Group
Games:
Sort/group items and recyclables in four or more ways.
Use items to make sets of 1 to 5. Give adult five items.
Order items first, second, last.
Match one to one up to eight or more.
Act out prepositions by using two objects.
Begin to talk about opposites.
Over several days, talk about why we like animals; dictate to make ongoing list.
Talk about what animals need; dictate/add to list or web.
Read/discuss appropriate book on the environment.*
Play "what does not belong," "what is missing".
Help plan a special end of the year event.*

Meals and Snacks:
Continue all prior experiences.

Self-Assessment Checklist

Appendix B is a self-assessment checklist for the teacher. This checklist will help ensure that you are covering all the bases in your lesson planning and program management, and will help you maintain compliance with state, federal, and/or program standards.

Self-Assessment Lesson Planning and Program Management Checklist

Lesson Plans (Based on accepted standards in the field)

_____ 1. Lesson planning provides a balance of adult-directed and child-initiated hands-on experiences.

_____ 2. Lesson plan shows that child-initiated (child-planned activity time) equals or predominates over adult-directed time excluding time for routines.

_____ 3. Lesson plans document the following:

    _____ a. child activity time for children
    _____ b. several large-group times of short duration
    _____ c. short small-group times either as scheduled or clearly seen during free choice time.

_____ 4. Outdoor play time is seen on the lesson plan and takes place daily whenever possible.

_____ 5. Documentation of individualizing is seen on the lesson plan and actually takes place each day.

_____ 6. Lesson plan shows that children are exploring and experimenting, and are attaining mastery with hands-on experiences and discovery learning.

_____ 7. Planned experiences provide both success and appropriate challenge to children.

_____ 8. Art and sensory experiences are open-ended.

_____ 9. Foods experiences and/or cooking occur regulary.

_____ 10. There is space on the lesson plan for parent comments and input.

_____ 11. Health and dental education experiences (other than routines) are planned regularly and are integrated in varied ways and areas of the setting.

_____ 12. Safety education experiences are regularly integrated and seen in the lesson plans.

_____ 13. Antibias and diversity experiences are regularly seen in the lesson plans.

_____ 14. Environmental awareness activities are regularly seen in the lesson plans.

_____ 15. A variety of literacy experiences are seen in the daily lesson plans.

_____ 16. Small-group experiences in the lesson plan are developmentally appropriate and reflect activities in all basic skill areas (motor, perceptual, literacy, memory, problem solving).

Setting

_____ 1. Children have personal, identified space.
_____ 2. Children's art and work are posted at their eye level and predominate over teacher-made or purchased items.
_____ 3. Photos of the children are posted at their eye level.
_____ 4. The setting encourages safe, self-directed movement and choice making.
_____ 5. Materials and equipment are safe and clean.
_____ 6. There is an attractive and clearly defined parent information area.
_____ 7. All required documents and emergency plans are posted.
_____ 8. If group rules are posted, they have been developed jointly with children and are stated positively.
_____ 9. Learning centers are easily defined and are labeled in some manner, by name and/or purposes.
_____ 10. Active, noisy areas are separated from quiet areas.
_____ 11. There are ample supplies and a variety of developmentally appropriate materials.

Observable Basic Classroom Experiences

_____ 1. Ample and varied choices of appropriate materials are available in each learning area.
_____ 2. Open-ended art media and other materials that can be used by all children in the group are available.
_____ 3. A variety of materials in various areas support the current theme or subtheme/unit.
_____ 4. Both planned and spontaneous activities occur in antibias approaches and in nurturing social competence.
_____ 5. Self-esteem-building experiences occur regulary.
_____ 6. Family-focused activities occur regularly.
_____ 7. Children are involved regularly in foods planning and preparation experiences; nutrition education is integrated.
_____ 8. Children are involved regularly in concrete safety and health education activities.
_____ 9. Use of the following areas occurs daily in a free-choice period with ample time for all chaildren to explore.

   _____ a. _Sensory_—sand, water, other
   _____ b. _Blocks_—units, hollow, other construction
   _____ c. _Art_—easel and other paint, clays, collage, and drawing materials
   _____ d. _Dramatic Play_—housekeeping, puppets, other
   _____ e. _Motor_—fine and gross motor materials/equipment
   _____ f. _Literacy_—writing center, computer, literature, tapes or listening center
   _____ g. _Science/Math_—tools, items to handle and count, plants, animals
   _____ h. _Music/Movement_—instruments, records, tapes
   _____ i. _Outdoor Area_—natural setting, equipment, environmental awareness materials

Readers are also referred to the book *Reaching Potentials: Appropriate Curriculum and Assessment for Young Children,* Volume 1, edited by Sue Bredekamp and Teresa Rosegrant. (Washington, DC: National Association for the Education of Young Children, 1992), for checklists and questions concerning curriculum that may be of further help to early childhood teachers.

References and Resources for Further Reading

Child Development

Ames, Louise Bates, & Ilg, Frances L. *Your Four Year Old: Wild and Wonderful.* New York: Dell, 1976, Reprinted 1994.

Ames, Louise Bates, & Ilg, Frances L. *Your Five Year Old: Sunny and Serene.* New York: Dell, 1979.

Ames, Louise Bates, & Ilg, Frances L. *Your Three Year Old: Friend or Foe.* New York: Dell, 1985.

Berk, Laura E. *Infants and Children: Prenatal through Early Childhood.* Boston: Allyn and Bacon, 1994.

Bredekamp, Sue, ed. *Developmentally Appropriate Practice in Programs Serving Children Birth through Age 8,* expanded ed. Washington, DC: National Association for the Education for Young Children, 1992.

Elkind, David. *A Sympathetic Understanding of the Child: Birth to Sixteen,* 3rd ed. Boston: Allyn and Bacon, 1994.

Elkind, David. *Images of the Young Child: Collected Essays on Development and Education.* Washington, DC: National Association for the Education for Young Children, 1971; 8th printing, 1994.

Katz, Lillian, Evangelou, Demetra, & Hartman, Jeanette. *The Case for Mixed-Age Grouping in Early Education.* Washington, DC: National Association for the Education for Young Children, 1990.

Kendrick, Abby, Kaufman, Roxanne, & Messenger, Katherine. *Healthy Young Children: A Manual for Programs,* rev. ed. Washington, DC: National Association for the Education for Young Children, 1994.

McAfee, Oralie, & Leong, Deborah. *Assessing and Guiding Young Children's Development and Learning.* Boston: Allyn and Bacon, 1994.

Thompson, Eleanor D. *Pediatric Nursing: An Introductory Text,* 5th ed. Philadelphia: W. B. Saunders/Harcourt Brace Jovanovich, 1987.

Early Childhood Education—General

Beaty, Janice J. *Skills for Preschool Teachers,* 4th ed. Columbus, OH: Merrill, 1992.

Beaty, Janice J. *Preschool Appropriate Practices.* Orlando, FL: Holt, Reinehart and Winston, 1992.

Bredekamp, Sue, ed. *Developmentally Appropriate Practice in Programs Serving Children Birth through Age 8,* expanded edition. Washington, DC: National Association for the Education of Young Children, 1992.

Bredekamp, Sue, & Rosegrant, Teresa, eds. *Reaching Potentials: Appropriate Curriculum and Assessment for Young Children,* Vol. 1. Washington, DC: National Association for the Education for Young Children, 1992.

Brewer, Jo Ann. *Introduction to Early Childhood Education, Preschool through Primary Grades.* Boston: Allyn and Bacon, 1995.

Brown, Janet F. *Curriculum Planning for Young Children.* Washington, DC: National Association for the Education for Young Children, 1982; 6th printing, 1992.

Dodge, Diane Trister, & Colker, Laura J. *The Creative Curriculum,* 3rd ed. Washington, DC: Teaching Strategies, Inc., 1988, 1992.

Elkind, David. *Images of the Young Child: Collected Essays on Development and Education.* Washington, DC: National Association for the Education for Young Children, 1993.

Flemming, Bonnie M., & Hamilton, Darlene S. *Resources for Creative Teaching in Early Childhood Education,* 2nd ed. Orlando, FL: Harcourt Brace College, 1990.

Forman, George, & Hill, Fleet. *Constructive Play: Applying Piaget in the Preschool.* Reading, MA: Addison-Wesley, 1984.

Fortson, Laura Rogers, & Reiff, Judith. *Early Childhood Curriculum: Open Structures for Integrative Learning.* Boston: Allyn and Bacon, 1995.

Goffin, Stacie G., & Stegelin, Dolores A., eds. *Changing Kindergartens: Four Success Stories.* Washington, DC: National Association for the Education for Young Children, 1992.

Hendrick, Joanne. *The Whole Child: Developmental Education for the Early Years,* 5th ed. Columbus, OH: Merrill/Prentice-Hall, 1992.

Hendrick, Joanne. *Total Learning: Developmental*

Curriculum for the Young Child, 4th ed. Columbus, OH: Merrill/Prentice-Hall, 1994.

Hohmann, Mary, & Weikart, David P. *Educating Young Children: Active Learning Practices for Preschool and Child Care Programs.* Ypsilanti, MI: High/Scope Press, 1995.

Jones, Elizabeth, & Nimmo, John. *Emergent Curriculum.* Washington, DC: National Association for the Education for Young Children, 1994.

Katz, Lilian, Evangelou, Demetra, & Hartman, Jeanette. The Case for Mixed-Age Grouping in Early Education. Washington, DC: National Association for the Education for Young Children, 1990.

Koralek, Derry G., Colker, Laura J., & Dodge, Diane Trister. *The What, Why, and How of High Quality Early Childhood Education: A Guide for On-Site Supervision.* Washington, DC: National Association for the Education for Young Children, 1993.

Larson, Nola, Henthorne, Mary, & Plum, Barb. *Transition Magician.* St. Paul, MN: Redleaf Press, 1994.

Mitchell, Anne, & David, Judy, eds. *Explorations with Young Children: A Curriculum Guide from Bank Street College.* Beltsville, MD: Gryphon House, 1992.

Montessori, Maria. *The Secret of Childhood.* New York: Ballantine Books, 1972; 17th printing, 1992. Original copyright Fides Publishers, Inc., 1966.

Morrison, George S. *Early Childhood Education Today,* 6th ed. Columbus, OH: Merrill, 1995.

Peck, Johanne T., McCaig, Ginny, & Sapp, Mary Ellen. *Kindergarten Policies: What Is Best for Children?* Washington, DC: National Association for the Education for Young Children, 1988.

Peterson, R., & Felton-Collins, V. *The Piaget Handbook for Teachers and Parents.* Williston, VT: Teachers College Press, 1986.

Phillips, Carol Brunson, ed. *Essentials for Child Development Associates Working with Young Children.* Washington, DC: CDA Professional Preparation Program, Council for Early Childhood Professional Recognition, 1991.

Schweinhart, Lawrence J., Barnes, Helen V., Weikart, David P., Barnett, W. Stevens, & Epstein, Ann S. *Significant Benefits: The High Scope Perry Preschool Study through Age 27,* Monograph Number 10. Ypsilanti, MI: Migh/Scope Press, 1993.

Spodek, Bernard, & Saracho, Olivia. *Right from the Start: Teaching Children Ages Three to Eight.* Boston: Allyn and Bacon, 1994.

Taylor, Barbara J. *A Child Goes Forth,* 8th ed. Englewood Cliffs, NJ: Prentice-Hall, 1994.

Thematic Planning—Horizontal Curriculum

Becker, Joni, Reid, Karen, Steinhaus, Pat, & Wieck, Peggy. *Themestorming: How to Build Your Own Theme-Based Curriculum the Easy Way.* Beltsville, MD: Gryphon House, 1994.

Berry, Carla F., & Mindes, Gayle. *Planning a Theme-Based Curriculum: Goals, Themes, Activities, and Planning Guides for 4's and 5's.* New York: Goodyear Books/HarperCollins, 1993.

Brewer, Jo Ann. *Introduction to Early Childhood Education—Preschool through Primary Grades.* Boston: Allyn and Bacon, 1995.

Fortson, Laura Rogers, & Reiff, Judith. *Early Childhood Curriculum: Open Structures for Integrative Learning.* Boston: Allyn and Bacon, 1995.

Gryphon House. *The Giant Encyclopedia of Theme Activities for Children 2 to 5.* Beltsville, MD: Gryphon House, 1993.

Jones, Elizabeth, & Nimmo, John. *Emergent Curriculum.* Washington, DC: National Association for the Education for Young Children, 1994.

Katz, Lillian, & Chard, Sylvia C. *Engaging Children's Minds: The Project Approach.* Norwood, NJ: Albex, 1989.

Kostelnik, Marjorie, Howe, Donna, Payne, Kit, Rohde, Barbara, Spalding, Grace, Stein, Laura, & Whitbeck, Duane. *Teaching Young Children Using Themes: Ages 2 to 6.* Glenview, IL: Good Year Books/Scott Foresman, 1991.

Schiller, Pam, & Rossano, Joan. *The Instant Curriculum.* Beltsville, MD: Gryphon House, 1990.

Sobut, Mary A., & Bogen, Bonnie Neuman. *Complete Early Childhood Curriculum Resource.* West Nyack, NY: Center for Applied Research in Education/Simon and Schuster, 1991.

Trostle, Susan, & Yawkey, Thomas D. *Integrated Learning Activities for Young Children.* Boston: Allyn and Bacon, 1990.

Warren, Jean. *Theme-A-Saurus.* Everett, WA: Warren Publishing House, Inc., 1989.

Assessment

Bondurant-Utz, Judith, & Luciano, Lenore B. *A Practical Guide to Infant and Preschool Assessment in Special Education.* Boston: Allyn and Bacon, 1994.

Bredekamp, Sue, & Rosegrant, Teresa, eds. *Reaching Potentials: Appropriate Curriculum and Assessment of Young Children,* Vol. 1. Washington, DC: National Association for the Education for Young Children, 1992.

Brewer, Jo Ann. *Introduction to Early Childhood Education, Preschool through Primary Grades.* Boston: Allyn and Bacon, 1995.

Kamii, Constance, ed. *Achievement Testing in the Early Grades: The Games Grown Ups Play.* Washington, DC: National Association for the Education for Young Children, 1990.

McAfee, Oralie, & Leong, Deborah. *Assessing and Guiding Young Children's Development and Learning.* Boston: Allyn and Bacon, 1994.

Meisels, Samuel J. *Developmental Screening in Early Childhood: A Guide,* 3rd ed. Washington, DC: National Association for the Education for Young Children, 1985, 1989.

The Early Childhood Setting

Dodge, Diane Trister, & Colker, Laura J. *The Creative Curriculum,* 3rd ed. Washington, DC: Teaching Strategies, 1992.

Forman, George E., & Kuschner, David S. *Piaget for Teaching Children: The Child's Construction of Knowledge.* Washington, DC: National Association for the Education for Young Children, 1983.

Hirsch, Elisabeth. *The Block Book,* rev. ed. Washington, DC: National Association for the Education for Young Children, 1984.

Kritchevsky, Sybil, & Prescott, Elizabeth, with Walling, Lee. *Planning Environments for Young Children: Physical Space.* Washington, DC: National Association for the Education for Young Children, 1977.

McCracken, Janet Brown. *Playgrounds Safe and Sound.* Washington, DC: National Association for the Education for Young Children, 1990.

NAEYC Information Service. *Facility Design for Early Childhood Programs Resource Guide.* Washington, DC: National Association for the Education for Young Children, 1991.

Vergeront, Jeanne. *Places and Spaces for Preschool and Primary: Outdoors.* Washington, DC: National Association for the Education for Young Children, 1988.

Vergeront, Jeanne. *Places and Spaces for Preschool and Primary: Indoors.* Washington, DC: National Association for the Education for Young Children, 1987.

Play

Elkind, David. "Work Is Hardly Child's Play." In *Images of the Young Child: Collected Essays on Development and Education* (pp. 21–29). Washington, DC: National Association for the Education for Young Children, 1993.

Fein, Greta, & Rivkin, Mary, eds. *The Young Child at Play: Reviews of Research,* Vol. 4. Washington, DC: National Association for the Education for Young Children, 1986.

Hughes, Fergus P. *Children, Play, and Development,* 2nd ed. Boston: Allyn and Bacon, 1995.

McKee, Judy Spitler, ed. *Play: Working Partner of Growth.* Wheaton, MD: Association for Childhood Education International, 1986.

Rogers, Cosby, S., & Sawyers, Janet K. *Play in the Lives of Children.* Washington, DC: National Association for the Education for Young Children, 1988.

Sawyers, Janet K., & Rogers, Cosby S. *Helping Young Children Develop through Play: A Practical Guide for Parents, Caregivers, and Teachers.* Washington, DC: National Association for the Education for Young Children, 1988.

Literacy

Adams, Marilyn Jager. *Beginning to Read: Thinking and Learning about Print.* Urbana-Champaign: Center for the Study of Reading. Reading Research and Education Center, University of Illinois, 1990.

Cazden, Courtney, B., ed. *Language in Early Childhood Education.* Washington, DC: National Association for the Education for Young Children, 1981.

Edwards, Sharon A., & Maloy, Robert W. *Kids Have All the Write Stuff: Inspiring Your Children to Put Pencil to Paper.* New York: Penguin Books, 1992.

Glazer, Susan Mandel, & Burke, Eileen M. *An Integrated Approach to Early Literacy: Literature to Language.* Boston: Allyn and Bacon, 1994.

Liggett, Twila C., & Benfield, Cynthia Mayer. *Reading Rainbow Guide to Children's Books: The 101 Best Titles.* New York: Citadel Press/Carol Publishing Group, 1994.

Ollila, Lloyd O., & Mayfield, Margie I., eds. *Emerging Literacy: Preschool, Kindergarten and the Primary Grades.* Boston: Allyn and Bacon, 1992.

Raines, Shirley, C., & Canady, Robert J. *Story Stretchers: Activities to Expand Children's Favorite Books.* Beltsville, MD: Gryphon House, 1989.

Raines, Shirley, C., & Canady, Robert J. *More Story Stretchers: More Activities to Expand Children's Favorite Books.* Beltsville, MD: Gryphon House, 1991.

Schickedanz, Judith A. *More Than the ABC's: The Early Stages of Reading and Writing.* Washington, DC: National Association for the Education for Young Children, 1986.

Strickland, Dorothy, S., & Morrow, Lesley Mandel, eds. *Emerging Literacy: Young Children Learn to Read and Write.* Newark, DE: International Reading Association, 1989.

Totline. *1001 Rhymes and Fingerplays.* Everett, WA: Warren, 1994.

Totline. *Cut and Tell Cutouts Series.* Everett, WA: Warren, 1994.

Trelease, Jim. *The New Read-Aloud Handbook.* New York: Penguin Books. 1989.

Wiener, Harvey S. *Talk with Your Child: Using Conversation to Enhance Language Development.* New York: Penguin Books, 1988.

Discovery and Problem Solving— Science, Math, Cooking

Association for Childhood Education International (ACEI). *Cooking and Eating with Children: A Way to Learn.* Washington, DC: ACEI, 1974, 1978.

Bittinger, Gayle. *Play and Learn with Magnets.* Everett, WA: Warren, 1994.

Bittinger, Gayle. *1, 2, 3 Science: Science Activities for Working with Young Children.* Everett, WA: Warren, 1993.

Bittinger, Gayle. *Teaching Snacks: Snacktime Learning Opportunities.* Everett, WA: Warren, 1994.

Brown, Sam Ed. *Bubbles, Rainbows and Worms: Science Activities for Young Children.* Beltsville, MD: Gryphon House, 1991.

Cohen, Richard, & Tunick, Betty Phillips. *Snail Trails and Tadpole Tails: Nature Education for Young Children.* St. Paul, MN: Redleaf Press, 1993.

Hill, Dorothy, M. *Mud, Sand, and Water.* Washington, DC: National Association for the Education for Young Children, 1977; 6th printing, 1993.

Hirsch, Elisabeth S., ed. *The Block Book,* rev. ed. Washington, DC: National Association for the Education of Young Children, 1984.

Hodges, Susan. *Healthy Snacks.* Everett, WA: Warren, 1994.

Holt, Bess-Gene. *Science with Young Children,* rev. ed. Washington, DC: National Association for the Education for Young Children, 1989, 1991.

Jense, Rosalie, & Spector, Deborah. *Teaching Mathematics to Young Children: A Basic Guide.* Englewood Cliffs, NJ: Prentice-Hall, 1984.

Kamii, Constance. *Number in Preschool and Kindergarten: Educational Implications of Piaget's Theory.* Washington, DC: National Association for the Education for Young Children, 1982.

McCracken, Janet Brown. *More Than 1, 2, 3 . . . The Real Basics of Mathematics.* Washington, DC: National Association for the Education for Young Children, 1990.

Rockwell, Robert, Williams, Robert, & Sherwood, Elizabeth. *Everybody Has a Body: Science from Head to Toe.* Beltsville, MD: Gryphon House, 1992.

Sherwood, E., Williams, R., & Rockwell, R. *More Mudpies to Magnets: Science for Young Children.* Beltsville, MD: Gryphon House, 0000.

Sprung, Barbara, Froschi, Merle, & Campbell, Patricia B. *What Will Happen If . . . Young Children and the Scientific Method.* New York: Educational Equity Concepts, 1985.

Wanamaker, Nancy, Hearn, Kristin, Richarz, Sherrill, & the Idaho-Washington AEYC. *More Than Graham Crackers: Nutrition Education and Food Preparation with Young Children.* Washington, DC: National Association for the Education for Young Children, 1979.

Williams, Robert A., Rockwell, Robert E., & Sherwood, Elizabeth A. *Mudpies to Magnets: A Preschool Science Curriculum.* Beltsville, MD: Gryphon House, 1987.

Ecology/Environment, and the Outdoors

Baker, Katherine Reed. *Let's Play Outdoors.* Washington, DC: National Association for the Education for Young Children, 1966; 14th printing, 1994.

Bittinger, Gayle. *Exploring Sand and the Desert.* Everett, WA: Warren, 1993.

Bittinger, Gayle. *Exploring Water and the Ocean.* Everett, WA: Warren, 1993.

McCracken, Janet Brown. *Playgrounds Safe and Sound.* Washington, DC: National Association for the Education for Young Children, 1990.

Miller, Karen. *The Outside Play and Learning Book.* Beltsville, MD: Gryphon House, 1989.

Petrash, Carol. *Earthways: Simple Environmental Activities for Young Children.* Beltsville, MD: Gryphon House, 1992.

Redleaf, Rhoda. *Open the Door, Let's Explore.* St. Paul, MN: Redleaf Press, 1983.

Rockwell, Robert E., Sherwood, Elizabeth A., & Williams, Robert A. *Hug a Tree and Other Things to Do Outdoors with Young Children.* Beltsville, MD: Gryphon House, 1983; 4th printing, 1986.

Sunderlin, Sylvia, ed. *Bits and Pieces: Imaginative Uses for Children's Learning.* Washington, DC: Association for Childhood Education International, 1967.

Warren, Jean. *Exploring Wood and the Forest.* Everett, WA: Warren, 1993.

Celebrating Diversity

Chandler, Phyllis A. *A Place for Me: Including Children with Special Needs in Early Care and Education Settings.* Washington, DC: National Association for the Education for Young Children, 1994.

Derman-Sparks, Louise, & the A.B.C. Task Force. *Anti-Bias Curriculum: Tools for Empowering Young Children.* Washington, DC: National Association for the Education for Young Children, 1989.

Hopson, Darlene Powell, & Hopson, Derek S. *Raising the Rainbow Generation: Teaching Your Children to Be Successful in a Multicultural Society.* New York: Fireside/Simon and Schuster, 1993.

King, Edith W., Chipman, Marilyn, & Cruz-Jansen, Marta. *Educating Children in a Diverse Society.* Boston: Allyn and Bacon, 1994.

National Black Child Development Institute. *African American Literature for Young Children.* Washington, DC: National Black Child Development Institute, 1992.

Neugebauer, Bonnie, ed. *Alike and Different: Exploring Our Humanity with Young Children.* Washington, DC: National Association for the Education for Young Children, 1992.

Saracho, Olivia N., & Spodek, Bernard, eds. *Understanding the Multicultural Experience in Early Childhood Education.* (Chapter 10 copyright held by Dean Corrigan, 1983). Washington, DC: National Association for the Education for Young Children, 1983; 6th printing, 1992.

Wolery, Mark, & Wilbers, Jan S., eds. Including Children with Special Needs in Early Childhood Programs. Washington, DC: National Association for the Education for Young Children, 1994.

Creative and Divergent Thinking

Brashears, Deya, with Brashears, Lea. *More Dribble Drabble: Process-Oriented Art.* Orinda, CA: Circle Time, 1992.

Hoffman, Stevie, & Lamme, Linda Leonard, eds. *Learnaing from the Inside Out: The Expressive Arts.* Wheaton, MD: Association for Childhood Education International, 1989.

Kohl, Mary Ann. *Mudworks: Creative Clay, Dough, and Modeling Experiences for Children.* Billingham, WA: Bright Ring, 1989.

Lasky, Lila, & Mukerji, Rose. *Art: Basic for Young Children.* Washington, DC: National Association for the Education for Young Children, 1980.

McDonald, Dorothy T. *Music in Our Lives: The Early Years.* Washington, DC: National Association for the Education for Young Children, 1979.

Ramsey, Marjorie, E., ed. *It's Music.* Wheaton, MD: Association for Childhood Education International, 1984.

Skeen, Patsy, Garner, Anita Payne, & Cartwright, Sally. *Woodworking for Young Children.* Washington, DC: National Association for the Education for Young Children, 1984.

Sullivan, Molly. *Feeling Strong, Feeling Free: Movement Exploration for Young Children.* Washington, DC: National Association for the Education for Young Children, 1982; 2nd printing, 1985.

Parent Involvement

Berger, Eugenia Hepworth. *Parents as Partners in Education:* The School and Home Working Together, 3rd ed. New York: Macmillan, 1991.

Galinsky, Ellen. *Between Generations: The Six Stages of Parenthood.* New York: Berkeley Books, 1982.

Hymes, James L., Jr. *Effective Home-School Relations.* New York: Prentice-Hall, 1953 (out of print).

Powell, Douglas, R. *Families and Early Childhood Programs.* Washington, DC: National Association for the Education for Young Children, 1989.

Quisenberry, James D., & Martin, Lucy Prete, eds. *Changing Family Life Styles: Their Effect on Children.* Washington, DC: Association for Childhood Education International, 1982.

Stone, Jeannetrte Galambos. *Teacher–Parent Relationships.* Washington, DC: National Association for the Education for Young Children, 1987.

Index